T0344428

Tools and Techniques for Software Development in Large Organizations:

Emerging Research and Opportunities

Vishnu Pendyala
Cisco Systems Inc., USA

A volume in the Advances in
Systems Analysis, Software
Engineering, and High Performance
Computing (ASASEHPC) Book Series

Published in the United States of America by
IGI Global
Engineering Science Reference (an imprint of IGI Global)
701 E. Chocolate Avenue
Hershey PA, USA 17033
Tel: 717-533-8845
Fax: 717-533-8661
E-mail: cust@igi-global.com
Web site: http://www.igi-global.com

Copyright © 2020 by IGI Global. All rights reserved. No part of this publication may be reproduced, stored or distributed in any form or by any means, electronic or mechanical, including photocopying, without written permission from the publisher.
Product or company names used in this set are for identification purposes only. Inclusion of the names of the products or companies does not indicate a claim of ownership by IGI Global of the trademark or registered trademark.

Library of Congress Cataloging-in-Publication Data

Names: Pendyala, Vishnu, 1968- editor.
Title: Tools and techniques for software development in large organizations
   : emerging research and opportunities / Vishnu Pendyala, editor.
Description: Hershey, PA : Engineering Science Reference, 2020. | Includes
   bibliographical references. | Summary: "This book examines the tools,
   techniques, and processes large organizations use in software
   development"-- Provided by publisher.
Identifiers: LCCN 2019034165 (print) | LCCN 2019034166 (ebook) | ISBN
   9781799818632 (h/c) | ISBN 9781799818649 (s/c) | ISBN 9781799818656
   (eISBN)
Subjects: LCSH: Application software--Development.
Classification: LCC QA76.76.D47 T656 2020 (print) | LCC QA76.76.D47
   (ebook) | DDC 005.3--dc23
LC record available at https://lccn.loc.gov/2019034165
LC ebook record available at https://lccn.loc.gov/2019034166

This book is published in the IGI Global book series Advances in Systems Analysis, Software Engineering, and High Performance Computing (ASASEHPC) (ISSN: 2327-3453; eISSN: 2327-3461)

British Cataloguing in Publication Data
A Cataloguing in Publication record for this book is available from the British Library.

All work contributed to this book is new, previously-unpublished material.
The views expressed in this book are those of the authors, but not necessarily of the publisher.

For electronic access to this publication, please contact: eresources@igi-global.com.

Advances in Systems Analysis, Software Engineering, and High Performance Computing (ASASEHPC) Book Series

ISSN:2327-3453
EISSN:2327-3461

Editor-in-Chief: Vijayan Sugumaran, Oakland University, USA

MISSION

The theory and practice of computing applications and distributed systems has emerged as one of the key areas of research driving innovations in business, engineering, and science. The fields of software engineering, systems analysis, and high performance computing offer a wide range of applications and solutions in solving computational problems for any modern organization.

The **Advances in Systems Analysis, Software Engineering, and High Performance Computing (ASASEHPC) Book Series** brings together research in the areas of distributed computing, systems and software engineering, high performance computing, and service science. This collection of publications is useful for academics, researchers, and practitioners seeking the latest practices and knowledge in this field.

COVERAGE

- Enterprise Information Systems
- Software Engineering
- Network Management
- Performance Modelling
- Metadata and Semantic Web
- Virtual Data Systems
- Human-Computer Interaction
- Computer Graphics
- Computer System Analysis
- Parallel Architectures

IGI Global is currently accepting manuscripts for publication within this series. To submit a proposal for a volume in this series, please contact our Acquisition Editors at Acquisitions@igi-global.com or visit: http://www.igi-global.com/publish/.

The Advances in Systems Analysis, Software Engineering, and High Performance Computing (ASASEHPC) Book Series (ISSN 2327-3453) is published by IGI Global, 701 E. Chocolate Avenue, Hershey, PA 17033-1240, USA, www. igi-global.com. This series is composed of titles available for purchase individually; each title is edited to be contextually exclusive from any other title within the series. For pricing and ordering information please visit http://www.igi-global. com/book-series/advances-systems-analysis-software-engineering/73689. Postmaster: Send all address changes to above address. © © 2020 IGI Global. All rights, including translation in other languages reserved by the publisher. No part of this series may be reproduced or used in any form or by any means – graphics, electronic, or mechanical, including photocopying, recording, taping, or information and retrieval systems – without written permission from the publisher, except for non commercial, educational use, including classroom teaching purposes. The views expressed in this series are those of the authors, but not necessarily of IGI Global.

Titles in this Series

For a list of additional titles in this series, please visit:
https://www.igi-global.com/book-series/advances-systems-analysis-software-engineering/73689

Cloud Computing Applications and Techniques for -Commerce
Saikat Gochhait (Symbiosis Institute of Digital and Telecom Management, Symbiosis International University, India) David Tawei Shou (University of Taipei, Taiwan) and Sabiha Fazalbhoy (Symbiosis Centre for Management Studies, Symbiosis International University, India)
Engineering Science Reference • © 2020 • 300pp • H/C (ISBN: 9781799812944) • US $245.00

Soft Computing Methods for System Dependability
Mohamed Arezki Mellal (M'Hamed Bougara University, Algeria)
Engineering Science Reference • © 2020 • 293pp • H/C (ISBN: 9781799817185) • US $225.00

Grammatical and Syntactical Approaches in Architecture Emerging Research and Opportunities
Ju Hyun Lee (University of New South Wales, Australia) and Michael J. Ostwald (University of New South Wales, Australia)
Engineering Science Reference • © 2020 • 351pp • H/C (ISBN: 9781799816980) • US $195.00

Fundamental and Supportive Technologies for 5G Mobile Networks
Sherine Mohamed Abd El-Kader (Electronics Research Institute, Egypt) and Hanan Hussein (Electronics Research Institute, Egypt)
Information Science Reference • © 2020 • 360pp • H/C (ISBN: 9781799811527) • US $225.00

Deep Learning Techniques and Optimization Strategies in Big Data Analytics
J. Joshua Thomas (KDU Penang University College, Malaysia) Pinar Karagoz (Middle East Technical University, Turkey) B. Bazeer Ahamed (Balaji Institute of Technology and Science, Warangal, India) and Pandian Vasant (Universiti Teknologi PETRONAS, Malaysia)
Engineering Science Reference • © 2020 • 355pp • H/C (ISBN: 9781799811923) • US $245.00

For an entire list of titles in this series, please visit:
https://www.igi-global.com/book-series/advances-systems-analysis-software-engineering/73689

701 East Chocolate Avenue, Hershey, PA 17033, USA
Tel: 717-533-8845 x100 • Fax: 717-533-8661
E-Mail: cust@igi-global.com • www.igi-global.com

To Kriti & Mahadyuti

Table of Contents

Preface

Succeeding is an art, even in the software industry. No amount of science can substitute for this art. For instance, the principles of Agile methodologies are known widely in the industry. But not every organization has practiced them successfully. Practice that comes with profound experience and intuition makes the difference. It is not easy to document the expertise so gained – it still needs to be practiced as an art. But can we at least get some insights into the successful practices? This book is an attempt at it. I sometimes wonder if the tribal knowledge in the corporate world, particularly on the operations side of things will probably run into millions of volumes in print. It remains in the organizations, largely untapped for application to common good. The open-source movement brought the source code into the open and contributed tremendously to the cross-organization synergies of software development. But the operations side of software development is still mostly within the closed doors. The motivation for conceptualizing this book was to present good insights into how the operations around software development can be successfully handled in large organizations, the best practices, opportunities, and challenges.

Having experienced how the software development landscape changed over the last several years, I took upon myself to share my experiences in a book. It then seemed more valuable if others also joined the efforts to cover more diverse topics, given the scope of the proposed work. I therefore announced the idea for a book on the "Innovation Challenge" portal within our organization, Cisco, mainly to see the response from my colleagues to the idea. Expressing expertise in words is not easy. I knew it was a daunting task. In the meantime, I also explored the option of opening up the authoring opportunity to a wider audience by submitting this book proposal to IGI publishers, which got accepted. My original idea of a joint authored book now got converted into that of an edited book, with the prospects of much broader scope and a more diverse authorship. Indeed, the authors of the chapters in this book come from multiple countries and multiple organizations and cover a much more diverse portfolio of topics.

Mere understanding solves many problems. One of the criteria for accepting the chapters for this book was its contribution to raising the level of understanding of the reader. Merely stating the facts will not suffice to improve the understanding. The treatise must also explain the motivation and philosophy behind the tools and techniques. The chapters are written by diverse authors spread all around the world. It is understandably hard to enforce a strict charter of expectations from the chapters, but through reviews and the process of selection, we tried to make sure that the chapters have certain common ingredients in terms of the purpose they serve, and their tone and tenor in general. As you will notice, the chapters have been written lucidly, providing substantial detail and sufficient inspiration to adopt the salient insights provided in each chapter.

The chapters are all written independently and can be read in any order. The first chapter serves as an introduction to the topic of the book, briefly tracing the evolution of the tools and techniques used for software development for the last 20 to 30 years, providing an introduction to various concepts. History should never be ignored, even if not everything in it was successful. Artificial Intelligence was almost written off a few years ago, but the same tools and techniques today are serving as the mortar of modernization. The chapter therefore provides some history of software engineering over the years. It explains how integration engineering used to be practiced several years ago, with multiple branches and merges between them to propagate changes and provides the motivation for today's continuous integration in a single-branch model. Agile methodologies have largely obsoleted much of the waterfall model concepts, paving way to the current day DevSecOps. As you will read, the area is still evolving and needs to be closely watched for more disruptions.

One of the early steps in the Software Development Life Cycle is collecting requirements. The second chapter is about determining and documenting requirements for a software project in a more pragmatic way that models the real world more closely. The chapter rightly starts with the statement that software quality depends on the effectiveness of the requirements collection phase and presents an interesting idea that can soon be an emerging trend in the software industry. Software requirements often come from teams that are not well-versed with software. The requirements tend to be stated loosely and imprecisely. One of the tools that is often used to model imprecision in the real world is Fuzzy Logic. Ontology provides the framework for capturing the knowledge in a given domain in a machine-interpretable way. The chapter proposes and discusses how a combination of both these tools, Fuzzy Ontology, can be used in the requirements phase of software development.

Once requirements are collected, the next step is to estimate the efforts required to develop the software that can meet the requirements. The third chapter is a comprehensive discussion on the process of estimating efforts, models that can be used, and challenges encountered in the process. Using diverse techniques such as Bayesian Belief Networks, Machine Learning, Case-Based Reasoning, and Multiple Linear Regression, the author explains how to estimate the efforts, evaluate the models used for estimation, and the limitation of the models. Using a number of illustrations, citations, and equations, the chapter details how the models can be used for different kind of software applications. The chapter is hoped to serve as a ready reference to anyone wanting to formally estimate the efforts needed in a software project.

Strength lies in the ability to quickly change in non-intrinsic ways, whether it is for an individual or an organization. Software development is all about changes – code changes, requirement changes, process changes, etc. DevOps provides the tools, techniques, and processes to manage change, particularly the code changes through their deployment in production. The various changes can cause the artefacts produced in the course of software development also to change, causing serious inconsistencies. In the fourth chapter, Dr. Meedeniya and her colleagues survey how artefacts are traced and their consistency is managed in the software development process. The chapter starts with the required background of the key concepts, explaining the importance of artefact traceability and the terminology involved. It then describes multiple tools like IBM DOORS and Rational RequisitePro, and techniques from areas like Information Retrieval that are used for artefact traceability. The chapter concludes with a discussion on the challenges, limitations, and future directions in artefact traceability.

Continuing the discussion, the authors of the previous chapter present their prototype tool for software artefact traceability in the fifth chapter. Through detailed flowcharts, pseudo-code, visualizations and architecture diagrams, the authors explain how their tool detects changes in the software artefacts, analyzes the impact of the changes, manages the consistency of the artefacts. The prototype tool that the authors propose uses NLP based Information Retrieval techniques and integrates with the DevOps tools stack. The chapter presents a case study and compares their work with other existing solutions. The fourth and fifth chapters together provide a comprehensive discussion on the important problem of software artefact traceability and serve as a ready reference to organizations wanting to establish the practice in their software development life cycle.

Next is an important chapter contributed by representatives of a few companies who discuss various aspects of Continuous Deployments in their respective organizations, every year, for the last few years, in a summit environment. I represented Cisco in the annual summit that is hosted each year by a different company such as Google and Twitter and considered it is important for the readers of this book to get insights into the salient points of discussion at the summit. The chapter presents a number of strategies and practices that helped the organizations succeed and/or learn. Did you know that at one point of time, Google determined that 84% of the times, a test failed because the test itself was flaky? Or that Netflix releases 4000 deployments in a day? Read the chapter to know more about such practices. The chapter covers diverse aspects of the DevOps tasks, providing valuable insights into how large organizations run their DevOps activities.

From multiple companies and diverse aspects of DevOps, in the next chapter, we narrow our focus to a single company, Cisco and to a single area, data. Data is often touted as the new oil. Just like the source code has all the ultimate answers to questions about the software product, answers to questions just about anything or anyone can be obtained by tracing the roots and probing the metadata about the source. The last chapter of the book talks about generating valuable analytics from the metadata associated with software development. The artefacts from running these data analytics can be used, particularly by the higher management to make decisions and fine-tune strategies. Data analytics also help in determining expert code reviewers, identifying areas for hardening, failure densities per module or engineer and so on. More details on how all this is done are presented in the last chapter.

Overall, the book provides some unique tools and techniques, plenty of ready-to-use best practices, and a general discourse on important and sometimes ignored topics related to software development. The references and additional reading suggested at the end of each chapter should help in further exploring the topics. It is sincerely hoped that the book will serve as a compendium for ready reference by the experts and the uninitiated, alike, for many years to come.

An effort like this will not be possible without the help of many individuals and organizations. First and foremost, I thank all my present and past employers, particularly Cisco and Synopsys for giving me the rich experience in the topical areas of this book. Fortunately, all the years of my industry experience have been with large organizations, who could afford time and resources for substantial processes, tools, and techniques for software development. Next, my thanks go to the authors of the chapters. They helped with the reviews of other chapters, some at a short notice, providing valuable suggestions and insights. Thank you, authors, for the excellent co-operation in bringing out the book. I also wish to express my gratitude to IGI Publishers, who have been supportive all through, amending the contract and accommodating my requests through the circumstantial changes over the months. Thanks to my children who consider me as their role model, for motivating me to live up to their expectations and for giving up quite a bit of their quality time with me during the weekends for this cause. Finally, and most importantly, thanks to my father, who set the standards high, but was not alive to see any of how I was executing on the goals he set for me.

Vishnu S. Pendyala
Cisco Systems Inc., USA
San Jose, CA, USA

Chapter 1

Evolution of Integration, Build, Test, and Release Engineering Into DevOps and to DevSecOps

Vishnu Pendyala
Cisco Systems Inc., USA

ABSTRACT

Software engineering operations in large organizations are primarily comprised of integrating code from multiple branches, building, testing the build, and releasing it. Agile and related methodologies accelerated the software development activities. Realizing the importance of the development and operations teams working closely with each other, the set of practices that automated the engineering processes of software development evolved into DevOps, signifying the close collaboration of both development and operations teams. With the advent of cloud computing and the opening up of firewalls, the security aspects of software started moving into the applications leading to DevSecOps. This chapter traces the journey of the software engineering operations over the last two to three decades, highlighting the tools and techniques used in the process.

INTRODUCTION

Software Engineering teams have traditionally been responsible for branching strategies, code merges, nightly and production builds, validation of the builds, image generation and posting in addition to serving as consultants in Software Engineering practices to the product development teams. These functions continue to exist but have been transformed to adapt to the growing needs of the industry.

DOI: 10.4018/978-1-7998-1863-2.ch001

Copyright © 2020, IGI Global. Copying or distributing in print or electronic forms without written permission of IGI Global is prohibited.

Globalization has come to stay. Teams operate in different time zones, often providing a seamless stream of development and operations activities round the clock. Software Configuration Management (SCM) tools such as Clearcase used for version control provided multi-site functionality to support code commits from all over the world – an excellent application of the distributed computing paradigm (Van Der Hoek, et al,1998). Software Engineering poses quite a few challenges when the code structure is complex, and the product dependencies are significant. Present day requirements of distributed teams and agile development add to these challenges.

Software Configuration Management (SCM) is key to effective product releases. The SCM tool employed to maneuver the Software Engineering processes of an organization should provide the necessary constructs to meet the requirements of the various releases. Interdependencies of the code and the volume of the code changes raise the complexity of the Software Engineering operations. With time, needs multiplied, operations scaled drastically, causing new tools, architectures, and patterns to be invented. From a handful of tools two decades ago, we now have a plethora of tools to manage Software Engineering operations. XebiaLabs recently came up with an entire periodic table of popular DevOps tools (Kaiser, 2018). The integration, build and release engineering discipline that existed originally has far transcended SCM related activities as its primary charter to a much broader DevSecOps role. This chapter traces through the journey of the Software Engineering discipline from the days of primarily performing builds, merges, releases, and tooling to the present day DevSecOps.

RELATED WORK

The DevOps area has predominantly been a domain of the industry than that of academia. Publishing articles is not as emphasized in the industry as it is in academia. This is one of the reasons for working on this book, so that insights into the tools, techniques, and processes employed in the industry, particularly, the large organizations are captured in the literature. Nevertheless, there is quite some literature already that captures the state-of-art in the DevOps and DevSecOps areas. The literature uncovered several interesting aspects of DevOps. This section captures a few of them. A framework for automated Round-Trip Engineering from development to operations and operations to development (Jiménez et al, 2018) is one of them. Round-Trip Engineering ensures that the Deployment and Configuration specifications are automatically ensured to be consistent with the system, thereby eliminating any technical debt on that count. This further confirms the need for tight integration of development and operations and automating the coupling as much as possible – one of the key points of this chapter.

Another channel of tight coupling between the development team and operations is through metrics. Metrics can provide an effective feedback mechanism in software organizations, which can be a substantial challenge in large organizations due to bureaucracy and cross-organizational environments (Cito et al., 2018). The authors identify feedback categories and phases and point to the tools that can help with the metrics generation. Culture plays an important role in DevOps (Sánchez-Gordón & Colomo-Palacios, 2018). Empathy is a critical component of the DevOps culture. Development teams and Operations teams must understand each other's perspectives and strive towards the overall productivity of engineers and the quality of the product. The authors survey the literature and summarize the trends about the DevOps culture. DevOps can be thought of like a Project Management methodology that fills in the lacunae in Agile methodology (Banica, et al, 2017).

Intertwined with culture is the skillset that the DevOps discipline demands. In the 26th European Conference on Information Systems, the authors (Wiedemann & Wiesche, 2018) categorize the skills needed to work in the DevOps area. The role of a Full-stack Engineer is gaining increasing relevance with the advent of DevOps. Full-stack engineering is particularly relevant in the Cloud Computing era (Li, Zhang, & Liu, 2017). Full-stack Engineers require broad skills covering all or most aspects of the software industry. Such skills are particularly important in fast-paced companies that produce several releases in a day. Describing such an environment where companies like Facebook release hundreds or even thousands of deployments into production daily, the authors (Savor et al, 2016) point out that it is possible to scale the teams and codebase several times without impacting the developer productivity.

Before the preceding work, excellent insights into the nature of software development at Facebook were provided by the authors of a different article (Feitelson et al, 2013). They point out that the differentiating characteristic of companies like Facebook is that the software they develop need not be "shipped" to customers as it runs on their servers. This enables rapid deployments of software updates in production. A different kind of domain is where software that is shipped is embedded. The complexity of embedded systems makes DevOps a formidable challenge in that domain (Lwakatare et al, 2016). Using multiple case studies, the authors explain why embedded systems are different when it comes to DevOps. The practice of DevOps in general, was surveyed and recommendations were made based on the survey (Erich et al, 2017). One such recommendation is to implement Continuous Delivery to the point of being able to release software updates on-demand.

From a software architecture perspective, microservices facilitate rapid deployability (Chen, 2018). Monolithic architectures, however modular they are designed to be, cannot scale-up to the level of microservices architecture when it comes to Continuous Deployment. Using microservices architecture, small teams can deploy their changes, without having to wait to merge changes from other teams. Because of the limited functionality in a microservice, deploying the software update is much faster as compared with monolithic architectures, which need to be deployed a whole. Changing to microservices architecture and adopting DevOps methodology requires substantial efforts. Designing a DevOps maturity model helps in the process (Bucena & Kirikova, 2017). The maturity model helps in identifying gaps in the current processes and goals for improvement.

DevOps brought-in a bunch of terms into the software engineering realm. Disentangling the terms and giving them a clear definition helps in better implementation of the DevOps practice. The authors of (Stahl, Martensson, & Bosch, 2017) survey the literature substantially to come up with definitions of the important terms used in the DevOps practice. One of the terms that is quite popular with DevOps is "Infrastructure-as-Code (IasC)" It is a tactic to speed-up the DevOps processes and is a good example of one of the many tactics that DevOps brought into the software engineering discipline to accelerate the pipelines (Artac, 2017). Software infrastructure typically comprises of several scripts and variable settings for setting up the infrastructure needed for the software to run. IasC treats these scripts and configuration files as source code as well, so that they can be versioned and treated as any other source code.

The evolution of DevOps is currently at the stage of encompassing security into DevOps and transitioning DevOps into DevSecOps. It has been observed that the increased automation of the processes that DevOps entails leads to improved product security (Rahman et al, 2016). The term, DevSecOps seems to have originated in 2012 in a blog post (Myrbakken et al, 2017) by a Gartner analyst. The key idea behind DevSecOps is to further break the barriers in the Software organization and make Security of the software product, everyone's business.

THE SOFTWARE ENGINEERING JOURNEY

Software Engineering organization in large companies traditionally comprises of some form of an Integration and Release Engineering team, a Platform Engineering team, a Tools team, and Program Management. The Platform Engineering team is typically responsible for porting the software across a wide variety of hardware and software platforms and maintaining the common code components of the software product. Porting involves making changes to the source code so that it works seamlessly across the platforms. Tools team makes the software to ensure developer productivity is high and processes run efficiently. Program management is responsible for managing software development projects. Integration engineering teams are responsible for builds, software configuration management, and sometimes, to some extent, quality assurance as well. The key component and highly visible role in Software Engineering organizations is still most often held by the team responsible for Builds, Release, and Integration engineering. The software development milestones have a huge dependency on the operations of this team. Let us start our journey by taking a closer look at this important function in its legacy form in the next subsection.

Integration Engineering

A typical large software organization has several products developed independently. Each of these products comprises of several features. Integration Engineering refers to the process of integrating these features and the individual changes that go into each of these products. Integration engineering is the interface between development and production. Interdependencies of the code and the volume of the code changes raise the complexity of builds and configuration management. The Integration Engineering team is responsible for branching strategies, code merges between product modules, nightly and production builds, validation of the builds, and image generation. Collecting metrics, creating dashboards, enabling access to the results of the builds and validation are the other activities that form the crux of Integration Engineering (Dyer, 1980).

A substantial portion of the source code is common to several products and product families. It would be chaos if the developers of each of these products check-into a single branch. Development is therefore segregated into more manageable '*development*' or '*dev*' branches. Developers check-in product-related changes into these '*dev*' branches which are periodically integrated into a '*release*' or '*rel*' branch. Each '*dev*' branch contains code changes contributed by the development team for a product or family of products. The '*rel*' branch incorporates the changes in all '*dev*' branches which merge to and from it periodically.

We, therefore, have the time-synchronized handshakes between the '*dev*' branches and the '*rel*' branch as shown in Figure 1. The merges to and from the '*rel*' branch are done against labels on the branches. Changes propagate to the '*rel*' branch and from the '*rel*' branch to the '*dev*' branches with every merge. Because of the interdependencies of the code on different '*dev*' branches, this is accomplished through a physical merge, not by just updating the config_spec with the new label, if using Clearcase for software configuration or similar means if using other tools for the software configuration.

Handoffs to and from the release branch occur in Δt cycles where Δt is statically determined for each release based on the rate of code changes on all branches and their interdependencies. The time length of a cycle, Δt is inversely proportional to the rate of code changes on all branches in Δt, which handoff to the release branch and their interdependencies. We can mathematically model this relationship as,

Figure 1. Branch integration

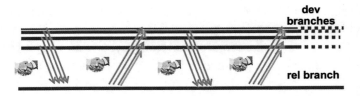

$$\Delta t \propto 1/[\ ^d\!/_{dt}(^n\!\!\int_{db=1}C)]\gamma_1\ \gamma_2\ \gamma_3\ ...\gamma_n ....(1)$$

where db = development branch, C= code changes, $^d\!/_{dt}(^n\!\!\int_{db=1}C)$ is the rate of code changes on all *'dev'* branches and $\gamma_1\ \gamma_2\ \gamma_3\ ...\gamma_n$ are the correlation coefficients of the *'dev'* branches. The formula is only a conceptual representation of the relationships. In practice though, Δt is determined empirically, based on experience.

Each cycle comprises of 3 distinct phases on the *'dev'* branch: development, merge and build, which includes testing. The release engineering team, which manages the *'rel'* branch also generates an image after consuming a handoff. As was mentioned before development happens only on the *'dev'* branch – merges, builds, regression testing, and generating images are the only actions that happen on the *'rel'* branch, other than the handoffs. A handoff is typically a label, a snapshot of the source code, and information about the criteria this snapshot meets, like the test pass %s, etc. The label from a *'dev'* team is a sparse label of the files on the *'dev'* branch only, while the label from release engineering is a complete label on all files. After consuming the label from the *'rel'* team, changes in all *'dev'* branches will be visible in each of the individual development views.

In all the above activities, automation is essential. Software Engineering is a process and human-memory intensive. There are too many steps, dependencies and other factors that make it difficult to remember and do them manually, without the aid of scripts, checklists, and other aides. Manual processes have proven to be error-prone and time-consuming. Automation is essentially programming human expertise into scripts. When automation is not possible in entirety, it is a good idea to generate checklists, messages, and other aides. The very nature of Software Engineering makes it imperative that we automate as much as possible. Quality and productivity demand automation.

From Waterfall to Agile

The traditional software development paradigm is referred to as the Waterfall model because SDLC happens sequentially, in cascading stages. Requirements are collected upfront; development happens as one big project and the feedback loop between the development teams and operations is usually long. Over time, the software industry realized the perils of following the Waterfall model and the need for agility in the development (Sureshchandra & Shrinivasavadhani, 2008). Long feedback cycles result in a substantial risk. Teams operate in silos and bugs are discovered late in the cycle. Therefore, there is a need to break the one big project into more manageable smaller chunks. The branching model discussed in the section on Integration Engineering also needs to change to facilitate shorter release cadence. Code changes need to be integrated more rapidly than wait for Δt time cycle, which typically runs into days or weeks.

In the waterfall model, testing typically starts after all development is done. It is often too late and too expensive to fix bugs that late in the cycle. It is imperative to "fail fast" and recover from the failure fast as well. The cycle needs to be shortened even if it takes several cycles for completion of the project. Overheads need to be minimized and simplified to get into this iterative, agile mode of operations. Agility calls for flexible and highly collaborative environments and an entire rethink of the software development activity. For instance, companies have moved away from having many feature branches as described in the section on Integration Engineering to a single branch model that avoids merges and the heavy processes involved in managing numerous branches. In large organizations, thousands of developers could be working on a single branch. The source code instead uses 'feature toggles' for selectively exercising the code. Agile methodologies resulted in substantial improvements for companies. Some form of the Agile methodology has been successfully practiced by most large organizations.

One of the popular flavors of the Agile methodology is Scrum. Much like in the rugby football game by that name, where players flock together into a tightly packed team to grab the ball, in the scrum framework, teams collaborate closely with each other to develop the product. The idea of scrum is simple to understand, but difficult to practice. It originated in 1986, from a paper in the Harvard Business Review and is inspired by processes in the manufacturing firms like in the automotive and the photocopier industries. Scrum defines only three roles: Product Owner, Scrum Master, and the Team. The Product Owner is responsible for funding the project, setting the vision and release dates for the product. The scrum master makes sure that the team is productive and works to remove any blockers that the team may run into during the execution of the project. Scrum master, as the name indicates, is a key role, crucial for creating and sustaining a high-performance team. The team typically comprises of 5 to 9 members who do the real work of building the product. The team does not have a hierarchy, sub-teams or titles and functions seamlessly.

The work-cycle in scrum is called the sprint, which typically lasts for two weeks and comprises of many tasks to be accomplished in that cycle. A task is a fundamental unit of work in a sprint. The product is developed in increments. The end of a sprint marks the completion of a useable portion of a product, which can be released to the customers. This iterative development results in agile release cycles and shortened time to market. The simple operating environment results in low process overheads and quick decision making. Quality improves because of frequent testing and feedback from the field. Teams feel empowered and work-life balance is better achieved. Agile methodologies are big on automation, thus enhancing productivity. During a sprint, the team meets daily for a short duration, typically 15 minutes, standing and discuss these 3 key questions: (a) What did you do yesterday? (b) What will you do today? (c) Are there any blockers impeding the progress? Any blockers or issues are not resolved during the meeting – scrum meetings are not to be used for problem-solving.

If there are blockers discovered during the meeting that cannot be resolved by the scrum master, instead of extending the time, the scope is reduced – some of the tasks are downsized or eliminated. It is therefore imperative that the scrum master is an excellent problem solver and be able to unblock the team through collaboration, coaching, and leadership. In terms of documentation, the tasks that need to be implemented are described in form of "user stories" with the syntax, "As a <some user>, I want <some goal>, so that <some reason>." For instance, a user story in a sales analysis application could be, "As a Regional Director for the Asia Pacific, I want to be able to drill down to the sales numbers for a particular country with a few clicks so that I can change the sales strategy for that country if necessary." Documentation need not be exhaustive – working software is prioritized over comprehensive documentation.

Agile planning happens at different levels – task-level, done daily, feature level, done for a sprint and at a strategic level for the entire release. The development happens using timeboxed, lightweight iterations aligned with the sprint. The scrum framework prioritizes individuals over tools or processes, making sure that there are limits on the work in progress and feedback loops. One of the techniques often used is pair programming, where programmers work in pairs, one of them writing the code and the other reviewing it as it is being written. The pair keeps switching roles and collaborate closely. A sprint retrospective is held after every sprint, also for a short duration, where the entire team participates in reviewing what went well and what did not. The retrospective also follows a simple process. The team collectively decides what they should start doing for the next sprint, stop doing and what the team should continue doing going forward.

There are simple tools that help in the process of the timeboxed, iterative development. The tools include burndown charts which show the remaining work plotted against the days in the sprint and sprint backlog that is updated by the scrum master with the time required to complete the remaining tasks. Commercial software packages like Rally or Jira incorporate these tools. A key aspect of the framework is a sense of urgency that is shared by the entire team. The scrum methodology can be viewed as a shift in coding culture and requires buy-in from all stakeholders. It is a different way of doing software product development and can prove to be a major shift in the organization's culture. It must also be noted that Agile or Scrum frameworks are not a silver bullet and are not suited for every software product development. Often, large organizations use some components of the agile framework in conjunction with other methodologies as a middle-ground.

DevOps

Software Engineering Operations teams continue to strive to provide a consistent environment for global development. They engineer the products from the hands of the developers to the hands of the customers. Agile methodologies proved that collaboration and people must be top priority in software development. An extension to that idea is to break the barriers between development and operations teams further, resulting in the concept of DevOps. In some ways, DevOps can be thought of as extending the principles of agile software development. Silos are further broken down and development, quality assurance, and operations teams all act without any barriers.

One of the best practices of DevOps is Continuous Integration (CI), an idea proposed by Grady Booch, the inventor of the famed Unified Modeling Language, UML. The idea is to provide immediate feedback to the developer about their code changes and almost always have a working product that can be tested and possibly released. The code changes need to meet several criteria such as being buildable, pass sanity tests, go through static analysis checks successfully, reviewed and approved by peers/module owners, and so on. Most of the checks happen automatically. The code can be integrated into the product only if all the checks pass. Thus, all integration issues are addressed immediately, in a sharp contrast with what was described in the section on Integration Engineering. Continuous Integration, therefore, becomes the basis for all subsequent operations and automation.

Unlike huge changesets getting propagated across branches through the handshakes described in integration engineering, the changesets in Continuous Integration are small, much more manageable, and iterative. The automation around CI is crucial for developers to remain productive. Hence the need for tools – several of them – so many that a periodic table can be filled with them and even more. The pivotal tool is the CI engine, which does much more than the traditional 'cron' on Unix machines that typically spun off the builds in the waterfall model. There are currently many tools that function as a CI engine today. Jenkins, Travis, and Bamboo are a few of such CI engines. These CI engines take the code changes from the developers through a series of checks to validate the code diffs. The sequence of checks can be envisioned as a 'pipeline,' quite analogous to the line of pipes that transport liquids and gases to a production area. Just like the commercial liquid and gas pipelines are equipped with the required control devices, the CI engine pipelines have the necessary mechanisms to control the processes that take the code changes through the validations.

Along with continuous integration, there is a need for continuous testing as well, so that the developers get feedback on quality aspects, continuously. When the product is continuously tested, it is ready for deployment in production continuously as well, resulting in hundreds or even thousands of releases in a day. Continuous Integration, Continuous Testing, Continuous Deployment, and Continuous Delivery lead to continuous improvement. All these continuous processes can be implemented using the 'pipelines' that the CI engines provide. As can be envisioned, the pipelines can easily grow in complexity. The trend now is to 'code' the CI engine pipelines, so that they can be maintained better and there is change history. 'Pipeline as Code' often resides in the same repository as the source code.

Cloud computing has come to stay. Today, most of the computing, including that which happens in the pipeline, run in a private or public cloud. Cloud computing and virtualization enable spinning up a 'virtual' machine (VM) in no time. Multiple VMs, possibly running different operating systems can run on the same bare metal hardware providing isolation and optimal usage. Cloud computing provides access to the VMs seamlessly across the network, even if the bare metal machines are miles away and are owned by a 3rd party. A lightweight model of a VM is a container, which can run on a VM, providing an isolated environment for an application to run. The container packages any given application along with all its dependencies including configuration files and libraries so that the application is ready to run as soon as the container is brought up – quite convenient for testing and deploying as part of the pipeline. A container image is immutable so that it can be run and rerun many times.

The container image contains everything that an application needs to run and serves as an immutable snapshot of the application's runtime environment. Multiple containers share the kernel running on physical hardware and provide isolated namespaces for the application to run. Therefore, a container includes its abstraction of memory, devices, network ports, processes, and filesystems, shielding the underlying kernel's resources from direct access. The containers resources eventually use the resources provided by the underlying kernel but do not let the applications access them directly. Containers provide great portability suitable for instant deployment, particularly when using a microservices architecture. As a general guideline, all builds should be reproducible. Reproducibility is particularly important for production builds or builds which go out to customers. Containerization can help in reproducibility of builds since a container image can effectively store the configuration needed for a build to be reproduced.

Some of the functions that the DevOps teams perform are shown in Figure 2. As can be seen, the DevOps teams are responsible for most of the operations in software development, starting with setting up the repository to deploying and shipping the releases. Each one of these functions needs to be automated and automation requires tools. Hence the explosion of tools. For instance, the number of artifacts that are needed for the build and produced by it has grown so much that we now have tools like Artifactory and Nexus to handle them. Source code itself is versioned in tools like Git and Subversion. Huge files like the binary artifacts are not usually versioned with the source code, hence separate tools for them. For testing, we have tools like Selenium, JUnit, and TestNG. ElectricFlow and Julu help with deployment. Metrics and dashboards play an important role in monitoring and improving productivity. In the DevOps world, it is said that if it is measured, it is bound to improve. Tools like Kibana and Nagios help in creating dashboards that can show metrics.

Docker and Kubernetes are popularly used tools for containerization and their orchestration respectively. Configuration and provisioning tools include Chef, Puppet, and Ansible. Coverity and SonarQube are two of the tools that help in static analysis of the source code to detect any vulnerabilities and potential bugs, without actually running the code. Tools like Cobertura, JaCoCo, and Valgrind are used for measuring code coverage statistics. As we saw, collaboration plays a crucial role in software development and is one of the main driving forces for the DevOps movement. Multiple tools like Slack, HipChat, and Webex Teams are popularly used for instant messaging and collaboration. In addition to these open-source or commercially available tools, most large organizations have their internal tools to handle several software development operations. For instance, Cisco has its huge bug tracking system called CDETS and release posting tool called IRT.

Code bloating and code obsolescence is quite common over time. As highlighted in Figure 2, the DevOps team needs to work on reducing the code footprint and explore other ways to reduce the build times to reduce the wait-time for the developers to get feedback about their code changes. In some cases, particularly when the software is embedded, there are strict limits on how much memory the software can consume at runtime, requiring a check to be placed on the incremental size of the image built from the code changes. This is an example of a policy that needs to be put in place. As can be seen, software development is a disciplined activity, which needs to be regulated by several policies. Some of the other policies could be to allow commits only after sufficient approving reviews, mandate a double-commit to the master branch before committing to a release branch, and so on. The DevOps team is responsible for enforcing the policies. Instrumenting such mechanisms and the software development environment in general requires plenty of tooling on part of the DevOps teams. It is not hard to see that DevOps is, therefore, a substantial charter requiring strong technical and analytical skills.

DevOps to DevSecOps

Security is everyone's business, even in the software industry. Application security is critical, given their usage profile. That part has not changed, but the way security is achieved has gone through substantial changes due to paradigm shifts in the development processes. Traditionally, as shown in Figure 3a, boundaries were secured using firewalls. Companies and applications operated in silos. Development and Operations too operated in silos and were not well orchestrated. DevOps fixed the broken collaboration mechanisms and provided for continuous, seamless operations. Security continued to be ensured by protecting the organization's borders.

The scenario is depicted in Figure 3b. However, as cloud computing gained in adoption, borders weakened, and computing happened across borders. It was no longer enough to protect the

corporate borders using firewalls. Security had to be built into the application, resulting in the "Security as Code" paradigm and the birth of DevSecOps, as depicted in Figure 3c.

Cloud computing and DevOps brought in a series of "…as a Service" and "…as Code" paradigms, such as "Infrastructure as a Service," "Infrastructure as Code," and "Pipeline as Code." DevSecOps continued the trend with the "Security as Code" paradigm, taking a holistic view of security. Like DevOps, DevSecOps has to do

Figure 2. Typical responsibilities of the DevOps team

Figure 3a. Security in legacy software systems

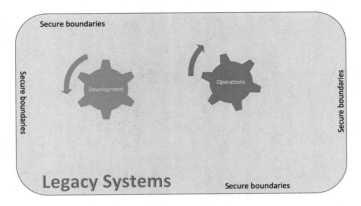

a lot with the corporate mindset and is a culture shift. It can be viewed as a set of tools, techniques, and processes to build security into software. It requires buy-in from all stakeholders and is a community-driven effort. DevSecOps is still evolving through learning and exploration. With security moving into the application, security infrastructure needs to be 'cloud-aware' and security features need to be published via APIs. Security aspects are now built into the CI engine pipeline and automation tooling as much as possible. Security is part of the software building process as illustrated in Figure 4.

Development, security, and operations are the new building blocks of a software organization.

Figure 3b. Security with the advent of DevOps

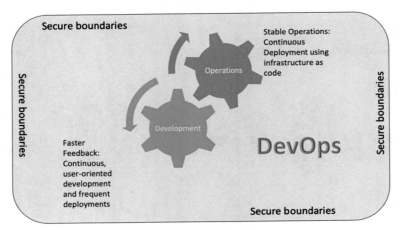

Figure 3c. Security in DevSecOps

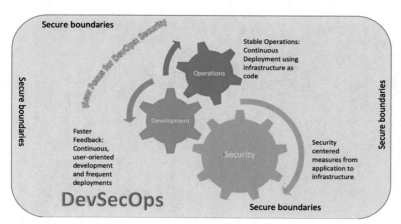

DevOps broke the silos between Development and Operations teams. DevSecOps extends the idea and broke the silos between the Security teams and the DevOps teams. DevSecOps orchestrates the workflows among the development, security, and operations teams to provide an integrated, seamless infrastructure for the development of the product. Security vulnerabilities in the code are continuously monitored and addressed paving way for "Continuous Security." Products are always security-ready, in addition to being deployable with every code commit. Product security is therefore tightly coupled with the pipeline controls. For instance, continuous testing now requires security aspects to be tested as well as part of the code commit validations in the pipeline. Security, which came into the picture in the later stages of software development, now needs to "shift left," to earlier stages of development as well, right from the beginning. There must now be at least a few agile user stories related to security in every sprint if agile methodologies are being used.

Figure 4. Building blocks of a software organization

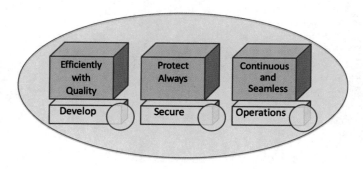

Issues, Controversies, Problems

The DevSecOps area is still evolving and poses multiple challenges. It is a culture shift and driving change across organizations continues to be a challenge. Roadshows within the organization, identifying security champions to serve as brand ambassadors for DevSecOps, and promoting the benefits of DevSecOps by other means are some of the techniques that can be used to make the culture shift. Security certainly raises the complexity of the applications. Architecture changes to accommodate security aspects as applicable to on-premises, cloud, and container deployments must be considered right from the beginning. A security mindset must be inculcated among cross-functional teams.

Skilled manpower continues to be a challenge in the DevSecOps area. The author personally interviewed scores of candidates for open positions in his team and found that many engineers have restricted themselves to mere tool configuration and usage, without much experience at all in writing substantial scripts and implementing tools from scratch or understanding the underlying principles. It is also observed that some engineers continue to work in older waterfall methodologies and tools, without much exposure to the latest trends in the industry. Organizations, particularly the large, well-established ones must learn to quickly adopt newer technologies and train their personnel for the change. It is hard to drive change, but the risk of obsolescence should be enough motivation to move with the industry.

Another major challenge is the budget allotted for DevSecOps. The higher management may not always see the value or the complexity of the DevSecOps tasks, resulting in understaffed DevSecOps teams and inadequate tooling infrastructure. In such cases, it may help if the first-line managers and technical leads of DevSecOps teams meet with the higher management to impress upon the critical value that the DevSecOps methodologies provide and the complexities involved in them. It is also helpful to standardize the tool and process usage across large organizations, so that interoperability if needed, is better achieved. Legacy tools can pose challenges in terms of scaling and adapting to growing needs. It is imperative to quickly identify infrastructure that is not able to keep up and replace it with the industry-standard tooling.

FUTURE RESEARCH DIRECTIONS

The Software Engineering journey will of course not stop at DevSecOps and full-stack engineering. A hot area that is still evolving is implementing DevSecOps for Artificial Intelligence products and using Artificial Intelligence for DevSecOps. Machine Learning is the mortar of modernization and is becoming more and more ubiquitous. Machine Learning approaches can be used to detect security vulnerabilities and bugs in general. Analyzing the logs from the tools using AI techniques can help improve the quality of the tools – an area that can benefit from more research. There is also ample scope for building tools to integrate security aspects into the pipelines.

CONCLUSION

This chapter briefly examined the evolution of the Software Engineering domain into today's DevSecOps, presenting important tools, techniques, and observations, all along. Several aspects of Software Engineering have transformed drastically over the last three decades. For instance, the simple 'cron' in the Unix systems has now become a full-blown Continuous Integration engine acting as the backbone of the DevSecOps revolution. The chapter also identified a few challenges and solutions to address them. The domain continues to evolve further and holds plenty of promise for the future.

ACKNOWLEDGMENT

The author gratefully acknowledges the experience gained from various software organizations that was instrumental in writing this chapter.

REFERENCES

Artac, M., Borovssak, T., Di Nitto, E., Guerriero, M., & Tamburri, D. A. (2017, May). DevOps: introducing infrastructure-as-code. In *2017 IEEE/ACM 39th International Conference on Software Engineering Companion (ICSE-C)* (pp. 497-498). IEEE. 10.1109/ICSE-C.2017.162

Banica, L., Radulescu, M., Rosca, D., & Hagiu, A. (2017). Is DevOps another Project Management Methodology? *Informações Econômicas*, *21*(3), 39–51. doi:10.12948/issn14531305/21.3.2017.04

Bucena, I., & Kirikova, M. (2017). Simplifying the DevOps Adoption Process. BIR Workshops.

Chen, L. (2018, April). Microservices: architecting for continuous delivery and DevOps. In *2018 IEEE International Conference on Software Architecture (ICSA)* (pp. 39-397). IEEE. 10.1109/ICSA.2018.00013

Cito, J., Wettinger, J., Lwakatare, L. E., Borg, M., & Li, F. (2018, March). Feedback from Operations to Software Development—A DevOps Perspective on Runtime Metrics and Logs. In *International Workshop on Software Engineering Aspects of Continuous Development and New Paradigms of Software Production and Deployment* (pp. 184-195). Springer.

Dyer, M. (1980). The management of software engineering, Part IV: Software development practices. *IBM Systems Journal*, *19*(4), 451–465. doi:10.1147j.194.0451

Erich, F. M. A., Amrit, C., & Daneva, M. (2017). A qualitative study of DevOps usage in practice. *Journal of Software: Evolution and Process*, *29*(6), e1885.

Feitelson, D. G., Frachtenberg, E., & Beck, K. L. (2013). Development and deployment at Facebook. *IEEE Internet Computing*, *17*(4), 8–17. doi:10.1109/MIC.2013.25

Jiménez, M., Castaneda, L., Villegas, N. M., Tamura, G., Müller, H. A., & Wigglesworth, J. (2018, March). DevOps round-trip engineering: Traceability from dev to ops and back again. In *International Workshop on Software Engineering Aspects of Continuous Development and New Paradigms of Software Production and Deployment* (pp. 73-88). Springer. 10.29007/gq5x

Kaiser, A. K. (2018). Introduction to DevOps. In *Reinventing ITIL® in the Age of DevOps* (pp. 1–35). Berkeley, CA: Apress. doi:10.1007/978-1-4842-3976-6_1

Li, Z., Zhang, Y., & Liu, Y. (2017). Towards a full-stack DevOps environment (platform-as-a-service) for cloud-hosted applications. *Tsinghua Science and Technology*, *22*(01), 1–9. doi:10.1109/TST.2017.7830891

Lwakatare, L. E., Karvonen, T., Sauvola, T., Kuvaja, P., Olsson, H. H., Bosch, J., & Oivo, M. (2016, January). Towards DevOps in the embedded systems domain: Why is it so hard? In *2016 49th Hawaii International Conference on System Sciences (HICSS)* (pp. 5437-5446). IEEE.

Myrbakken, H., & Colomo-Palacios, R. (2017, October). DevSecOps: a multivocal literature review. In *International Conference on Software Process Improvement and Capability Determination* (pp. 17-29). Springer. 10.1007/978-3-319-67383-7_2

Rahman, A. A. U., & Williams, L. (2016, May). Software security in DevOps: synthesizing practitioners' perceptions and practices. In *2016 IEEE/ACM International Workshop on Continuous Software Evolution and Delivery (CSED)* (pp. 70-76). IEEE. 10.1145/2896941.2896946

Sánchez-Gordón, M., & Colomo-Palacios, R. (2018, October). Characterizing DevOps Culture: A Systematic Literature Review. In *International Conference on Software Process Improvement and Capability Determination* (pp. 3-15). Springer. 10.1007/978-3-030-00623-5_1

Savor, T., Douglas, M., Gentili, M., Williams, L., Beck, K., & Stumm, M. (2016, May). Continuous deployment at Facebook and OANDA. In *2016 IEEE/ACM 38th International Conference on Software Engineering Companion (ICSE-C)* (pp. 21-30). IEEE. 10.1145/2889160.2889223

Stahl, D., Martensson, T., & Bosch, J. (2017, August). Continuous practices and DevOps: beyond the buzz, what does it all mean? In *2017 43rd Euromicro Conference on Software Engineering and Advanced Applications (SEAA)* (pp. 440-448). IEEE. 10.1109/SEAA.2017.8114695

Sureshchandra, K., & Shrinivasavadhani, J. (2008, August). Moving from waterfall to agile. In Agile 2008 conference (pp. 97-101). IEEE. doi:10.1109/Agile.2008.49

Van Der Hoek, A., Carzaniga, A., Heimbigner, D., & Wolf, A. L. (1998). *A reusable, distributed repository for configuration management policy programming.* Univ. Colorado, Boulder, Tech. Rep. CU-CS-864-98.

Wiedemann, A., & Wiesche, M. (2018). Are you ready for DevOps? Required skill set for DevOps teams. *Proceedings of the European Conference on Information Systems.*

ADDITIONAL READING

Allen, L., Fernandez, G., Kane, K., Leblang, D., Minard, D., & Posner, J. (1993). ClearCase MultiSite: Supporting geographically-distributed software development. In *Software Configuration Management* (pp. 194–214). Berlin, Heidelberg: Springer.

Bartusevics, A., & Novickis, L. (2015). Models for implementation of software configuration management. *Procedia Computer Science*, *43*, 3–10. doi:10.1016/j.procs.2014.12.002

Dyck, A., Penners, R., & Lichter, H. (2015, May). Towards definitions for release engineering and DevOps. In *2015 IEEE/ACM 3rd International Workshop on Release Engineering* (pp. 3-3). IEEE. 10.1109/RELENG.2015.10

Mohan, V., & Othmane, L. B. (2016, August). SecDevOps: Is it a marketing buzzword?-mapping research on security in DevOps. In *2016 11th International Conference on Availability, Reliability and Security (ARES)* (pp. 542-547). IEEE.

Rahman, A. A. U., & Williams, L. (2016, May). Software security in DevOps: synthesizing practitioners' perceptions and practices. In *2016 IEEE/ACM International Workshop on Continuous Software Evolution and Delivery (CSED)* (pp. 70-76). IEEE. 10.1145/2896941.2896946

Schwägerl, F., Buchmann, T., Uhrig, S., & Westfechtel, B. (2015, February). Towards the integration of model-driven engineering, software product line engineering, and software configuration management. In *2015 3rd International Conference on Model-Driven Engineering and Software Development (MODELSWARD)* (pp. 1-14). IEEE.

Ur Rahman, A. A., & Williams, L. (2016, April). Security practices in DevOps. In *Proceedings of the Symposium and Bootcamp on the Science of Security* (pp. 109-111). ACM. 10.1145/2898375.2898383

Wiedemann, A., Forsgren, N., Wiesche, M., Gewald, H., & Krcmar, H. (2019). The DevOps Phenomenon. *Queue*, *17*(2), 40.

Williams, L. (2018, May). Continuously integrating security. In *Proceedings of the 1st International Workshop on Security Awareness from Design to Deployment* (pp. 1-2). ACM.

Yasar, H. (2017, August). Implementing Secure DevOps assessment for highly regulated environments. In *Proceedings of the 12th International Conference on Availability, Reliability and Security* (p. 70). ACM. 10.1145/3098954.3105819

KEY TERMS AND DEFINITIONS

Artificial Intelligence: An area of Computer Science that involves writing programs that can do things that would otherwise require human intelligence.

Everything as Code: A concept that everything that is needed to implement the software lifecycle can be treated as code, for example, pipeline as code.

Machine Learning: A branch of Artificial Intelligence which involves writing programs that can identify patterns, learn from data, and make predictions.

Pipeline as Code: Use a programming language to specify what needs to happen in the pipeline and version the file containing this 'pipeline program' along with the source code, so that it is much more maintainable.

Shift-Left: Assuming that the software lifecycle is drawn from left to right in chronological order, move certain aspects such as testing and security, which were previously done towards the end, to the earlier phases of the software development lifecycle.

Source Code Branch: An artifact in a version control system such as Git that allows parallel and independent development in the same files, unbeknownst to each other, until the branches merge.

Workflow: A series of processes through which software code changes need to go through from conception to product completion.

Chapter 2
Fuzzy Ontology for Requirements Determination and Documentation During Software Development

Priti Srinivas Sajja

 https://orcid.org/0000-0002-9676-0885
Sardar Patel University, India

Rajendra A. Akerkar
Western Norway Research Institute, Norway

ABSTRACT

Every business has an underlying information system. Quality and creditability of a system depend mainly on provided requirements. Good quality requirements of a system increase the degree of quality of the system. Hence, requirements determinations is of prime importance. Inadequate and misunderstood requirements are major problems in requirements determination. Major stakeholders of the requirements are non-computer professional users, who may provide imprecise, vague, and ambiguous requirements. Further, the system development process may be partly automated and based on platform such as web or Semantic Web. In this case, a proper ontology to represent requirements is needed. The chapter proposes a fuzzy RDF/XML-based ontology to document various requirements. A generic architecture of requirements management system is also provided. To demonstrate the presented approach, a case of student monitoring and learning is presented with sample software requirements specifications and interfaces to collect requirements. The chapter concludes with advantages, applications, and future enhancements.

DOI: 10.4018/978-1-7998-1863-2.ch002

Copyright © 2020, IGI Global. Copying or distributing in print or electronic forms without written permission of IGI Global is prohibited.

INTRODUCTION

The quality of any software depends on the requirements considered during the development of the software. Requirements generally provide a basic skeleton of the software. The document containing well-formed requirements serve the basis for all phases of the software development activity. The inclusion of good quality requirements in the software requirement specifications leads towards good quality software. After proper analysis phase, once requirements are collected, analyzed and documented; a Software Requirements Specification (SRS) will be prepared. The SRS will be useful at the beginning of the design phase as well as at the end of the design phase to test whether the specified requirements are accommodated in the proposed design or not. Coding, testing and evaluation of the software are also done according to the requirements.

The requirements often contain imprecision and vagueness within them. Further, the importance of each requirement is different and affected by various parameters such as requirement initiator's (who has initiated the requirement) mindset, cost of adding the requirements, loss due to missing of the requirements, the priority of the requirements, etc. Such important but vague criteria can be added as a fuzzy tag to each requirement while documenting the requirements with the help of fuzzy logic. Fuzzy logic, with the virtue of fuzzy membership function, can efficiently handle such vagueness and impression in computer systems. In this scenario, there is a need for a documentation ontology that documents requirements on the Web platform and manages the fuzziness associated with it. In contrast to traditional knowledge-based approaches, e.g. formal specification languages, ontologies seem to be well suited for an evolutionary approach to the specification of requirements and domain knowledge (Wouters, Deridder, & Van Paesschen, 2000). Moreover, ontologies can be used to support requirements management and traceability.

Besides, varying requirements and evolving solutions are important challenges during the software development process. Agile software development is the way to tackle these challenges by adopting methods based on iterative and incremental development. The challenges are similar in the area of ontology engineering. Several situations ontology development is a continuous and collaborative task.

The proposed chapter introduces the current scenario and sets the necessary technical background of ontology, knowledge engineering and fuzzy logic in section 1 and section 2. After that, the chapter documents related work in the area of ontology, fuzzy logic, and use of ontology in software development activities with general observations and limitations. The related work is documented in section 3 of the chapter. The section also summarizes the survey on work done by presenting the observations and characteristics. Section 4 of the chapter proposes a fuzzy ontology for requirements determination. The section introduces various components of requirements with the necessary description along with the graphical representation of the components to highlight the relationship between them. An RDF/XML structure is proposed for the requirements documentation in section 4. A generic architecture to manage the fuzzy ontology repository along with a knowledge base and other components are also illustrated here. Section 5 discusses a case of a student's learning and monitoring system and presents sample software requirements specification with the requirements documented in the RDF/XML format and an interface screen for the acquisition of requirements. Section 5 also presents the fuzzy membership functions used for the experimental system. Section 6 presents advantages, applications and future directions based on the proposed approach.

FUNDAMENTALS

Software Engineering, Knowledge Engineering and Ontology

Ontology deals with the study of various objects, attributes and relationships that exist in the domain of interests. Ontology can be considered as the representation and explicit conceptualization of vocabularies such as entities, sub-entities, relations and properties in a domain of interest. With the help of such a formal definition, it is possible to represent a situation in an efficient manner. Proper designing of ontology in a given domain does not help only in the conceptualization of the domain entities but also provides a framework/structure to store knowledge about the domain. Ontology is a great tool not only for describing the domain but also for managing the domain knowledge. The ontology can be considered as a formal set of vocabularies, symbols and/or a model/schema in a predefined framework with linked data. Both computer science and philosophy domain identify ontology as *"the nature of being"*. In 1995, computer scientist Tom Gruber (1995) used the term ontology and introduced it as a means of specification of conceptualization. A formal definition of ontology as given by Mike Uschold and Michael Gruninger (1996) is quoted below:

Ontology is the term used to refer to the shared understanding of some domain of interest which may be used as a unifying framework to solve the above problems in the above-described manner.

For ontology representation in a machine-interpretable way, different languages exist. Ontology languages are typically declarative languages based on either first-order logic or on description logic. Ontology languages based on first-order logic have high expressive power, but computational properties such as decidability are not always achieved due to the complexity of reasoning. The most popular language based on description logic is OWL DL, which has attractive and well-understood computational properties (Akerkar R., 2009). Another relevant language in Ontological Engineering is the Resource Description Framework (RDF). RDF was originally meant to represent metadata about web resources, but it can also be used to link information stored in any information source with semantics defined in the ontology. The basic construction in RDF is an <Object, Attribute, Value> triplet: an object O has an attribute A with value V. A RDF-triplet corresponds to the relationship that could be written as <O, A, V>.

Importance of Ontology

Well defined vocabularies about entities, their types and their inter-relationships are always helpful in avoiding misunderstanding and communicating the basic objectives of the business. Ontology helps in enhancing communication between key-objects and key people of the organization. This is one of the major reasons to develop ontology. An ontology defines the requirements, situations and goals in a formal manner; which is easy to follow and communicate. Especially, requirements documented in proper ontology support and accelerate the system development process also. Further, the interoperability of the entities and concepts is also supported by ontology. Once an ontology is defined, tested and utilized, it can be reused in a similar situation for future decision making, problem-solving and learning. Various advantages of ontology are illustrated in Table 1.

Software Engineering and Knowledge Engineering

The field of software engineering provides guidelines for the development of software. There are many models and approaches suggested for the development of software systems as described in a review paper of Isabel M. del Aquila et al. (2014). In spite of the help offered by the established approaches and models, systems development is partly an art. Higher-level systems dealing with tacit knowledge such as expert systems and other intelligent systems face many problems related to the acquisition of domain knowledge, representing and inferring the knowledge for problem-solving. Many researchers have provided development models for such a knowledge-based system (Akerkar & Sajja, 2009). A new disciplined also has evolved namely knowledge engineering in the field of knowledge engineering which considers the application of various software development techniques as well as knowledge acquisition, knowledge representation and its use in co-operative form (Studer, Benjamins, & Fensela, 1998). The field considers the techniques, approaches, and models for software development for knowledge-based systems development. It

Table 1. Various advantages of using ontology

Documentation and consistency	Ontology helps in modeling domain knowledge by modeling concepts, entities and their relationships.
Communication	An ontology may be formally defined and shared among the beneficiaries with clear understanding thus leaving a little scope of miscommunication. Meaning of objects, a possible relationship between the objects, and intended applications of the ontology are well defined at the time of ontology development; which leads to filling the gap of communication.
Inter-operability	Well documented ontology enables easy and smooth machine processing and helps in exchanging data without ambiguity.
Reusability and future use	Content once documented in a form of a suitable ontology, can be used for predefined applications and also can be extended or reused for similar applications without much change. It is advisable to go for modular and loosely coupled representation of content, so a component (or a module) can easily detach/attached as per need. Well documented concepts represented in the proper ontology can be reused many times in the future for learning, training, knowledge representation, and machine processing. Another key factor is the flexibility of ontologies. With information integration as a major use case, ontologies are well-suited to combine information from various sources and infer new facts based on this. The flexibility permits to widen existing ontologies very straight forward, thus fostering the reuse of existing work.
Ease of use and testing	An Ontology component undergoes thorough testing while its development phase and an integrated higher level ontology are built using such well-tested modules resulting in a good quality upper-level ontology. Concepts described via such ontology are comparatively error-free and have good quality.

can also consider the knowledge-oriented development of a typical (non-knowledge based) system. Figure 1 represents the relationship between the fields.

Software engineering as knowledge-based systems together can be applied in many ways. The broad categories for the same can be given as (i) use of software

Figure 1. Knowledge engineering

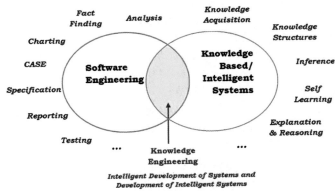

engineering guidelines to develop knowledge-based/intelligent systems; (ii) use of intelligent systems to invent new guidelines for software engineering; and (iii) a true hybrid manner, where intelligent systems are developed in an intelligent manner. It should be noted that both the fields have some similarities, which can help each other in evolving better for mutual advantages. Further, most of the systems use Web as a platform, where ontology can be considered as an effective tool for content representation. Considering these facts, in this chapter, we proposed the use of ontology as a knowledge representation tool, which will be helpful in systems development, specifically for the determination and management of the requirements related to the software system.

Fuzzy Logic

The term fuzzy logic was proposed by Lotfi Zadeh (1965). Fuzzy logic is a logic-based on fuzzy sets. Fuzzy sets are the special sets without a rigid boundary or sets without boundaries. Belongingness of an entity to a set is generally well defined and crisp in nature. That is, a given item belongs to a set is determined by the definition of the set; and there is no vagueness in it. An element, if belongs to a set, then it completely belongs to the set. Otherwise, it completely does not belong to the set. In any case, the belongingness is crisp and Boolean. That is the nature of a typical crisp set. However, the fuzzy sets talk about the partial or graded membership of an element to a set; hence incorporating multiple values between two extreme crisp values 0 and 1. To determine such partial membership, a specially designed function is utilized; which is known as fuzzy membership function.

An example of crisp and fuzzy membership functions for various fuzzy membership functions such as "Hot Temperature", "Cold Temperature", etc. is illustrated in Figure 2.

Figure 2 illustrates the crisp set of hot temperature which is by definition bivalent. That is, if the temperature is greater than or equal to 25 (in degree centigrade), then the temperature is 'Hot' otherwise not. That means temperature value 24.99-degree centigrade is not 'Hot', and similarly temperature value 13 degree centigrade is also not 'Hot'. The major difficulty with such typical bivalent logic is that, both the temperature values are considered in the same 'not hot' category and treated at par. The first value of temperature, 24.99-degree is nearly 25-degree and we normally considered that as a 'Hot'! Fuzzy logic helps to reduce such rigidness in belongingness of the candidate into a given set by considering set without boundary and suggest partial or graded membership to the set. As shown in the membership function illustrated in Figure 2, the 'Hot' temperature considers temperature values from 25-degree centigrade to 35-degree centigrade and provides multiple degrees of belongingness for various temperature values provided within the range.

Figure 2. Crisp and fuzzy membership functions for temperature

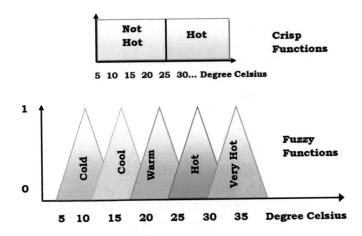

Figure 2 also illustrates other fuzzy function for 'Cold', 'Cool', 'Warm', and 'Very Hot' temperature using triangular membership functions. Since all the functions are about the Temperature in a common domain and return values between 0 and 1, they can be presented as an integrated chart. Slight change in the triangular membership function for 'Hot' temperature, 'Slightly Hot' membership function can be generated. Similarly, many other variations of the previously defined membership functions can easily be generated.

It is obvious that human beings are very comfortable with such linguistic representation of situations such as 'Hot temperature', 'High speed' and 'Tall man'; however, machines do not welcome such linguistic and native words. Machines are more comfortable with values. Because the membership functions are efficiently converting the linguistic parameters into its equivalent values, a human can use such native words in decision making. A linguistic variable can be defined as follows.

*A **linguistic variable** on a fuzzy set defined on universe U is characterized by a four-tuple (X,T,U,G,S) where X is the name of the **variable**, T is the set of terms of X, U is the universe of discourse, G is a grammar to generate the name of the terms, and S is a semantic rule for assigning meaning to a term.*

Use of the linguistic words in logic opens up the possibility to interact with machines like human beings. This is possible with the help of fuzzy rules. Figure 3 illustrates some simple fuzzy rules associated with the fuzzy sets and membership functions illustrated in Figure 2. Figure 3 also shows a general form of fuzzy rule.

Such multiple rules are encoded and used as the major content of the knowledge base of the fuzzy logic-based system. Along with such knowledge base and meta-data for the fuzzy membership functions (for the meaning of linguistic variables used in fuzzy rules), the user interface, inference mechanism, reasoning and explanation facilities are also available with the fuzzy logic-based systems.

Exemplifying Fuzziness in Ontologies

Formalisms regarding fuzzy ontologies were introduced to represent semantic knowledge-based on vague concepts and relations (Straccia, 2006). A number of approaches have developed to implement those formalisms into OWL-based ontologies. Some approaches emphasize on building precise OWL ontologies formally defining the common elements of fuzzy set theory to be later populated with instances representing the fuzzy axioms and elements of specific domain ontology. Extending the OWL language to support fuzzy definitions is one strategy for building fuzzy ontologies. While some approaches (Stoilos, Stamou, & Pan, 2010) propose extending the standard building blocks of the OWL language, others use the OWL standard tools to represent such fuzzy information. However, the work on Fuzzy OWL2 (Bobillo & Straccia, 2011) is the most prominent effort in this area. It uses OWL2 annotation properties to encode fuzziness. The use of annotation properties makes fuzzy ontologies compatible with OWL2 management tools (editors, programmatic environments, etc.) and enables crisp OWL-based reasoners to compute inferences over this sort of ontologies discarding the fuzzy elements. Moreover, Fuzzy OWL2 also offers a general Java parser as a base for building specific parsers for translating from Fuzzy OWL2 syntax to the syntax of any fuzzy DL reasoner.

RELATED WORK

Requirements determination in software engineering plays a vital role. Well determined requirements are the skeleton of the systems being developed. The quality

Figure 3. Sample fuzzy rules

```
If {Temperature is 'Hot'} then { Switch on AC_machine on 'High' mode}
If {Temperature is not 'Hot'}  then { Switch on AC_machine on 'Fan'
mode}

The general form is
If { X is 'A' }  then { Y is 'B' }
```

of the system directly depends on the quality of the requirements finalized for the system under devolvement. If the right requirements are considered for software, the purpose of the development will be served and users will get the required software. The requirements and other knowledge are acquired from multiple users and various sources in different forms/structures. Most of the software development projects suffer from the problem of communication and getting the right requirements from various categories of users. The following are the major common problems while the determination of requirements.

- Users are not aware of the requirements or users are not ready to provide the requirements- because of a lack of knowledge of advanced technology, lack of domain knowledge, and inability to foresee the change required in the business. Further, users may not know about their own requirements. They are habituated with exiting systems and technologies; so they do not want to change the working of the system.
- Users can not articulate their requirements correctly - users may want to share their requirements and expectations from the system; but cannot explain their needs effectively to the systems analyst.
- Requirements are not understood correctly- the requirements provided by the users may not be properly understood by the systems analyst in its intended manner. He may understand something else and communicate different requirements to the team of programmers. Programmers and other developers can also get the requirements in the wrong manner.

Above these, if the platform used for the development is Web or the semantic web, problems related to representation and documentation of the requirements also arise. Shared conceptualization of ideas (here requirements) can be helpful. This leads to the utilization of suitable ontology to document and communicate requirements. If software requirements are specified using a proper ontology, not only for experts and users but for machines also it would be easy to work with such requirements. Documentation, sharing, using and matching of requirements (with similar requirements of the other software project), etc. operations would become efficient and fruitful with the adaption of ontology in requirements engineering.

A lot of work is done in this area to resolve the above-mentioned issues and to use ontology as a requirements determination tool. Ontology for documentation of requirements is used by Jinxin Lin, et al., (1996) for the engineering domain. The authors have proposed ontology for engineering design with an objective to provide a common and generic ontology that can be used by many experts. A tool is also proposed by Michael Lang and Jim Duggan (2001) to manage requirements in a collaborative manner. In this work, the major importance is given to the communicability of the software requirements specification between various developers. An experiment on creating domain ontology in the area of public administration is proposed by Graciela Brusa, et al., (2008). The paper also discusses the problem of semantic heterogeneity while working in a large domain such as public administration.

A broad architecture of ontology-based engineering of requirements is also proposed by Katja Siegemund, et al., (2011). As per the claim of the authors, it is a meta-model capable of representing requirements into suitable ontology and checking for consistency. S. Murugesh and A. Jaya (2015) represented requirements in a suitable ontology and presents a mechanism to check the consistency of the requirements represented in the OWL DL form. The domain of interest considered for experimenting with the proposed research work is Automatic Teller Machine transactions. Hans-Jörg Happel and Stefan Seedorf (2006) have demonstrated the use of ontology during various phases of software engineering. The authors could prove that the use of ontology may be costly at the initial stage and also requires high efforts in the development of the ontology; however, later it is proved as cost-beneficial with its reusability.

To encode security-related requirements, many authors have used ontology. Their contributions can be seen in a survey paper by Amina Souag, et al., (2012). The paper articulates the work of more than 40 researchers in the field of ontologies for security requirements. The authors could classify the requirements into 8 different groups and discusses sample ontology for the groups. The work also presents a summary of various types of requirements ontologies with their comparative analysis.

The use of ontology for knowledge representation has started way back. Nicola Guarino and Pierdaniele Giaretta (**1995**) studied ontologies and large knowledge base together and explained the application of ontology in the domain of knowledge representation. The incorporation of fuzzy logic in ontology is experimented by Silvia Calegari and Davide Ciucci (**2006.** They have proposed a mechanism to generate a fuzzy value and assigning it to a suitable label used in the ontology by software. The authors have suggested the fuzzy modeling in two ways: linguistic and precise. Chang-Shing Lee, et. al., (**2005**) have used fuzzy ontology for news summarization. Jeff Pan, et al., presented the use of fuzzy logic in SWRL ontology. Verónica Castañeda, et al., (**2010**) have proposed the use of ontology in requirement engineering. However, fuzzy logic is not incorporated in their work. Priti Srinivas Sajja (**2014**) has also used fuzzy logic for XML based ontology to represent knowledge for a web-based expert system. A method for automatic extraction of attributes of concepts, leading to the automatic creation of ontologies was proposed by G. Cui, et. al., (**2009**). On the other hand, P. Alexopoulos, et al., (**2012**) proposed a method to convert a "crisp" ontology in a fuzzy one. Ismail Muhammad (**2016**) proposed a framework to create ontology in a semi-automatic manner and use it for requirements testing. This is a case of post-conversion of the available requirements documents into suitable ontology. Further, test case generation is also possible with the help of ontology as claimed by Tarasov et al. **(2016).** The ontology layer cake model is also proposed to deal with the specified ontology in natural language as mentioned by Abel Browarnik and Oded Maimon **(2015).**

Verification of requirements via pre-specified ontology is experimented by Dong, Q. et al. **(2012),** in which verification of the requirements is done from the acquired and documented requirements in a proper ontology. Work by Dzung, D. V., and Ohnishi, A **(2009)** extracts the key elements form the set of requirements and verifies them for their practical feasibility using natural language processing. The latest work in the ontology domain is done by Rizvi, S et al. **(2018),** which restricts itself to technical documents information to identify users' behavior using the virtue of ontology. However, the approach does not handle vagueness and imprecision. Work of Oriol X., Teniente E. **(2018)** describes a framework of the ontology-based discovery of various data services. This is purely related to data retrieval.

From the above mentioned related work and the discussion on underlying concepts, the observed advantages of using ontology for requirements determination are as follows:

- Documentation of requirements
- Communication of requirements
- Sharing of requirements
- Traceability of requirements
- Automatic use and matching of requirements
- Automatic testing the software product and cross-verification of requirements with developed source code
- Partial management of ambiguous requirements
- Dynamic requirements

These advantages are more strengthened with the use of fuzzy logic. As the field of software development is an art as well as science, it deals with more linguistic, uncertain and ambiguous knowledge related to the process of software development. The situation is manageable in comparison with the earlier scenarios, where software development was more art and less science. Currently, it has become a bit systematic and sophisticated because of available tools and technological advancements. Further, users have also become familiar with various systems/software in a given domain. Still, the major requirement providers are non-computer professionals. Though they may not aware of the automation and popular computing advancements, it is comparatively difficult for them to provide a clear requirement. Inadequate specification, changing requirements and requirements that are not completely defined (and may have chances to be interpreted in different ways) can be handled with the notion of a linguistic fuzzy variable. Section 4 proposes how fuzzy logic can be incorporated with ontology to determine requirements.

FUZZY ONTOLOGY FOR REQUIREMENTS DETERMINATION

Requirements determination typically involves requirements anticipation, requirements investigation through fact-finding techniques and requirements specification in suitable representation structure. Anticipated requirements are common and standard requirements that are ordinary and typical in nature. The anticipated requirements save time and effort, which is normally spent at the investigation phase. For requirements investigation time and effort must be given for the acquisition of requirements through fact-finding methods such as interviews, questionnaires, record reviews and observations. However, this effort will earn some extraordinary requirements. Whether anticipated or investigated, requirements once acquired need to be specified in various structures and ontology for its safekeeping, communication for further development and other future uses. To document requirements in ontology following components may be considered.

- **Requirements Statement:** Description about the requirements in textual format. The text may use one or more fuzzy linguistic variables, which later on can be interpreted with the help of associated fuzzy membership functions.
- **Requirement Author:** Name of the expert or user who has suggested the requirements.
- **Requirement Subject:** Subject or the requirement suggested.
- **Requirement Section:** The suggested requirements may be applicable to a particular section or a block of the organization/business. It may also be possible that more than one section can be benefited by the requirements or the requirement is truly generic in nature.
- **Requirement Identification Number:** A unique identification number needs to be given to each specified requirement for ease of access and documentation. The identification number can be made by combining subfields/parts of the above-mentioned components such as requirement author, subject and sections.
- **Requirement Class Hierarchy:** The suggested requirement may be part of or type of upper level/generic requirements.

- **Requirement Type:** The suggested requirement may be an anticipated requirement, quality requirement, a security requirement, network requirement, interface requirement, etc. Further, it can be generic, multi-disciplinary or hierarchical in nature.
- **Requirement Date of Last Used:** The last used date of the requirement suggested. This will be helpful in auto-delete and back up procedures. Requirements that are no longer in use can be automatically shifted to the back up to create additional space to accommodate more latest requirements and temporary workspace, if required.
- **Frequency of Uses:** This is a simple counter. Each time the requirement is utilized, the counter is incremented. The requirements with the maximum utilization (as per the value of the counter for each requirement) can be proactively presented to the users/developers for consideration.
- **Effect of the Requirement Use:** This is really a fuzzy field. In many cases, it is difficult to describe the effect of the use of a requirement in values but description. Fuzzy linguistic variables can be used here for demonstrating the effect of using the requirements at an organizational level as well as the individual level.

Besides the above components, the requirements ontology may encompass sub-section names, product/service for which the requirement is meant, identification numbers of other similar requirements and some important comments on the requirements.

The above components are organized and represented in an RDF/XML structure to demonstrate the requirements ontology as shown in Figure 4.

The RDF is known as Resource Description Framework, which is used to represent information on the Web platform. The World Wide Web Consortium (W3C.org) has published a recommended set of syntax and specification for the use of RDF/XML[1]. We have added fuzzy tags within the RDF/XML schema as per the need and nature of the application. With such use of fuzzy RDF/XML, not only ontology-based advantages for knowledge engineering can be achieved, but advantages of the Web and semantic web platform can also be achieved. The graphical representation of the structure of the proposed requirement ontology is shown in Figure 5.

As per the structure shown in Figure 4, many requirements are documented with the required fuzzy variable embedded in it. All the requirements are placed at a common repository for centralized access on a need to multiple users. Along with the requirements repository, there is a need for a fuzzy rule base and fuzzy membership function definitions. Fuzzy membership definitions are used in conjunction with the fuzzy linguistic variables used within requirements. Fuzzy rules are needed to access and manage requirements within the centralized repository. The fuzzy

Figure 4. RDF/XML structure to demonstrate the requirements ontology

```
<?xml version="1.0"?>

<!-- RDF Schema Candidate Recommendation (27 March, 2000)
Section 2.3.2.1 -->

<rdf:RDF xml:lang="en"
        xmlns:rdf="http://www.w3.org/1999/02/22-rdf-syntax-ns#"
        xmlns:rdfs="http://www.w3.org/2000/01/rdf-schema#">
<rdf:Descriptionrdf:>
<dc:Title>Requirements Obntology</dc:Title>
<dc:Req_Id> Requirements Identification </dc:Req_Id>
<dc: Req_Author> Requirements Author </dc:Req_Author>
<dc: Req_Subject> Requirements Subject </dc:Req_Subject>
<dc: Req_Section> Requirements Section</dc:Req_Section>
<dc: Req_Class> Requirements Class </dc:Req_Class>
<dc: Req_Type> Requirements Type</dc:Req_Type>
<dc: Req_Date_Use> Requirements Date _Used </dc:Req_Date_Use>
<dc: Req_Frequency> Requirements Frequency </dc:Req_Frequency>
<dc: Req_Effect> Requirements Effect </dc:Req_Effect>
<dc: Req_Path> Requirements Path </dc:Req_Path>
<dc: Req_Alt_Path> Requirements Alternative Path </dc:Req_Alt_Path>
<dc: Req_Trgg> Requirements Trigger </dc:Req_Trgg>
<dc: Req_Pre> Requirements Precondition </dc:Req_Pre>
<dc: Req_Exe> Requirements Exceptions </dc:Req_Exe>
<dc: Req_Other> Requirements Other Information Path </dc:Req_Other>
.......
.......
</rdf:Description>
</rdf:RDF>
```

Figure 5. Graphical representation of the requirements ontology

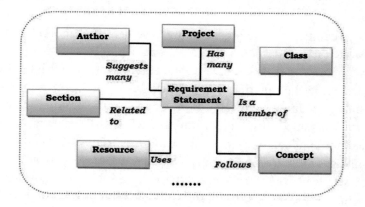

inference mechanism is also required in conjunction with the fuzzy rules. Users such as manager, developer, programmer and testers can use the requirements for the typical development purposes such as documentation of requirements, cross-verification of requirements, reuse of requirements, testing the final product as per the requirements documented, etc. Optionally, an interface facility may be made

Figure 6. General architecture of the requirements ontology management system

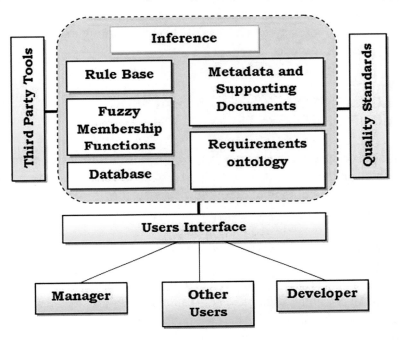

available besides the major components mentioned here. The general architecture of the system is shown in Figure 6. Such an ontology management system keeps track of users, development procedures and resources associated with the development procedures besides the management of the requirements.

As shown in Figure 6, the two major components of the requirements ontology management are namely: (i) the repository of the requirements and (ii) fuzzy rule base. The requirements repository, as stated earlier, acts as a repository of the requirements in the ontology structure presented in the RDF/XML format proposed in this chapter. Independently, it is mere formal documentation of the requirements of the systems being developed. To efficiently access the requirements, to proactively suggest its possible uses and re-uses, and to automatically keep track of the development activities fuzzy rules can be designed. These fuzzy rules are application-specific and can be developed after considering the nature of the systems being developed and requirements are documented. Similarly, the fuzzy membership functions should be defined after documentation of the requirements is completed and the repository of the requirements is developed in a selected ontology. After that, the fuzzy linguistic variables used in the requirements can be defined formally and stored in fuzzy membership functions definition utility for automatic interpretation of fuzzy variables in requirements ontology as well as fuzzy rules. Necessary metadata, quality standards and other requirements of the organization also should be considered while finalizing requirements for the use. To clearly demonstrate the working of the proposed system, a case of students learning monitoring system is discussed in the next section.

DEVELOPMENT OF STUDENTS LEARNING AND MONITORING SYSTEM

In a classical teaching and learning system, students are manually monitored for their learning and understanding. An expert teacher always has an eye on students' ability to learning and applying the knowledge for day to day problem-solving. Teachers know about positive as well as weak points of the students and can provide personalized attention to the required students. To fast-learners, new challenges are also provided with the necessary guidance and to weak-students support during learning is also extended. In the case of distance learning, e-learning and sometimes typical classroom learning, where a number of students is high; such a personalized approach is not possible. A sample set of requirements is articulated for an effective e-learning system that can handle the automatic selection of content with the help of users' profiles and monitors the learning process of students. The general working of the system is as per the architecture shown in Figure 6.

The sample requirements specification with selected fields for the proposed system is given below along with the necessary fuzzy membership functions.

Sample Software Requirements Specification

Purpose of the system: The system documents various learning material as well as users and presents customized learning material as per the users' need and level.

1. **Users:** Administrator, instructor, learner, evaluator and guest (description of each with aliases can be made available here...)
2. **Glossary:** .....Glossary related to the system....
3. Basic functional requirements:
    a. **Management of course material:**
        i. Add course:
            Title Add Course
            Reference Reference if any
            Trigger Request from administrator to add a course with one or more material files
            Precondition The administrator login and no such course is existing

Basic Path A new entry is made in database and path for the material is set

Links between the material and the course are set

Material is assigned categories such as 'High', 'Average' and 'Low'

Access rights for edit and view are provided to the course

Necessary validations are made

Alternative Paths If the course already exists, then a direct path to the course is given

Required validations are made

Post-condition The Reviewer has been added to the database

Exception Paths The operation may not be granted if the course has already existed

The operation may be abandoned at any time

Other Course code, title, prerequisites, author name and material types are added within the necessary database/files

b. Registrations of users
  i. Add user: as per the format shown in add course, this requirement can be documented.
  ii. etc.

c. Report on masters
  i. Reports on learners' strength with their details
  ii. Reports on authors who have added material
  iii. Topic wise list of material added between given dates
  iv. etc.

d. Reports on transactions
  i. ....

e. Present a course material to a learner (as follows)

Title Present Material

Reference Reference if any

Trigger Request from users to see material on an eligible topic

Precondition The users have access to the requested material

Basic Path The requested topic is searched from the database

Users level is determined through a fuzzy membership functions

If users level is low then the material with 'low' label is fetched and presented to the user

Necessary validations are made.

Alternative Paths Users log may be accessed for the last material category seen

Post-condition Users feedback is taken on the material

The material tag may be changed as per the users' feedback by the administrator. A call is raised for the same.

Exception Paths The message is passed to the authors if no such material for the learner's(user's) category is available.

Other --

 f. Learner wise reports

 g. etc.

4. Quality requirements:

  ....

5. Database requirements:

  .....

6. Interface requirements

  .....

7. etc.

The XML/RDF representation of the above requirements is as follows:

```
< ? xml version = "1.0"? >
< !-- RDF Schema .... -->
< rdf:RDF xml:lang = "en"
xmlns:rdf="http://www.w3.org/1999/02/22-rdf-syntax-ns#"
xmlns:rdfs=http://www.w3.org/2000/01/rdf-schema# >
< rdf:Descriptionrdf: >
< dc:Title > Add Course </dc:Title >
< dc: Req_Id > Add_course_01 </dc: Req_Id >
< dc: Req_Author > Administrator </dc: Req_Autho r>
< dc: Req_Subjec t> Functional Add_Course </dc: Req_Subject >
< dc: Req_Section > Functional _General </dc: Req_Section >
< dc: Req_Class > Class_Master </dc: Req_Class >
< dc: Req_Type > Functional </dc: Req_Type >
< dc: Req_Date_Use > "27/07/2016" </dc: Req_Date_Use >
< dc: Req_Frequency >14 </dc: Req_Frequency >
< dc: Req_Effect > Good </dc: Req_Effec t>
< dc: Req_Path > Requirements Path </dc: Req_Path >
< dc: Req_Alt_Path > "path.txt" </dc: Req_Alt_Path >
< dc: Req_Trgg > "trigger_add_course01.txt" </dc: Req_Trgg >
< dc: Req_Pre > "Pre_trigger_add_course01.txt" </dc: Req_Pre >
< dc: Req_Exe > "Exe_trigger_add_course01.txt" </dc: Req_Exe >
< dc: Req_Other > "Other_ trigger_add_course01.txt" </dc: Req_Othe r>
.....
```

.....
< /rdf:Description >
< /rdf:RDF >

The fuzzy membership function used in the above-mentioned sample requirements is about the learner's level and material level. These functions are defined as follows.

Learners' level can be identified as "High", "Average" and "Low". The learners are presented with general questions from the domain for quick answers. Based on the number of correct answers given to the rapid questions in a given time, the speed correctness ratio is calculated. The initial set of questions fired to the users contains questions that are generic and above average level from the domain selected by the users. If the user cannot answers these questions to some efficiency, lower level questions can be selected otherwise higher-level questions are provided. From such exercise, the level of users can be calculated. See Figure 7.

The above requirements with necessary definitions of fuzzy membership functions are well documented in the software requirements specification, which is used as a base to carry out further systems development process. The initial requirements acquisition interface is as shown in Figure 8.

ADVANTAGES, APPLICATIONS AND FUTURE DIRECTIONS

The main stakeholders of the requirements determination about a system are the users of the system. The users, who have requested for system development and who are directly benefited by the system are generally domain experts and not the developers. Such non-computer professionals are key entities (major stack holders) in providing requirements about the system. Many times the requirements are fuzzy, incomplete and uncertain in nature. To correctly acquire requirements, to correctly specify them, to use them in throughout the development process, etc.

Figure 7. Fuzzy membership functions for learner's level

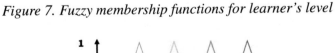
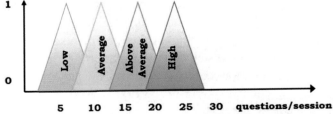

Figure 8. Initial requirements acquisition interface

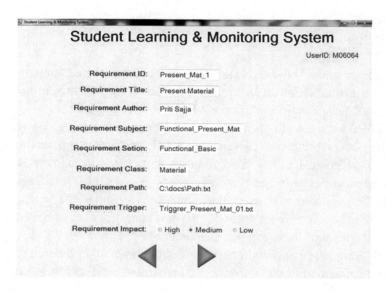

needs an effective representation of the requirements. The use of fuzzy logic helps in documenting requirements in more native form as well as easy to understand them by non-computer professionals. This is the way to directly include the users in the determination of the requirements. Advantages related to the fuzzy logic such as covering a large number of requirements into a small, manageable set of requirements and simultaneously handing of the vagueness of the requirements can be achieved with the proposed approach. Further, if the platform of the semantic web is available, such requirements can be stored and accessed on the web platform automatically with the help of the metadata (semantic) associated with them. Once the requirements are in fuzzy ontology format, not only effective and machine-based assess of them is possible, but automatic searching, merging, interpretation and reuse of such requirements are also possible. Further, the documentation of the requirements specification is more native in nature and hence easy to handle.

In future the interface can be enhanced that interacts with the users, developers and other requirements providers and acquires useful requirements automatically. The system can also provide an auto-generated output of the software requirements specification (SRS) in standard formats such as IEEE. Various innovative algorithms can be developed for automatic matching of the requirements and control the software development procedures on the semantic web platform. It may lead to a general-purpose knowledge acquisition tool that acquires knowledge about a project under development and documents finding in the fuzzy ontology. One may propose a model for guiding software engineering using a fuzzy ontology.

REFERENCES

Akerkar, R. (2009). *Foundations of the semantic web*. London: Alpha Science International Ltd.

Akerkar, R. A., & Sajja, P. S. (2009). *Knowledge Based Systems*. Sudbury, MA: Jones & Bartlett Publishers.

Alexopoulos, P., Wallace, M., Kafentzisi, K., & Askounis, D. (2012). IKARUS-Onto: A methodology to develop fuzzy ontologies from crisp ones. *Knowledge and Information Systems*, *32*(3), 667–695. doi:10.100710115-011-0457-6

Aquila, I., Palma, J., & Tunez, J. (2014). Milestones in software engineering and knowledge engineering history: A comparative review. *The Scientific World Journal*, *2014*, 10. PMID:24624046

Berners-Lee, T., Hendler, J., & Lassila, O. (2001). The Semantic Web. *Scientific American*, *284*(5), 29–37. doi:10.1038cientificamerican0501-34 PMID:11234503

Bobillo, F., & Straccia, U. (2011). Fuzzy ontology representation using OWL 2. *International Journal of Approximate Reasoning*, *52*(7), 1073–1094. doi:10.1016/j.ijar.2011.05.003

Browarnik, A., & Maimon, O. (2015). Departing the ontology layer cake. In J. Zizka, & F. Darena (Eds.), Modern computational models of semantic discovery in natural language (pp. 167-203). IGI Global. doi:10.4018/978-1-4666-8690-8.ch007

Brusa, G., Caliusco, L., & Chiotti, O. (2008). Towards ontological engineering: A process for building a domain ontology from scratch in public administration. *Expert Systems: International Journal of Knowledge Engineering and Neural Networks*, *25*(5), 484–503. doi:10.1111/j.1468-0394.2008.00471.x

Calegari, S., & Ciucci, D. (2006). Integrating fuzzy logic in ontologies. *18th International Conference on Enterprise Information Systems: Databases and Information Systems Integration*, Paphos, Cyprus.

Castaneda, V., Ballejos, L., Caliusco, L., & Galli, R. (2010). The use of ontologies in requirements. *Global Journal of Researches in Engineering*, 2-8.

Chang-Shing, L., Zhi-Wei, J., & Lin-Kai, H. (2005). A fuzzy ontology and its application to news summarization. *IEEE Transactions on Systems, Man, and Cybernetics*, *35*(5), 859–880. doi:10.1109/TSMCB.2005.845032 PMID:16240764

Cui, G., Lu, Q., Li, W., & Chen, Y. (2009). Automatic acquisition of attributes for ontology construction. In L. Wenjie, & M.-A. Diego (Eds.), Computer Processing of Oriental Languages. Language Technology for the Knowledge-based Economy (pp. 248-259). Springer. doi:10.1007/978-3-642-00831-3_23

Dong, Q., Wang, Z., Zhu, W., & He, H. (2012). Capability requirements modeling and verification based on fuzzy ontology. *Journal of Systems Engineering and Electronics*, *23*(1), 78–87. doi:10.1109/JSEE.2012.00011

Dzung, D. V. (2009). Ontology-based reasoning in requirements elicitationon. In *Software Engineering and Formal Methods, 2009 Seventh IEEE International Conference* (pp. 263–272). IEEE.

Gruber, T. (1995). Toward principles for the design of ontologies used for knowledge sharing. *International Journal of Human-Computer Studies*, *43*(5-6), 907–928. doi:10.1006/ijhc.1995.1081

Guarino, N., & Giaretta, P. (1995). Ontologies and knowledge bases: Towards a terminological clarification. In N. Mars (Ed.), Towards Very Large Knowledge Base: Knowledge Building and Knowledge Sharing (pp. 25-32). Amsterdam: IOS Press.

Happel, J., & Seedorf, S. (2006). Applications of ontologies in software engineering. *2nd International Workshop on Semantic Web Enabled Software Engineering*, Athens, USA.

Ismail, M. (2016). Ontology learning from software requirements specification. In *Knowledge engineering and knowledge management* (pp. 251–255). Springer.

Lang, M., & Duggan, J. (2001). A tool to support collaborative software requirements management. *Requirements Engineering*, *6*(3), 161–172. doi:10.1007007660170002

Lin, J., Fox, M., & Bilgic, T. (1996). *A requirement ontology for engineering design*. Toronto: Enterprise Integration Laboratory, University of Toronto.

Murugesh, S., & Jaya, A. (2015). Construction of ontology for software requirements elicitation. *Indian Journal of Science and Technology*, *8*(29). doi:10.17485/ijst/2015/v8i29/86271

Oriol, X. T. E. (2018). An Ontology-Based Framework for Describing Discoverable Data Services. In *Advanced Information Systems Engineering. CAiSE 2018*. Cham: Springer. doi:10.1007/978-3-319-91563-0_14

Pan, J., Stamou, G., Tzouvaras, V., & Horrocks, I. (2005). f-SWRL: A fuzzy extension of SWRL. *Notes in Computer Science*, 829-834.

Rizvi, S. M. (2018). Ontology-based Information Extraction from Technical Documents. In *Proceedings of the 10th International Conference on Agents and Artificial Intelligence (ICAART 2018)* (pp. 493-500). SCITEPRESS – Science and Technology Publications, Lda. 10.5220/0006596604930500

Sajja, P. S. (2014). Knowledge representation using fuzzy XML rules in web based expert system for medical diagnosis. In *Fuzzy Expert Systems for Disease Diagnosis* (pp. 138–167). Hershey, PA: IGI Global.

Siegemund, K., Thomas, E., Zhao, Y., Pan, J., & Assmann, U. (2011). Towards ontology-driven requirements engineering. *10th International Semantic Web Conference*, Bonn, Germany.

Souag, A., Salinesi, C., & Wattiau, I. (2012). Ontologies for security requirements: A literature survey and classification. In *24th International Conference on Advanced Information Systems Engineering*, (pp. 61-69). Gdansk, Poland: Academic Press. 10.1007/978-3-642-31069-0_5

Stoilos, G., Stamou, G., & Pan, J. (2010). Fuzzy extensions of OWL: Logical properties and reduction to fuzzy description logics. *International Journal of Approximate Reasoning*, *51*(6), 656–679. doi:10.1016/j.ijar.2010.01.005

Straccia, U. (2006). A fuzzy description logic for the semantic web. *Capturing Intelligence*, *1*, 73–90. doi:10.1016/S1574-9576(06)80006-7

Studer, R., Benjamins, V., & Fensela, D. (1998). Knowledge engineering: Principles and methods. *Data & Knowledge Engineering*, *25*(1-2), 161–197. doi:10.1016/S0169-023X(97)00056-6

Tarasov, V., Tan, H., Ismail, M., Adlemo, A., & Johansson, M. (2016). Application of inference rules to a software requirements ontology to generate software test cases. In M. Dragoni, M. Poveda-Villalón, & E. Jimenez-Ruiz (Eds.), OWL: Experiences and directions – Reasoner evaluation (pp. 82-94). Springer.

Uschold, M., & Gruninger, M. (1996). Ontologies principles methods and applications. *The Knowledge Engineering Review*, *11*(2), 93–136. doi:10.1017/S0269888900007797

Wouters, B., Deridder, D., & Van Paesschen, E. (2000). The use of ontologies as a backbone for use case management. *14th European Conference on Object-Oriented Programming*, Cannes, France.

Zadeh, L. (1965). Fuzzy sets. *Information and Control*, *8*(3), 338–353. doi:10.1016/S0019-9958(65)90241-X

ADDITIONAL READING

Sure, Y., Staab, S., & Studer, R. (2003). On-To-Knowledge Methodology. In S. Staab & R. Studer (Eds.), *Handbook on Ontologies* (pp. 117–132). Berlin: Springer-Verlag.

KEY TERMS AND DEFINITIONS

Fuzzy Logic: It is a multi-valued logic based on sets without boundary and offers graded membership of an element to such set. Crisp logic always gives binary values say 0 or 1; however, the fuzzy logic provides many values between 0 and 1.

Fuzzy Membership Functions: Fuzzy membership function determines the graded membership of an element to the base fuzzy set.

Fuzzy Ontology: The ontology which uses fuzzy linguistic variables to demonstrate relationships between various objects and attributes.

Ontology: It is a study of various objects, attributes and their relationships that exist in the domain of interests. Ontology can be considered as the representation and explicit conceptualization of vocabularies such as entities, sub-entities, relations and properties in a domain of interest. With the help of such a formal definition, it is possible to represent a situation in an efficient manner.

Ontology Engineer: Ontology engineer is an expert, who is responsible for identifying, acquiring, conceptualizing and representing ontology. He also keeps track of the above-mentioned ontology cycle.

Ontology Life Cycle: Life cycle for typical phases of ontology development such as setting an objective, collection of knowledge, conceptualization, determination of suitable ontology model, knowledge representation into the ontology, evaluation of the ontology, documentation of ontology and sharing ontology.

Requirement Determination: It is the process of anticipating, investigating and specifying the necessary and important features about the system being developed in a predetermined format.

XML/RDF: The RDF is known as Resource Description Framework; XML is defined as eXtensible Markup Language. These tools are used to represent information on Web/Semantic Web platform. The World Wide Web Consortium (W3C.org) has published a recommended set of syntax and specification for the use of RDF/XML.

ENDNOTE

[1]   https://www.w3.org/TR/REC-rdf-syntax/

Chapter 3
Software Effort Estimation for Successful Software Application Development

Syed Mohsin Saif

https://orcid.org/0000-0001-7237-8828
Islamic University of Science and Technology, India

ABSTRACT

The recent advancements in information and communication technology (ICT) have inspired all the operational domains of both public and private sector enterprise to endorse this technology. Software development plays a crucial role in supporting ICT. Software effort estimation serves as a critical factor in software application development, and it helps application development teams to complete the development process on time and within budget. Many developmental approaches have been used for software effort estimation, but most of them were conventional software methods and therefore failed to produce accurate results when it came to web or mobile effort estimation. This chapter explains different types of software applications, software estimation models, the importance of software effort estimation, and challenges faced in software effort estimation.

INTRODUCTION

The current age is the era of information and communication technology (ICT). The diverse ICT enabled modalities has inspired almost all the operational domains of both public and private sector enterprise to endorse this technology. All these advancements made in the field of Information and Communication Technology is

DOI: 10.4018/978-1-7998-1863-2.ch003

Copyright © 2020, IGI Global. Copying or distributing in print or electronic forms without written permission of IGI Global is prohibited.

deployable when there is an appropriate underlying software framework to make it functional. In real essence, it is this software component that has revolutionized the modern age and has also facilitated humankind with its sophisticated serviceability at every corridor of humanity.

The Merriam-Webster dictionary defines software as a set of programs, procedures and related documentation associated with a system known as a computer program (Merriam-Webster). The most critical and challenging aspect is to design a mechanism to develop these computer programs. The design and development of these computer programs remain a challenging aspect in the software development industry. Identification, selection, and implementation of a particular development strategy have a direct relationship with quality and successful development and deployment of these computer programs more broadly the software application. The identification and selection of a particular development process solely depend on the overall experience and understandability of the developer in specific and software project management in general.

Diverse people in the development industry have different opinions related to various models available to develop software applications, and some were optimal; some were contradictory; some were localized, and some were lacking specific parameters. To streamline this development process and to design a benchmark standard with universal acceptability, a collaborative deliberation among various individuals related to software development was he, and the outcome was an approach that can guarantee to deliver versatile, scalable and quality products. This improvised software development approach is now a systematic sequence of various processes known as software engineering (Mills H. D., 2010). Fritz Bauer defines software engineering as; "A systematic design and development of software products and the management of the processes (Fritz, 1968). The main objective of Software Engineering is to meet the specifications & demonstrate accurateness in completing the development process of a software system on time and within budget". The main practice of various fundamentals prescribed through software engineering as a discipline was to development conventional or traditional standalone software applications. With the advent of time, the cost of hardware technology drastically came down and subsequently, the usage of soft systems increased. The conventional software applications also saw evolutionary changes in both nature and scope. Therefore, in addition to traditional software applications, web-based and mobile based software applications came into existence. The introduction of these soft variants has almost redefined both horizontal and vertical dimensions of software engineering practices and principles.

The fundamental approach defined by software engineering to develop software based applications is known as "software development life cycle (SDLC)". SDLC describes the more lucid and systematic procedure to guide successful software development on time and within resources. With time the popularity of these soft variants increased and therefore, the use also shown exponential trends. This popularity resulted in increasing demand for software applications in general and application features & functions in particular. This rapid demand for both application and the features/functionality has made the software development process more and more complex. This growing complexity and to manage the successful development became challenging for software project management as many times project management failed to deliver the project on time or sometimes failed to develop within the allotted budgets or even were unable to understand and management development positively and progressively.

TYPES OF SOFTWARE APPLICATIONS

Software-based applications are broadly categorized into three types: traditional or conventional software applications, web-based applications, and mobile based application. All these application variants do share certain similarities, but holistically are different from one another in their nature, scope, and dimensionality. The brief description of these types in mentioned as under.

- **Traditional or Conventional Software Application:** They are generally known as software applications; they are designed, developed and deployed as standalone software systems to deliver services and operations related to a particular group or organization. This works within the boundary of that working domain only outside access is restricted, and also its scope is geographically localized and developed by more professional developers only, e.g. Banking software, UMS, etc.
- **Web-Based Applications:** Web application is any hypertext rich program with both technical and non-technical features, developed to serve some purpose accessed inside a web browser by specifying a particular URL over the network using HTTP. Web application services a vehicle to fulfill the client request by acquiring information(say internet or WWW), structures it, build a packed presentation and delivers it to serve the purpose(Web engineering, 2014).

In a broader perspective, one can say web application is a software system based on the technologies and standards of World Wide Web Consortium (W3C) that provides Web-specific resources such as content and services through a user interface, the Web browser.

Figure 1. Different types of software applications

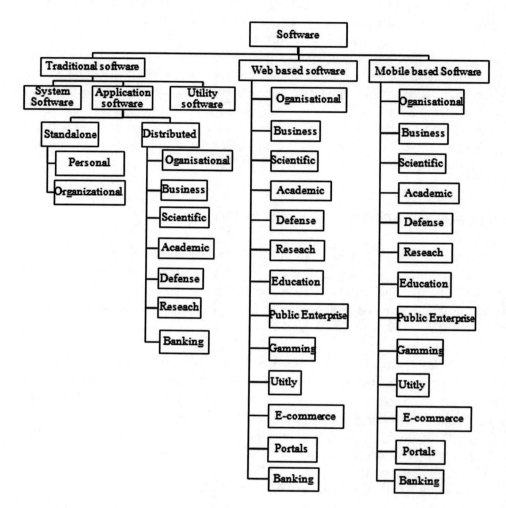

- **Mobile-Based Applications:** These applications are similar to that of web applications. However, they are different in some aspects. These are specially designed to run on a small display with almost no geographic restriction meant for diverse people. Similar to web applications, a user downloads a client program to run these mobile applications and also can browse through mobile browsers to request for content on the internet. Nowadays, the trend for acquiring mobile applications is heavy increasing, and most of the services and practices that were delivered through conventional or web applications are now available as mobile applications.

EFFORT ESTIMATION

Effort estimation has been a pivotal domain for software project management that irregularities of which may lead to developmental or delivery failures. Effort estimation helps the project management team to draw budgetary estimates required to carry out successful software development on time and within budget. It is this effort estimation that generates insights about the cost of development. The inaccurate effort estimation process can result in inaccurate effort estimates or inaccurate resource identification and elicitation, which always lead to failure. This failure can sometimes completely abandon the development industry from software development market. Therefore, it is very much essential to design an efficient, effective and productive mechanism to perform effort estimation before the actual software application development is conceived.

Software effort estimation is defined as a systematic and structured approach to approximate the amount of human efforts required to perform software application development successfully on time and within budget. This development can be the development of any software application falling under traditional, web or mobile application domains. The Effort estimation processes have a direct relationship with the size of software development, and subsequently, the cost of the development is approximated. The more accuracy and perfection in size always guides to get more accurate effort estimates and therefore, the cost (Jørgensen, M., 2007). However, the approximation of the overall cost is obtained after integrating the efforts, overhead cost and profit margins with the estimated efforts (Boehm, B. 1981), inaccuracy in effort estimates can cause overestimation or underestimation which will result in miss management of projects. Accurate effort estimation not only helps the development industry to leverage its client base but also edges the development industries benchmark ahead of other similarly situated developers in the market. Positive and perfect effort estimates help the software development team to draw a clear view of all the fundamental requirements that are required to perform successful software development on time and within budget. That means effort estimation prescribes profitable budgetary schedulers for all related and relevant constructs that are subjected to be consulted or used by the development team during the software development process. The size of software development depends on various functional and non-functional requirements that are expected to be delivered by the software application when deployed in the candidate system. Therefore, it is essential and equally a crucial step in effort estimation to identify all the requirements and then map them into their respective functional or non-functional size measure to arrive at the approximate size and subsequently the cost (Briand, L., 1998).

ACTUAL AND ESTIMATED EFFORTS

To perform successful effort estimation, different techniques or models have been introduced by many researchers to be used by practitioners for successful software development and delivery. The amount of efforts that are obtained during the effort estimation process is called as estimated efforts. The amount of efforts that are actually spent on the development of software application is called as actual efforts. Actual efforts can be either same as that of estimated efforts or sometimes it can be either more or less. This difference in the value of actual and estimated efforts is called as deviation or estimation gap and can be defined as the difference between the value of actual efforts and estimated efforts. The deviation of estimated efforts from their corresponding actual efforts may cause either overestimation or underestimation. The deviation can be defined as the difference between the actual efforts and estimated efforts. Overestimation is the situation in effort estimation when the amount of estimated efforts is found to be more than the amount of actual efforts incurred in the development. While as underestimation is the situation when the observed amount of estimated efforts is found to be out less in comparison to actual efforts spent on software development. Both underestimation and overestimation are not considered as good signs for successful project management.

IMPORTANCE OF EFFORT ESTIMATION IN SOFTWARE DEVELOPMENT

The growing demand and increasing complexity in different types of software applications have resulted in several issues for software project management to perform successful software development on time and within budget. Effort estimation plays an important role to ensure adequate software development and to carry out different developmental assignments on time and within a budget Effectiveness in effort estimation always helps development industry to establish new benchmarks of success and quality product delivery. Both cases of deviation that is either overestimation or underestimation have always proved disastrous for the development industry like the development industry may fail to retain its reputation, competition and market space resulting in less profitable outcome, unsuccessful delivery, erroneous development, less user acceptance, delayed delivery and budget overruns, etc. Selection of a proper effort estimation approach and accuracy in efforts obtained before the actual development is made have greater chances of success in comparison to vague estimation and software development. Therefore, this has always been a critical task for software project management to indentify the best possible effort estimation approach to predict the efforts required to perform successful software development on time and by utilizing the allocated resources efficiently. The importance of effort estimation can be understood by drawing a simple analogy of prediction the fuel (gasoline) needed by an airplane for successful departure and arrival. If the aero-engineers failed to guess the amount of fuel there are chances that the airplane may either fail to reach the destination or may have to make emergency landing somewhere between source and destination. The accurate estimates of fuel have higher chances of successful arrival. Therefore, the technique on the basis of which the fuel consumption is predicted is very much critical.

To ensure that the effort estimation process will deliver better outcomes, it is very much preliminary for project manager to identify an experienced team to perform effort estimation. The experienced team of estimators has probably greater dynamism and wider understandability of problem domain, requirements identification and analysis thereby leading to have arrived at accurate estimates for efforts. The ill understanding of problem domain by inexperienced project management has greater chances of failure. In conclusion it can be said that the successful software development is possible only when the effort estimation team equipped with both experience and knowledge to understand the problem domain thereby designing estimation approach or select best suitable in-line with problem context. The decision making that is involved at every single stage of effort estimation process is very critical and challenging to manage when requirements are not clear, or analysis is not done scientifically.

EFFORT ESTIMATION PROCESS

As effort estimation is a systematic process, it consists of many interrelated and interdependent steps to arrive at the final estimated value for efforts required to perform successful software development. Every step in effort estimation process is meant to deliver a specific functionality needed to approximate the overall amount of efforts needed by project management. Effort estimation begins with the requirements specification, followed by the identification of functional and non-function measures. The size of the software application development depends on various functional and non-functional measures; the detailed discussion on functional and non-functional measures is provided in the subsequent parts of this chapter. Software development size has a direct relationship with the amount of efforts that may be required to accomplish a successful software development. Therefore, the accuracy of effort estimation lies on the accuracy of size approximation. Software project management always needs to contemplate on the perfection and effectiveness of the effort estimation process holistically. The group of individuals who are assigned the job of performing effort estimation needs to have much diverse knowledge and experience

51

of the nature and scope of the development domain. The experienced team always has the potential to identify various functional and non-functional requirements attributed to a particular development to arrive at much accurate size approximation and subsequently the efforts. The demand for software applications has increased with much-unprecedented pace. Most of the organizations have endorsed software applications for delivering their diverse functions. The growing use and demand for features embedded in these software applications have made software application development much complex, and subsequently, the effort estimation processes have also become difficult for management to deal with. The abstract view of the effort estimation process is described in figure 2 below and figure 3 represents a generic effort, estimation model.

There is an array of techniques that can be selected and used to perform software effort estimation. However, each effort estimation method has got different background mechanism to deal with particular type of software effort estimation using distinguished estimation approach. The selection of a particular technique does also impact the accuracy of both size and efforts. Various effort estimation techniques used across literature are discussed under section effort estimation models later in this chapter. The best effort estimation approach helps project management to minimize the gap between actual and estimated efforts.

Figure 2. Abstract view of effort estimation model

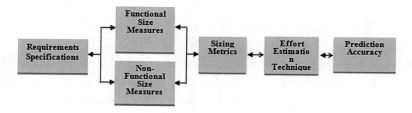

Figure 3. Components of generic effort estimation model

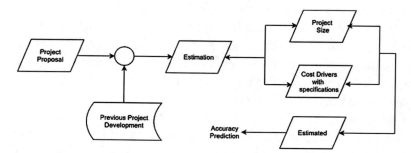

EFFORT ESTIMATION METRICS

Software application development in general and web or mobile application development, in particular, is an integrated activity of different processes. The nature, scope, and complexity of various software-based application developments depend upon several functional and non-functional requirements. These requirements have a direct relationship with software development size, and more requirements mean more software size. To quantify software application size, different functional and non-functional measures were identified, and based on these measures, the aggregate size could be approximated. Therefore, software development metrics are used to measure and then quantify application size in a standard metrics unit or sizing unit. Metrics can be product metrics, process metrics, complexity metrics, effort metrics, etc. which helps project managers to measure, monitor and control web development or software development (S. M. Saif, 2017) These metrics are inputs to the system where approximated efforts are obtained as output. More precisely the activity of measuring these developmental parameters is called as software metrics or and are calculated by establishing empirical relationships between functional, non-functional and complexity measures like LOC, No. of web pages, No. of new web pages, No. of media objects, etc. Web application development metrics can be broadly seen as size metrics and effort metrics.

- **Functional Size Measures:** These are those measuring constructs that directly specify the functional aspect of the development. They depend on the services and functionality of the application. Like in case of function point analysis, these functional measures can be related to external input, external output, logical interface, internal logic files or external queries.
- **Non-Functional Measures:** These are those measuring constructs that directly do not contribute towards size but have an indirect influence on the development. These include the parameters that actually impact the development environment, the technical aspect of the development. Their presence or absence may either increase developmental efforts or may even decrease. E.g., Knowledge of development, the experience of the development team, code reusability, reliability, Difficult Programming Language, project methodology, testability, etc.

EFFORT ESTIMATION STAKEHOLDERS

As mentioned above, effort estimation is a systematic process involving diverse activities to reach out at final estimates. In order to accomplish these diverse activities related to effort estimation at different levels of project management, many individuals are directly or indirectly involved. These individuals are called as effort estimation stakeholders. Below are few prominent stockholders that are a party with effort estimation process.

- **Estimation Process Owner (EPO):** responsible identification, introduction, and maintenance of activities required in the estimation process like methods, process, models, functional and non-functional entities and the data are emanating in whole management. EPO is usually an experienced person in management who has got sufficient knowledge related to effort estimation and this position within an organization is usually a sustentative position.
- **Estimator:** An individual in project management who implements various available effort estimation models to perform effort estimation for software developments.
- **Domain Expert:** They are the experienced people in the project manager who can train or model different modalities to perform the effort estimation when sample data is limited, or there is skewness or outliers in data. By virtue of their knowledge, they guide project management to find and identify various factors that have a potential influence on effort estimation process. They have a significant role when it comes to expert-based or judgment based effort estimation.
- **Decision Marker**: A stockholder with a unique role as decision maker have indirect control or influence on effort estimation process. Whenever the estimation team arrives with the estimates that are to be provided to complete the development, in some cases, the estimated budget and the budget that the project owner (Sponsor) is willing to provide contradicts than the role of decision maker comes into practice to decide whether to accept the value from sponsor or to reject his proposal. The decision maker can also guide the estimators to revise or modify specific estimation criteria to minimize some budget to please the project owner so that the development work can be retained.

CHALLENGES TO SOFTWARE EFFORT ESTIMATION

The growing demand and increasing complexity in various types of software applications (like web or mobile applications) have raised several issues in software project management for the successful development of software application on time and within budget. These issues have resulted into developmental failures, less user acceptance, delayed delivery, and budget overruns. Effort estimation plays an important role in effective software development and helps project managers to perform development within budget and delivery on time by predicting or guessing the extent of resources of various types required for the successful and on time completion of software development. There has been several effort estimation approaches used by practitioners to perform software effort estimation however, the implementation and various methods could not be as significant as it would have been. Therefore, the failures still continued to be there in software development, delivery and deployment. The use of various effort estimation approaches across these application types to perform effort estimation has failed to deliver much-required results acceptable to both project sponsor and developer and subsequently caused many challenges in development and management of software projects.

The overall success and accuracy of software development rely on how good and perfect the efforts were estimated. As mentioned earlier effort estimation is a systematic process and to perform it, there are various approaches designed by several researchers to ensure more accuracy and perform in the said process. The identification and selection of a particular approach are very much difficult, critical and challenging for project management. The ill selection of approach definitely will lead to unsuccessful development. There is no unanimous agreement among researchers that which particular model performs effort estimation perfectly in all situations (Boehm B., Abts C. and Chulani S., 2000).

The importance of software effort estimation has been justified by many researchers in the literature. A report by Cutter Consortium in 2000 (Emilia M., 2000)shows some alarming statistics which was derived from a large database of effort estimation related to software projects in general and web-based projects in particular and is given below:

- 79% of the studied projects presented schedule delays;
- 63% of the studied projects exceeded budgets;
- 84% of the studied projects did not meet requirements;
- 53% of the studied projects did not provide the required function; and
- 52% of the studied projects had a poor quality of deliverables.

According to the study performed by the International Society of Parametric Analysis (ISPA) (Eck D., Brundick B. and Fettig ., 2009) and the Standish Group International(Lynch J., 2009), two-thirds of software projects fail to be delivered on time and within budget. And according to them the two main reasons that cause these failures are: (1) improper estimation in terms of project size, cost, and staff needed and (2) uncertainty of software and system requirements.

As there exits different types of software applications (conventional software application, web application, mobile application) and these applications are different from one another in several aspects: nature, scope, functionality, development, deployment, usage spectrum, etc. Therefore, each of these applications needs a tailor-made approach to perform effort estimation. The use of model developed for one type may be useful in some cases but cannot be a holistically successful approach. Theref0re, the deployment of ad-hoc methods will only increase the chances of failure and not a success.

It is an inevitable requirement to understand the differences between various types of software applications so that a proper type of approach can be either identified or developed to ensure accuracy in effort prediction. The project management not only needs to differentiate the type of development then has to identify and select if available a proper approach to pursue effort estimation and land in a good result. The whole success of the development industry relies on its best estimation policy and reliable estimation team. The sensitivity and seriousness of this domain make it challenging, important and critical. The literature review performed in (S. M. Saif, 2017b) describes in length the various approaches developed and used for effort estimation. These models continue to be revisited and modified to cater to more desirous demands of estimates to achieve more effectiveness and accuracy in the estimation process. Therefore, it is pretty crucial for a project manager to perform efficient effort/cost estimation in early stages of software development. As the perfection in estimation will help the development industry to perform better over bidding process, since overestimation will lead to bidding loss and underestimation will cause the company to lose money.

EFFORT ESTIMATION MODELS

Measurement and accuracy in effort estimation process is a very important and critical activity for software project management to ensure that their development is successful and effective. The identification and selection of an efficient and reliable estimation process always help the development team to obtain accurate size estimation and consequently, the cost of application development. Therefore, it is inevitable for project management to select a best suitable and reliable method to perform effort estimation at early stages of software development to draw realistic budgetary for required to accomplish a successful software development (Jacky K. and Ross J., 2008). In order to approximate software efforts estimation, several approaches or methods were introduced. Most of these approaches were developed to perform effort estimation for conventional software applications. However, they were also used to perform effort estimation for mobile and web applications, and the results obtained were not as good and promising as were obtained for conventional software's. The main reason behind this failure is purely on the nature and type of the applications, as we know, all these types of applications are different from one another. Therefore, the approaches developed for one type cannot prove out to be successful for other as well. Therefore, there is need to have tailor-made and specific effort estimation approaches specific to the particular type of application development then only successful development and accurate estimates are possible.

Different researchers have put effort estimation methods were put into several categories like Trendowicz and Jeffery (Back, T., Hammel U. and Schwefel H, 1997),(Burgess, Colin J., and Martin L., 2007) and Shepherd C. et al. (Shepherd M, and Kadoda M., 2001).However, effort estimation methods can be broadly categorized as Expert based, Algorithmic and Machine learning based models or Algorithmic and non-algorithmic models. Figure 4 represents various effort estimation methods and their corresponding sub-category. The models or approaches mentioned below have been developed for either conventional applications or mobile applications or web application.

ALGORITHMIC MODELS

Algorithmic models also called as parametric models as they use mathematical equations between dependent and independent variables or empirical models to estimate efforts required for software in general and web or mobile application development in particular. These are the most popular and commonly used effort estimation approaches as they are easier and simpler to use (R D Banker, 1994).

Figure 4. Classifications of effort estimation methods

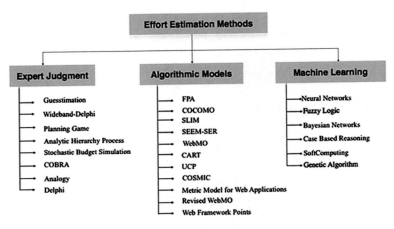

However, to make them more effective, they need calibration or adjustment with most circumstances. Algorithmic model is purely based on the state and degree of various variables required in the development process; LOC, function points, web objects, no. of web pages, no. of links, no. of multimedia files, etc. In addition to these direct parameters, there are other factors that also have an impact on the efforts and are called as cost drivers. These cost drivers correspond to all those factors that are associated with an environment where the web application is developed, and the technical resources are required to fulfill the pragmatic development process. These factors are typically called as Environmental Factors and Technical Factors. This relationship between parameters cost drivers is formalized by framing a mathematical equation between them. Equation 1 below structures such relation.

$$Estimated\ Effort = a\ Size\ of\ New\ Proj \times EAF \tag{1}$$

where, a and b are parameters chosen based on certain criteria like; type of project being developed, EAF is Effort Adjustment Factor. The relationship between effort and size can either linear or non-linear; such representation can be expressed by equation no 2 and 3 respectively obtained after applying regression analysis on past project data. Equation 2 issues the relationship as linear and equation 3 as non-linear (E. Mendes, N. Mosley and S. Counsell, 2006)

$$Estimated\ Effort = C + a_0 Estimated\ Size\ of\ New\ Proj + a_1 CD_1 + ... + a_n CD_n \tag{2}$$

$$Estimate\ Effort = C \times EstimatedSizeofNewProj^{a0}CD_1^{a1} + ... + CD_n^{an} \tag{3}$$

where, C is constant denoting initial estimated effort (assuming the size and Cost drivers to be Zero) derived from past project data (Putnam, L. H., 1978) and a_0... a_n denote parameters derived from past project data.

The most popular algorithmic models used to perform effort estimation for conventional/ web/mobile applications are briefly discussed below:

Putnam's Model/ Software Life Cycle Model

The Putnam's model, developed by Larry Putnam in the 1970s, is also called as Software Life Cycle Model (SLIM) (Fenton N.E. and Pfleeger, S.L., 1997). This model was used for estimating the efforts for projects exceeding 70,000 lines of code (LOC). Putnam's model describes the time and efforts required to complete a software project development of certain size and complexity. The time-effort curve required to accomplish development is performed by using the Rayleigh Curve function or Rayleigh distribution. Putnam Suggests that staffing rises smoothly during the project and then drops sharply during the acceptance testing. The SLIM method is expressed by two variants equations: Software equation and Manpower-Buildup equation. Software equation is expressed by equation 4, states that effort is proportional to the cube of the size and inversely proportional to the fourth power of time (Albrecht A. J., 1979) and Manpower-Buildup equation represented by equation 5, states that effort is proportional to the cube of the development time.

$$Size = E \times Effort^{\frac{1}{3}} \left(t_d\right)^{4/3} \tag{4}$$

where, E is Environment or technical factor; t_d is software delivery time in years. Efforts are total project efforts in person-years. Size is an effective source lines of code (SLOC).

$$D = E/t^3 \tag{5}$$

where, D is constantly called as manpower accelerator, E is total project effort in years and 't' is a delivery time in years.

The total efforts required to develop software projects are represented by equation 6 below.

$$E = \left(\frac{\left(CE^{1/3}\right)t^{4/3}}{C} \right)^{9/7} \left(\frac{E}{t^3} \right)^{4/7} \tag{6}$$

SLIM is applied to almost all types and sizes of software projects. It computes schedules, efforts, cost, staffing for all software development phases and reliability for the main development phase.

SLIM takes SLOC, Function Points and other valid measures of functions to be created as its primary input metrics to generate efforts. Putnam's model can be used to plot software development effort as a function of time, as shown in figure 4.

Figure 5. Software development effort as a function of time in Putnam model
Source: Fenton N.E. and Pfleeger S.L., 1997

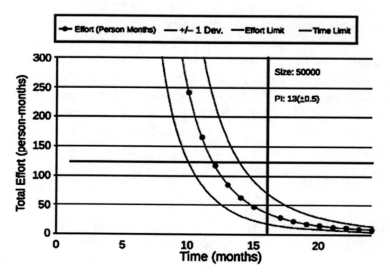

FUNCTION POINT ANALYSIS

Function point analysis (FPA) an effort estimation model developed by Allan Albrecht of IBM in 1979 (Boehm B. W., 1981). In FPA, the project management implements basic operational units known as function points to represent individual function to be delivered through a software application. In more precisely, these function points indicate different functional user requirement desired by the client from the application. Therefore, FPA approximates the overall functional complexity of application by identifying all functional size measures corresponding to each function. In FPA, five types of functional components were identified to obtain functional size measurement: external input file, external output file, external inquiry, internal logic file, external interface file. In addition to functional components, 14 value adjustment factors (VAF) or general system characteristics (GSC) are used to normalize the size. These factors are also called as cost drivers. Functional components can be either data functions or transactional functions.

The functional complexity of the web application development is directly proportional to the number of functional user requirements and there corresponding basic functional units such as record element type (RET), data element type (DET) and file type referenced (FTR). International Function Point Users Group (IFPUG), an independent organization have developed a universal standard for proper elicitation, identification, and counting of function points present in any software application development.

Once the identification of the function points is done, they are classified into simple, average and complex categories. These categories have their specific weighting factor associated to it is shown in table 1. The behavior of these function types are described in figure 6,

The overall function points are calculated by obtaining by multiplying function count by an adjustment factor that is defined by considering 14 technical attributes called as General system characteristics (GSC) given in table 2. The aggregate impact of these GSC is calculated as Summation of all the individual parameters, as shown by equation 7 and total function points by equation 8.

$$VAF = (TDI \times 0.01) + \sum_{i=1}^{14} F_i \tag{7}$$

Figure 6. Function point model: a high-end view

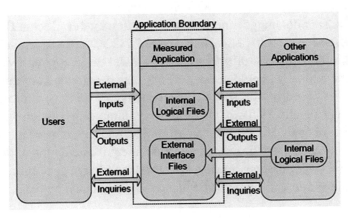

Table 1. Overview of function point analysis

Parameter description	Count		Weight Factor			Count
			Simple	Average	Complex	
Number of Inputs		×	3	4	6	
Number of Output		×	4	5	7	
Number of Inquiries		×	3	4	6	
Number of Internal Files		×	7	10	15	
Number of External Interfaces		×	5	7	10	
Function Count (Unadjusted)						

where TDI is the total degree of influence and has the lowest value, 0.65 and highest value as 70. F is particular VAF

$$FP = Function_{count} \times \left[0.065 + 0.01 \times \sum_{i=1}^{14} F_i \right] \tag{8}$$

These calculated Function points are used to predict the efforts required for the development of any software application in general and web applications in particular.

Table 3 shows the effort estimate (man-month), the actual effort (man-month), and percentage MRE data of the 15 software projects using Function Point Analysis (FPA) for the effort estimation performed by (Kemerer C.F., 1987).

COCOMO

The Constructive Cost Model (COCOMO), developed by Barry Bohm in 1980s, is one of the most popular algorithmic cost estimation model (Boehm B. W., C. Abts, A.W. and Brown S., 2000). This is also called a COCOMO 81 model. COCOMO was aimed to be a generic effort estimation model to be applied by any software development company to predict early efforts. The development of this algorithmic technique was based on the study of 63 software development projects at TRW Aerospace during the 1970s. COCOMO uses simple regression formula where parameters have been derived from a past project and are adjusted based on current developmental characteristics. The most fundamental calculation in the COCOMO model is the use of effort equation to estimate the number of person-months required for project development. The effort equation is represented by equation 9 and 10.

$$Effort = A \times (Est\ Pro\ Size)B \tag{9}$$

where, A is proportionality constant, B represents economy or dis-economy of scale, B depends on development mode or class (Organic, Semidetached, and Embedded). Project size is in source lines of code (SLOC)

$$Effort = a(Est\ Pro\ Size)^b EAF \tag{10}$$

where, *Effort* is estimated project effort, and *EstProSize* is the size of an application measure in thousand of delivered source instructions (KDSI), a and b are constants that determine the class of the projects to be developed(Organic, Semidetached, and Embedded), EAF is an effort adjustment factor, calculated from cost drivers.

Table 2. Functional complexity parameter

S No	Description of Parameter	Value Range	Lowest values	Highest Values
1	Data Communication	0-5	0	5
2	Distributed data communication	0-5	0	5
3	Performance	0-5	0	5
4	Heavily used configuration	0-5	0	5
5	Transaction rate	0-5	0	5
6	Online data entry	0-5	0	5
7	End user efficiency	0-5	0	5
8	Online update	0-5	0	5
9	Complex Processing	0-5	0	5
10	Reusability	0-5	0	5
11	Installation ease	0-5	0	5
12	Operation ease	0-5	0	5
13	Multiple sites	0-5	0	5
14	Facilitate changes	0-5	0	5
	Total degree of influence -TDI		0	70
	VAF=(TDI*0.01) + 0.65		0.65	1.35

Table 3. Details of the software projects from Kemerer

Project	Estimated Effort (man –month)	Actual effort (man –month)	MRE (%)
1	344.30	287.00	19.97
2	92.13	82.50	11.67
3	731.43	1,107.30	33.94
4	192.03	86.90	120.98
5	387.11	336.30	15.11
6	61.58	84.00	26.69
7	52.60	23.20	326.73
8	264.68	130.30	103.13
9	477.81	116.00	311.91
10	2.83	72.00	103.93
11	484.24	258.70	87.18
12	192.21	230.70	16.68
13	157.36	157.00	0.23
14	390.63	246.90	58.21
15	282.91	69.90	304.74
		MMRE (%)	**102.74**

- The organic model incorporates small and less complicated projects, and projects are familiar, stable. The project developed is similar to previously developed ones. They are developed by highly experienced teams with similar past development experience.
- Semi- Detached model incorporates projects that have intermediate characteristics (either too small or too easy). The development team has a mixed experience. This is also known as Basic COCOMO.
- Embedded Model, development is characterized by tight, inflexible constraints and interface requirements. This mode requires a great deal of innovation.

COCOMO can be applied at different stages of development to estimate the effort or cost of development at early stages of development where requirement elicitation is not clear or when detailed requirements have been specified or at later stages when application design has been finalized. These three different stages or approaches are called as Basic COCOMO, Intermediate COCOMO and Advanced COCOMO models(Nassif, A. B., Ho, D. & Capretz, L. F. (2011), RD Banker, H. Chang, C. Kemerer, 1994).

COCOMO-II

It is an enhanced variant of basic COCOMO in which new cost drivers were introduced to achieve better estimation accuracy. It uses LOC and Function Points as sizing metrics to calculate project size. COCOMO-II has three sub-models, Application composition, Early Design and Post-Architecture(R D Banker, H. Chang, C. Kemerer, 1994).The COCOMO II effort estimation model is summarized in equation 11:

$$Effort = A \times (size)^E \prod_{i=1}^{17} EM_i \tag{11}$$

where, Effort is expressed in person-months (PM). 'A' is a calibration factor, approximates productivity constant in (PM/KSLOC), it is 2.94 for COCOMO II 2000. Size is measured in KSLOC and unadjusted function points (UFP), converted to SLOC or UFP divided by one thousand. EM is effort multiplier (Table 2.3) with complexity classified into categorized into six ranking orders: very low, low, nominal, high, very high and extra high with their respective weighting factor. Exponent 'E' is an aggregation of five scale factors(SF) that accounts for the relative economics, and diseconomies of scale countered for software development of different sizes(Barry W. Bohm, 2000, Karner, G. (1993).

- if E<1.0, then project exhibits economy of scale
- if E=1.0, then project have both economy and diseconomy of scale in balance and
- if E>1.0, then project exhibits diseconomy of scale.

Kemerer C.F.,1987, analyzed many COCOMO models. COCOMO Intermediate showed the least Mean Magnitude of Relative Error (MMRE). The effort estimate (person month), the actual effort (person month), and percentage MRE of the 15 software projects are shown in Table 4.

TOP-DOWN ESTIMATION

This can be considered as specialization approach where total efforts/cost required for the software development is obtained by fine-graining the main problem into its constituent components that collectively attribute to overall efforts. Top-down

Table 4. Details of the software projects from Kemerer

No.	Estimated Effort (person month)	Actual Effort (person month)	MRE (%)
1	917.56	287.00	219.71
2	151.66	82.50	83.83
3	6,182.65	1,107.30	458.35
4	558.98	86.90	543.25
5	1,344.20	336.30	299.70
6	313.36	84.00	273.05
7	234.78	23.20	911.98
8	1,165.70	130.30	794.63
9	4,248.73	116.00	3,562.70
10	180.29	72.00	150.40
11	1,520.04	258.70	487.57
12	558.12	230.70	141.82
13	1,073.47	157.00	583.74
14	629.22	246.90	154.85
15	133.94	69.90	91.62
		MMRE	583.82

Source: (Kemerer C.F.,1987)

Estimation is more beneficial in the early stages of software development because detailed information is not available during this stage (Kusuma B. M., 2014) (Leung H and Fan Z, 2001). Putnam's Model is an example of this technique.

BOTTOM-UP ESTIMATION

Bottom-up estimation is opposite of Top-down estimation method. This can be treated as a generalization approach wherein all the attributes that are expected to play role in effort estimation are indentified and later converged into a single collective variable. These attributes are also called as cost drivers and the cost of each software component (drivers) is combined to achieve the overall cost of the software. Goal is to derive system estimate from the accumulated estimate of the small component (Leung H and Fan H., 2001).

USE CASE POINT ESTIMATION

Objective oriented software development has now become a development strategy of choice. In objective oriented programming paradigm, use-case diagrams are considered as basic information units modeled through unified modeling language (UML) and are usually prepared at preliminary stages of software development. The behavior of use case diagrams portrays the functional strength of the application development. The interaction between user and system in use case modeling is described through use case points in general and by using actors and use cases in particular. Each use-case is represented by the use case scenario diagram. The use case scenario is mainly composed of a success scenario and an alternative scenario.

Use Case Point (UCP) model for software effort estimation based on the use case diagrams was first developed by (Karner G., 1993) to establish an estimation framework to perform early and accurate effort estimation. In the UCP model, the software size is calculated according to the number of actors and use cases in a use case diagram and every number multiplied by their corresponding complexity factor. The complexity of the use-case is determined by the strength of the transactions incurred therein to complete a specific function.

ACTORS

The actors in the use-case point model are categorized as simple, average or complex depending on the complexity of the use-case. A weight is assigned to each actor category as specified in table 5. An actor can be defined as 'simple' if interaction with the system through application programming interfaces (API). An actor can be defined as 'average' if it interacts through protocols (like TCP/IP). The actor is defined as 'Complex' if an interaction is through a Graphical User Interface (GUI). The weight assigned to them is 1, 2 and 3, respectively, and the same is given in table 5.

The total unadjusted actor weight (UAW) is calculated by totaling the number of actors in each category and multiplying by its specified weight factor. All the products are added to get unadjusted actor weight. The equation for calculating unadjusted actor weight (UAW) is given as:

$$UAW = \Sigma(No.\ of\ factors \times their\ respective\ weight\ factor) \tag{12}$$

USE CASES

The use-cases are categorized as simple, average and complex, categories depending on the number of transactions including the transactions in alternative flow within a use-case. Use-case is categorized as 'simple' if the number of transactions is less than 3, a use-case is categorized as 'average' if the number of transactions is between 4-7 and use-case is categorized as 'complex' if the number of transactions is more than 7 within a use-case. The corresponding weight assigned to simple, average, complex categories are 5, 10 and 15, respectively, and the same is given in table 6.

Unadjusted use case weight (UUCW) is calculated from the number of use-cases in all the three categories simple, average and complex. The number of use-cases in the corresponding category is multiplied by its corresponding weight factor, and at the end, all values are summed to calculate unadjusted use case weight. The equation for calculating UUCW gives as:

$$UUCW = \Sigma(No.\ of\ use\ cases \times their\ respective\ weight\ factor) \tag{13}$$

Table 5. Actor complexity and their respective weighting factor

Actor Complexity	Categorization criteria	Weight
Simple	through an API	1
Average	through TCP/IP protocol	2
Complex	through Graphical User interface (GUI)	3

Table 6. Use case complexity and their respective weighting factor

Use Case Complexity	Number of Transactions	Weight
Simple	<=3	5
Average	4 to 7	10
Complex	>7	15

Different researchers have observed that both use cases and actors have their discrete behavior and accordingly contribute to the nature of transactions. In the UCP method of software effort estimation, the following three steps are carried out to calculate efforts required for a software project:

- Calculate the number of Unadjusted Use Case Points (UUCP).
- Calculate the total number of adjusted Use Case Points (UCP).
- Calculate the overall effort based on the total man-hours needed for the development of the project.

In order to calculate UUCP, the values for UAW and UUCW are required. Both the UAW and UUCW values are used to calculate UUCP, and the equation for the calculation is given as.

$$UUCP = UUCW + UAW \qquad (14)$$

where UUCP is unadjusted use case points, UUCW is unadjusted use case weight, and UAW is unadjusted actor weight. After calculating UUCP, the UCP (use case point) value needs to be calculated using the following equation.

$$UCP = UUCP \times TCF \times ECF \qquad (15)$$

where TCF is technical complexity factor, ECF is environmental complexity factor

TECHNICAL COMPLEXITY FACTORS

These are non-functional parameters that impact the development, implementation, and maintenance of web application development. These factors influence the technical characteristics associated with software application development like architecture, internal processing, interoperability, scalability, user training, etc. The technical complexity factor (TCF) is used to adjust the UCP estimate based on the perceived technical complexities of the project to be developed. TCF corresponds of thirteen (13) different parameters which are rated using a scale from 0 to 5 where value '0' implies that the parameter is 'irrelevant' and the assigned value will increase with the increase in significance and value '5' implies significance of the corresponding parameters is treated as 'essential'. The details of all the 13 technical complexity parameters with their relative weight are given in table 7. For each technical complexity factors, the influence estimate is multiplied by the corresponding weight factor, and the summation of all the calculated value is the Technical Complexity Factors (TCF) value.

The value of the TCF is calculated using the following equation.

$$TCF = 0.6 + 0.01 \sum_{i=1}^{13} Ws_i \times S_i \tag{16}$$

ENVIRONMENTAL COMPLEXITY FACTOR

These factors are related to various characteristics associated with the development team like developers experience, skills, knowledge of technology, etc. To what extent a person possesses these attributes makes its influence proportionally on web development in general and effort estimation in particular.

Table 7. Technical factor and weight

Factor	Description	Weight (W_i)
T1	Distributed system	2
T2	Response or throughput performance objectives	1
T3	End-user efficiency (online)	1
T4	Complex internal processing	1
T5	Code must be reusable	1
T6	Easy to install	0.5
T7	Easy to use	0.5
T8	Portable	2
T9	Easy to change	1
T10	Concurrent	1
T11	Includes special security features	1
T12	Provides direct access for third parties	1
T13	Special user training facilities are required	1

Environmental complexity factor is directly dependent on software development team experience in the software project to be developed. More experienced teams will have a greater impact on the UCP computation in comparison with less experienced software teams. The software development team determines the impact of each factor on the project with respect to different parameters of ECF. The influence of eight (8) environmental complexity factor parameters on the software development effort is estimated using a scale from 0 to 5 where '0' means 'irrelevant and '5' is for 'essential'. All the eight environmental complexity factor parameter with their corresponding weights are given in table 8.

The weight assigned based on the software project to be developed for different parameters of environmental complexity factor is multiplied with the corresponding weight of the parameter. All the eight (8) values calculated after multiplying corresponding weight are summed together to get the value of EF, which is used to calculate ECF. The environmental complexity factor (EF) can be calculated as:

$$ECF = 1.4 + 0.03 \sum_{i=1}^{8} Ws_i \times S_i \tag{17}$$

After calculating the value of UUCP (unadjusted use case points), ECF (Environmental Complexity Factors) and TCF (Technical Complexity Factors) the values for UCP use case points is calculated using the following equation:

$$UCP = UUCP \times TCF \times ECF$$

Table 8. Environmental factor and weight

Factor (E_i)	Description	Weight (W_i)
E1	Familiarity with the project	1.5
E2	Application Experience	0.5
E3	OO Programming Experience	1
E4	Lead Analyst Capability	0.5
E5	Motivation	1
E6	Stable requirements	2
E7	Part Time Staff	-1
E8	Difficult Programming Language	-1

In order to estimate the effort in person-hours the UCP value is multiplied by 20, as was suggested by (Karner G., 1993) to calculate efforts:

$$Effort = UCP \times 20 \text{ person-hours} \tag{18}$$

As use-cases based effort estimation are based on the object-oriented methodology where unified modeling language (UML) has emerged as the dominant technique for structuring requirements (Alves R., Valente P. and Numes N. J., 2013) The UCP became very popular due to its relative simplicity and applicability at early stages of software development process. The use case point method of software effort estimation has gained wide popularity due to its easy-to-use characteristic and use-case. The present state of software development is mostly using object-oriented approaches for software development, which make the availability of use-case diagrams a necessity. The use case diagrams are prepared by developers at the early stages of development, which further make the UCP effort estimation method as a suitable approach keeping in mind the present state of the software industry.

Table 9 shows the effort estimate (man-hour), the actual effort (man-hour), and percentage MRE data of the 15 projects obtained by Frohnhoft and Engels (S. Frohnhoff, and G. Engels, 2008) in thiere study.

Web Objects Model

Web Objects developed by Donald J. Reifer in 2000 used for sizing a web application, Web Objects are considered as the first metric specially developed for a web application. The size of the web application is measured as a total number of web objects, a particular web application exhibits. It is an extension to function points in the sense that four more web related components were added to it (Reifer J. D., 2000). These added four components make it sizing method for a web application. web objects consist of nine component: i) external input, ii) external output, iii) external interface, iv) internal logic file, v) external quires, vi) multimedia files, vii) web building blocks, viii) scripts and ix) links.

Web Objects computes the size by considering each and every possible element of the web application by using Holsters equation (equation 19) for volume, the measurements obtained in a language independent and related to the vocabulary used to describe it in terms of operands and operators.

$$V^* = Nlog_2(n) = \left(N_1^* + N_2^*\right)log_2\left(n_1^* + n_2^*\right) \tag{19}$$

where,

Table 9. Details of the 15 software projects from frohnhoft and engels

Project	Industry	Effort estimates (Man-Hour)	Actual Effort (Man- month)	MRE (%)
1	Apparel industry	1,205	728	65.52
2	Automotive	11,667	15,500	24.73
3	Automotive	114,023	136,320	16.36
4	Finance	1,002	2,992	66.51
5	Finance	3,301	3,680	10.30
6	Insurance	2,115	4,800	55.94
7	Logistics	1,406	944	48.94
8	Logistics	1,751	2,567	31.79
9	Logistics	8,840	7,250	21.93
10	Logistics	52,219	61,172	14.64
11	Public	39,030	46,900	16.78
12	Public	19,442	13,200	47.29
13	Telco	3,588	2,456	46.09
14	Telco	3,186	2,432	31.00
15	Telco	1,518	1,056	43.75
			MMRE	36.10

Source: Frohnhoff S and Engels G., 2008

N : number of total occurrences of operands and operators
n : number of distinct *operands* and *operators*
N_1*: total occurrences of *operand* estimator
N_1*: total occurrences of *operator* estimator
n_1*: number of unique *operand* estimator
n_2*: number of unique *operand* estimator
V* : volume of work involved represented as Web Object

In order to estimate the overall size of the web application, Reifer developed "Web Object Calculation Worksheet(WOCW)". WOCW consists of all the predictors with their corresponding weighting factor assigned to low, Average or High complexity level. The worksheet and size measurement metrics became the first step in developing a model, this model is called as WebMo or Web Model that accurately estimates the size and simultaneously the cost and optimal schedule required for the development of web application.

The mathematical foundation of WebMO depends on the parameters of COCOMO II and SoftCost-OO software cost estimating models (Donald J. R., 1993). The mathematical representation of WebMo is given in equation 20 and 21 below.

$$Effort = A \prod_{i=1}^{9} cd_i \left(size \right)^{P1} \tag{20}$$

$$Duration = B(Effort)^{P2} \tag{21}$$

where

An effort is expressed in person-months and duration in calendar months
A and B are constants
P1 and P2 are power laws
cd_i are cost drives, *Size* is the number of Web Objects,

The duration was calculated based on a square-root relationship with effort based upon built-in scaling rules. The validity of this estimation equation was performed on web applications like e-commerce, financial applications, business-to-business application, and web-based information utilities.

Table 10 shows the effort estimation results obtained by Ruhe (Ruhe M., Jeffery R and Wieczorek I., 2004) for web application development using Function Points and Web Object Counts with OLS regression based effort prediction models.

COSMIC-FFP

COSMIC-FFP (COSMIC stands for Common Software Metrics Consortium, while FFP stands for Full Function Points) is a widely adopted effort estimation approach

Table 10. Results of effort estimation of web application development using FP, WO and Allette's expert method

Estimation Method	Min MRE	Max MRE	Mean MRE	Pred
OLS regression(FP)	0.02	0.84	0.33	0.42
OLS regression(WO)	0.00	0.60	0.24	0.67
Allette's Expert Opinion	0.12	0.68	0.37	0.25

Source: M. Ruhe, R. Jeffery, I. Wieczorek, 2003

used for sizing software applications. It came into existence to address the challenges faced by measurement experts while using existing functional sizing methods. It was later approved as an International Standard (ISO/IEC 19761:2003 and now revised as ISO/IEC 19761:2011)(ISO/IEC 19761:2011). Data movements or transactions that correspond to any software application are fundamental identifiers for this sizing method. The basic idea underlying this approach is that, for usual software development, the biggest programming efforts are being devoted to handling data movements, and thus the number of these data movements can provide a meaningful insight of the development size (De Marco L., Ferrucci F and Gravino C., 2013). These data movements can be "to and from" persistent memory or between different users. The presence of these data movements in any application, whether core software application or web application has a direct contribution towards the size and complexity of the application. COSMIC standardize the mechanism to identify different data movements and other characteristic aspects related to them(Costagliola G., Di Martino S., Ferrucci F and Vitiello G., 2006).

COSMIC -FFP measures the functionality of the web application in terms of cosmic functional size units (CFSU). These CFSU are identified after applying a set rules, and procedures to Functional User Requirements to obtain a numerical value of CFSU's, which represents the functional size of the software. COSMIC-FFP model consists of two models: the context model and the software model(Costagliola G., Di Martino S., Ferrucci F and Vitiello G., 2006).

Figure 7. Generic flow of data attributes from functional perspectives (a) and generic software model for measuring software functional size(b)
Source: Bruegge B., Dutoit A. H., 2003

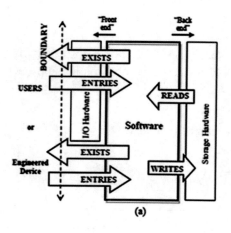 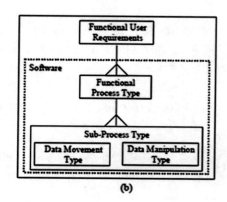

Context model establishes the boundary that separates software application from its host operating environment. It illustrates the generic functional flow of data attributes from a functional perspective. This data flow is characterized by two directions, front-end, and back-end, representing four different data movements (see Figure 6.a) entries and exits, read and write, respectively. Entries and exists allow data exchanges with the user and read and writes, which allow the exchange of data with the persistent storage hardware.

Software model assumes that software to be mapped and measure either takes input or produces useful output to users. It can also manipulate pieces of information designated as data groups, which consist of data attributes.

Software model allows us to consider that these functional user requirements are implemented by a set of functional processes, each of which represents a unique set of sub-processes performing either a data movement or a data manipulation (see Figure 6b). Four different sub-processes can be executed: entry, exit, read, write.

- Entry moves a data from user across the boundary into the functional process
- Exit moves data from the functional process across the boundary to a user
- Read moves a data from persistent storage to the functional process and
- Write moves data from the functional process to persistent storage.

The implementation of COSMIC functional measurement method takes three important aspects into consideration: measurement strategy phase, mapping phase, and measurement phase. After these phases are rendered, it becomes possible to determine the functional size that is a total number of CFP's of software application and is represented by equation 22.

$$Size(FP_i) = \sum Size(Entries_i) + \sum Size(Exits_i) + \sum Size(Reads_i) + \sum Size(Writes_i)$$
(22)

Similarly, the size of software in terms of COSMIC is then the sum of the sizes of all functional processes that occur in the measured software application and is expressed in equation 23.

$$Size(software) = \sum Size(FP_i)$$
(23)

The application of COSMIC in web application sizing was first adopted by Rollo after he faced difficulties in sizing Internet Bank System with FPA method (Rollo T., 2000). The application of the COSMIC method to size Web applications was further analyzed by(Costagliola G., Di Martino S., Ferrucci F and Vitiello G.,

2006) (Mendes E., Counsell S., and Mosley N., 2002)(Rollo T., 2000). The COSMIC method was found to be a suitable method for sizing web applications (Costagliola G., Di Martino S., Ferrucci F and Vitiello G., 2006).

Anda B. and Dreiem H., 2001, performed effort estimation using COSMIC-FFP and the details of estimated efforts (11,859.88 man-hour), the actual effort (6,308 man-hour), and percentage MRE (88.01%) data of the case study and the results obtained are shown in table 11 below.

EXPERT JUDGMENT

The estimation approach to predict the effort required for software application development by means of subjective expertise of an expert on similar development projects. The estimation of the new project involves that the expert must possess the developmental experience and knowledge of similarly situated project development. Later on, the estimates are drafted by these experts accordingly on the basis of their similarity with exiting projects. The expert estimation methods can be a single expert estimates, or it can be more than one experts consulting before forwarding the final estimates. The accuracy of this method is directly proportional to the experience, competence, skill set, environmental and technical knowledge of the expert or experts (Melanie R., Ross J., and Isabella W., 2003). There is no doubt that these methods are widely used in software and web development industry (Emilia M., Mosley N., and Steve C., 2006), and 70-80% of the industrial estimates made by experts are being performed without using any formal estimation models. The effectiveness of this approach is reduced because of bias, inter expert conflicts, political pressure, and expert centric approach. The simplest instance of this method is also known as guesstimation approach as a single expert provides final estimates. Expert-based estimation is adaptable at certain stages of software development and in situations where the development team lacks quantified and empirical data from

Table 11. Details of the software projects from

Case	Estimated Effort (Man-Hour)	Actual effort (Man-Hour)	MRE (%)
1	3,670	2,550	30.52
2	2,860	3,320	16.08
3	2,740	2,080	24.09
		MMRE	27.30

Source: Anda B. and Dreiem H., 2001

the previously computed projects (Kirmani, M.M. and Wahid, A., 2015). Expert estimation method has a limitation in quantifying and determining the factors that have been used to derive an estimate so that this can be used as a pattern of further estimation prediction. Expert estimation can produce much more efficient and accurate estimates when used in combination with other algorithmic models (Gray R., MacDonell S.G., Shepperd M.J., 1999)(Myrtveit I. and Stensrud E., 1999). Despite of its usefulness expert judgment have some drawbacks (Leung H. and Fan, Z., 2002) (Heemstra J. F., 1992)

- Depends highly on expert opinion.
- Very difficult to reproduce and use the knowledge and experience of an expert
- The estimation is not repeatable and means of deriving an estimate are not implicit.

Delphi Technique

Delphi was originally developed for the purpose of making future predictions about some issues by guiding the individuals involved in decision making to propose better prediction after carrying out an assessment on each individual opinion. This constitutes the preliminary stage in the Delphi technique. This assessment is performed by the coordinator to generate a tabular report. In the next stage, this tabular report is distributed among the participants to revisit and reassess the various interpretations mentioned in the report. The feedback from the participants is collected and further analyzed by the coordinator to project better estimation outcome. In original Delphi, there is no group consultation or deliberation on the assessment of issues, but in more open type of Delphi, Wideband Delphi accommodates group discussions between the participants in different assessment rounds(Boehm B., 1981) (Jørgensen M., 2007). The Wideband of Delphi technique can be used for software effort estimation in the following manner;

1. A coordinator begins by providing every expert a project's specification chart and a response sheet.
2. The experts will anonymously respond to various fields mentioned in the response sheet to nullify any bias.
3. The coordinator collects responses and summarizes them to prepare projections for effort estimation.
4. In case the skewness among responses is very high or unusual, the coordinator invites experts for further discussion to get a more aligned opinion.

This methodology is relatively easier to implement, less-expensive, and accurate in comparison to other techniques only when the experts have good expertise in the problem domain for which efforts are being estimated. The main disadvantage of this method is the lack of sensitivity analysis, dependency on experienced estimators; human error and pessimistic approach or unfamiliarity with key aspects of the project (Boehm B., 1981)(Jørgensen M., 2007).

Work-Breakdown Structure Approach

In this approach, software development is divided into modules or sub-processes therefore, and this is also known as the divide-and-conquer approach. To further fine-grain the work-breakdown structure, these sub-processes are further divided into smaller units. The efforts required to develop these sub-processes are estimated by experts on the bases of the previously completed similar software projects. This estimation of this sub-process is fewer errors prone in comparison to estimating the efforts for the whole project at once. The overall effort is estimated by aggregating the efforts corresponding to these sub-processes. A WBS actually consists of two hierarchies, one representing the software product itself, and the other representing the activities needed to build that product (Boehm B., 1981).

COBRA

COBRA (Cost estimation, Benchmarking and Risk Assessment), a hybrid cost modeling technique introduced by Briand in late 1990s (Briand L., El Emam K. and Bomarius F., 1998) to overcome the limitations floating from existing cost estimation methods. COBRA is based on both expert knowledge and quantitative project data. This particular technique frees measurement experts by allowing the usability of any functional size measure and data model to estimate cost. COBRA is actually a framework of activates that are required for the development of the COBRA model.

The fundamental objective of this method is to develop a productivity estimation model by clubbing overhead cost estimates with the productivity model. Productivity model estimates productivity from cost overheads. In other words, the COBRA model has two core components. The first component is a casual model that produces overhead cost estimates and the second component uses data from past completed projects o the basis of similarity in characteristics (Melanie R., Ross J., and Isabella W., 2003).

- **Causal Model**: to calculate the overhead cost estimate, the causal model considers local cost factors or drivers that have a direct relationship with the cost overhead of the project. This particular relationship can be either direct or interaction between any two cost drivers (Briand L., El Emam K. and Bomarius F., 1998) and shown in figure 8. All those factors need to be identified that have an additive effect on the cost of the project. This particular activity of estimating overhead is carried out by expert knowledge acquisition.

- **Estimation Cost Overhead**: The estimation of cost overhead begins with the identification of most relevant cost drivers among the available drivers in the literature that have a direct role in the cost of the project. The list of identified 39 and 12 was retained to have a greater impact on overhead cost estimation. Cost drivers were grouped into four categories: Product, Process, Project and Personnel (Syed M. S. and Abdul W., 2017a). The qualitative causal model was developed to further investigate the impact of individual cost factor on cost estimation and their relative complexity. The implementation of the causal model is followed by a reliable questionnaire to measure and validate the impact of cost factors on the cost estimation. Frequency scale, Evaluation scale, and Agreement scale were used to collect responses regarding cost factors (Syed M. S. and Abdul W, 2017b). After the acquisition of this conceptual, qualitative model, the experts were asked to "quantify" the effect of each of these cost factors on the development cost, by expressing in the percentage of overhead above an "optimal" application that each factor may induce, called as overhead multipliers. The next step ahead is to express the relationship and the estimates of multipliers and project questionnaire variables in the form of equations. The relationship between these variables can be direct, two way or three-way interaction and are expressed in (Briand L., El Emam K. and Bomarius F., 1998). These are then translated into parameters of triangular distribution (minimum, most likely or maximum). Monte Carlo simulation is used to obtain an overhead cost estimate by considering a sample from each triangular distribution. The same is shown in figure 9. This procedure is repeated 1000 times to obtain the distribution of cost overhead of the project. During these multipliers from all the experts are combined. The mean of this distribution can be randomly selected as the estimated value of cost overhead for the project.

Figure 8. Causal model example

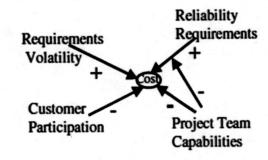

Figure 9. Overview of the productivity estimation model

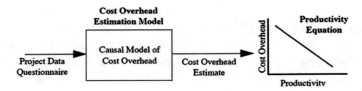

WEB-COBRA

The combinative nature of COBRA: expert opinion and formal modeling, increases its scope to perform effort estimation of web application development. The adoption of COBRA for estimating efforts was performed by Ruhe by developing a web-specific version of COBRA, the Web-COBRA (Melanie R., Ross J., and Isabella W., 2003). Web-COBRA has been modified in several aspects to make it suitable for estimating efforts for web applications. The working framework of Web-COBRA was obtained after conducting personal interviews with the experts of Allete Systems using open questions (Ruhe M., 2002)(Jacky K. and Ross J., 2008). In contrast to COBRA, the quality causal model developed had only direct relationships of cost factors with a cost. Further in Web-COBRA interactions were avoided by deriving a minimum set of independent cost factors. Quantification of relationships within the causal model was refined by conducting personal interviews with Allete System experts to obtain multipliers, in addition to this experts were in command to discuss and understand the cost factors and the multipliers together to improve and validate the quantitative causal model. To aggregate the multiple responses from experts for cost overhead a measure of "central tendency" was used and no weighting was done as Allete System experts were very similar in experience (Banker R D, Chang H. and Kemerer C., 1994).

Machine Learning

These are the most recent methods developed to estimate the efforts for software applications in general and web and mobile applications in particular. Machine learning models are based on computational intelligence extended from human problem-solving characteristics. These models were developed to overcome the challenges faced using expert and other algorithmic models. The irony is that there is yet no "silver bullet" method for estimating the efforts. Machine learning based methods do have both strengths and limitations as well. They largely depend on their context where they are applied. Machine learning methods have the characteristic feature to get trained, and then it automatically recognizes the complex pattern of variables to predict estimates by adopting intelligent decision making. There are different machine learning estimation methods like; Genetic algorithm (Back, T., Hammel U. and Schwefel H.,1997)(Burgess, Colin J., and Martin L., 2007), fuzzy logic(Kumar S., Krishna B. A. and Satsangi P. S., 1994), regression trees(Schofield C., 1998), neural networks (Shepperd M. J., Schofield C. and Kitchenham B., 1996) and case-based reasoning(CBR) (Shepperd M. J., and Kadoda G., 2001). The brief discussion on few popular machine learning based effort estimation methods is given under;

Neural Network

Neural network based model for estimating software efforts has been conceived from the work behavior of the human nervous system. The human nervous system acquires or perceives certain input from the environment through its distinguished perceptions and later activates desired actuators to deliver by responding through proper action. As processing/responding power of the nervous system is instant and fast, based on the same logic, an effort estimation algorithm is designed to perform fast, accurate and instant effort estimation. A simple neuron model is provided in figure 10. The neural network has become the most common and popular software effort estimation model-building technique and is a computer-assisted learning process that inherits the working principles of the human brain. Neural networks are massively parallel and complex and have the capability to solve complex problems with much speed and accuracy. Neural network based effort estimation model works by feeding neural network with historical data of previously completed software projects or web application to get it trained to learn the future course of data on the similar patterns to generate corresponding output. The trained neural network automatically configures or adjusts algorithmic parameters and corresponding weights in order to generate more significant and optimal solution(here in this case estimates)

Figure 10. A neural network estimation model

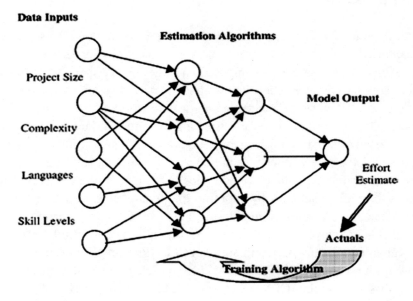

The actual design of the neural network model begins with the development of an appropriate layout, intermediate levels and links between neural nodes. These neural nodes compute the weighted sum of their corresponding input to generate output. If the sum of the weights exceeds a certain threshold, then this output can be either excitatory or inhibitory input to neuron or nodes of intermediate levels. This passing of input from one node to another in intermediate level continues till the final output is generated (Mair C., Gada K. and Martin L., 2000). The applicability of neural networks for estimating software efforts was extensively studied by Mair and Aggarwal (Gray A. and MacDonell S., 1996)(Aggarwal K.K., Singh Y.and Chandra P., 2005). The performance of the neural network is pretty sensitive to the training date set the feed to it.

Analogy Based Effort Estimation

Estimation by analogy is a systematic method where the estimation of efforts primarily involves characterization of features for the software project for which estimates are required. On the basis of these identified features, similar or analogous projects from already completed past projects are extracted. This characterization, identification of analogous projects forms the basic framework for analogy based effort estimation (ABE) method. The efforts of these completed projects are used to construct estimates for new but similar projects. This method of estimation is also called a systematic form of expert judgment since both involve the identification of similar projects to obtain estimates (Martin, 1996). Analogy Based Effort Estimation method has been widely used for developing software effort estimation models based upon retrieval by similarity among the projects effectively (Azzeh M., Neagu D. and Cowling P., 2010). The main challenging issue that needs further elaboration is "how to find similar projects ?", identification and prioritization of features.

The data driven ABE method involves four primary steps (Shepperd M and Schofield C., 1997) (1) select k nearest analogies using Euclidean distance or Manhattan distance. (2) Reuse efforts from the set of nearest analogies to find out the effort of the new project. (3) Adjust the retrieved efforts to bring them closer to the new project. Finally, (4) retain the estimated project in the repository for future prediction.

To find analogous projects and to perform effort estimation, an automated tool like ANGEL is used. It automatically finds the best combination of attributes used to find a similar score.

The main disadvantage of analogy method is that it requires considerable amount of computation to reveal similarity done previous projects like using Euclidian distance, etc. Walkerden and Jeffery (Walkerden F. and Jeffery R., 1999)," have compared few techniques for analogy-based software effort estimation with each other furthermore with a linear regression model. The outcomes demonstrated that human brains work superior than tools at selecting analogies for the considered dataset.

Case Based Reasoning

It is another variant of analogy based effort estimation approach, wherein estimates for the new project is initiated by adapting efforts of the most similar and relevant projects from the project pool of successfully completed projects. The process of Case-Based Reasoning (CBR) begins with the detection of most relevant characteristics of the project, called as cost drivers. These cost drivers give a real sense of project size. The similarity between the two projects is found by using Euclidean Distance to obtain distance metrics.

CBR is actually based on the principle that "new problems are often similar to previously dealt problems". Similarly, the estimates obtained for previously developed projects can be a solution to a new project to develop. CBR can be accomplished in four steps (Trendowiz A. and Joffery R., 2014):

1. Retrieve those projects that are similar to new projects to be estimated form projects completed already (historical data).
2. The solution of the identified projects in step 1 above means the efforts and attributes are reused to generate a solution for the current estimation problem.

3. The results obtained for new project estimates can be revisited against the actual estimate.

4. After successfully evaluating the estimates, that is to find the deviation either positive or negative between the actual and estimated efforts and the results are retained for future reference.

The estimation process in CBR is more or less similar to that of analogy based effort estimation. The implementation of CBR in order to obtain effort estimates for software applications in general and web application, in particular, is performed after taking following decisions in order (Shepherd M, and Kadoda M., 2001):

- Selecting attributes
- Scaling attributes
- Identifying analogies
- selecting analogies and
- Adapting analogies

Bayesian Belief Networks

Bayesian belief network (BBN) or simply Bayesian network is a directed acyclic graph in which nodes represent random variables, these variables can either be discrete or continuous. The edges of the graph express the probabilistic dependency among the connected nodes with different variables. Therefore, each of these nodes is associated with a conditional probability table(CPT) that quantifies its probability distribution. Relationship between two nodes is represented by an arrowhead stating from influencing variable and terminating on an influenced variable that is the direction from a child node to a parent node.

Figure 11 represents the believed causal dependencies between size and selected web application sizing metrics that is "no. of pages" and "no. of multimedia files". In this case, root node "size" has two child nodes: "no. of pages" and "no. of multimedia files". These kinds of topologies represent the belief that the size of the

Figure 11. Bayesian belief network

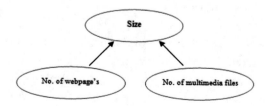

web application is influenced by "no. of pages" and "no. of multimedia files". BBN actually represents a model that supports reasoning with uncertainty and is mainly used in the situation where the knowledge of unknown events is obtained from the knowledge of observed events and are updated accordingly (Emilia M., 2012) (Jensen F.V, 1996). BBN can have broadly two events, Hypothesis and Evidence. Hypothesis(H) are those events which are yet to be explored, and Evidences(E) are those events that have been observed. The interpretation of these events is performed by probability calculus and Bayes theorem, and it continues across the belief to explore the entire hypothesis and update them to evidences, the observed events. To build BBN for estimating the efforts for software applications in general and web applications in particular, the number of issues surface (Emilia M, 2012)

- As BBN in context of the web application is concerned, the datasets used to build belief network needs to be large enough to capture all the possible relationships and the respective states of nodes so that probabilities can be easily mapped.
- Identification of variables that represents all the factors within a specific domain.
- Different structure and probability learning algorithms lead to different prediction accuracy (Mendes E., and Mosley N., 2008).To differentiate between the models is time-consuming.
- Implementation of hybrid BBN model the structure of these models needs to be jointly elicited by more than one domain expert to generalize its diverse applicability.
- The probabilities used by data-driven and hybrid models need to be investigated by at least one domain expert. this may sound like to check the probability of all the nodes of BBN, which is almost not feasible.
- The choice of variable discretization, structure learning algorithms, parameter estimation algorithms, and a number of categories used in the discretization all affect the accuracy of the results, and there is no proper guideline to make the best choice.

Regression Based Estimation Techniques

Regression analysis is a statistical method to investigate the relationship between two variables. One variable is regarded as independent or response/outcome and the second one regarded as dependent or predictive/explanatory. This technique is used to predict the relationship that exists between these variables. It is an important tool for modeling and analyzing data. The main advantages of using regressions analysis are: it indicates the significant relationships between the dependent and independent variable, it also indicates the behavior, impact of multiple independent variables on the dependent variable. In the case of estimating efforts, efforts are a dependent variable, and it depends on various independent variables that collectively make the size of particular software or web application.

Regression analysis can be pursued in different ways, depending on the number and behavior of its predictors or independent variables, few popular regression-based techniques implemented to predict effort estimates are mentioned and described briefly

Linear Regression

It is one of the most widely known modeling techniques. In this technique, the dependent variable is continuous, the independent variable(s) can be, and the nature of the regression line is linear.

Linear Regression establishes a relationship between the dependent variable (Y) and one or more independent variables (X) using a best fit straight line (also known as a regression line).

It is represented by an equation 24

$$Y = a + b * X + e, \tag{24}$$

where a is intercept, b is the slope of the line and e is error term. This equation can be used to predict the value of the target variable based on a given predictor variable(s).

MULTIPLE LINEAR REGRESSIONS

The relationship between dependent variable (Y) and independent variables (Xi) in multiple linear regression (MLR) is expressed by equation 25

$$Y = \beta_0 + \beta_1 X_1 + \beta_1 X_1 + ... + \beta_n X_n + \varepsilon \tag{25}$$

where, $X_1, X_2, ..., X_n$ are repressors or predictors; β_0 is the intercept parameter; β_1, $\beta_2, ..., \beta_n$ are the regression coefficients; and ε is the error component.

MLR technique is usually employed when: (i) the number of cases is significantly higher than the number of parameters to be estimated; (ii) the data has a stable behaviour; (iii) there is a small number of missing data; (iv) a small number of independent variables are sufficient (after transformations if necessary) to linearly predict output variables (also transformed if necessary), so as to enable an interpretable representation (Gray A. R. and MacDonell S. G., 1997). Application of the MLR method requires verification of the associated assumptions. The major assumptions to be considered are (Freund R. J. and Wilson W. J., 1998)(Ott R. L. and Longnecker M., 2010):

- **Linearity:** The relationship between each Xi and Y is linear. Thus the model adequately describes the behavior of data;
- The error component is an independent and normally distributed variable with constant variance and means value zero.

The difference between simple linear regression and multiple linear regression is that multiple linear regression has (>1) independent variables, whereas simple linear regression has only 1 independent variable. Now, the question is "How do we obtain the best fit line?"

Stepwise Regression

This form of regression is used when we deal with multiple independent variables. In this technique, the selection of independent variables is done with the help of an automatic process, which involves no human intervention.

This feat is achieved by observing statistical values like R-square, t-stats and AIC metric to discern significant variables. Stepwise regression basically fits the regression model by adding/dropping co-variates one at a time based on a specified criterion. Some of the most commonly used Stepwise regression methods are listed below:

- Standard stepwise regression does two things. It adds and removes predictors as needed for each step.
- Forward selection starts with the most significant predictor in the model and adds variable for each step.
- Backward elimination starts with all predictors in the model and removes the least significant variable for each step.

The main approach of implementing regression-based modeling is to find the set of independent variables that best explains the variation in the dependent variable. The goal of regression is to find the function $f(x)$ that best models the data. In linear regression, this is done by finding the line that minimizes the sum squares error on the data.

Evaluation Criteria

To investigate the effectiveness and accuracy of various effort estimation approaches that are being used by practitioners to perform software effort estimation, various evaluation criteria are used. Evaluation of effort estimation models is carried out by using data sets of past projects developed by the various organizations in the past. Using these datasets on these various models gives the idea about the effectiveness and accuracy in effort estimation by just looking on the deviation obtained(Actual efforts-estimated efforts using different models) The evaluation criteria statistically analyse the results using various mathematical or statistical/ probability distributions like Magnitude of Relative Error(MRE),Mean Magnitude of Relative error(MMRE), Median Magnitude of Relative Error(MdMRE), Mean Absolute error (MAE), Median Absolute Error(MdAE), Standard Deviation, PRED(x), Skewness, Significance tests(Z-test, t-test, chi-square test etc)(Syed M. S., Abdul W., 2017a).

LIMITATIONS OF EFFORT ESTIMATION MODELS

Different effort estimation approaches that have been introduced from time to time by several researchers to perform effective effort estimation have got both advantages and disadvantages with them. The most common limitations and advantages of few popular effort estimation models is provided in table 12.

CONCLUSION

Importance and usability of software applications are continuously increasing. Therefore, it is inevitable for project management to ensure security, reliability, and effectiveness in various software projects. Overriding the benefits of soft systems, most of the organizations are using software-based applications as an interface to access or deliver a multitude of services. To manage growing complexity and demand for quality of services, there is much-required need to have good software application development approach. Better development methodology helps project managers to develop software applications on time and within budget to meet user requirements effectively. Effort estimation plays a major role in effective web application development by predicting the efforts required for web development and subsequently, the cost of development. Accuracy in effort estimation helps project management to draw efficient budgetary estimates so that web development can be monitored and carried out in a systematic manner.

Table 12. Advantages and disadvantages of effort estimation models

Type	Approach	Advantages	Disadvantages
Algorithmic Method	LOC	Very easy in implementation to Estimate the size of software	Prediction of line is tough in early stages, not good for very large project and language dependent
	Putnam's Model	Time, Size and Effort are easily collected for past projects	It does not consider the other phases of SDLC
	FPA	Tools, methods and language are independent to achieve the fast result	Time, Quality and manual work are not considered
	SEER-SEM	Used in very large projects	50 input parameters are required which increased the complexity and uncertainty
	COCOMO	Estimating the cost is simple and gets the clear result	Details of past project are required
	COCOMO II	It provides more support for modern software development processes and an updated project database. Provide support to mainframe, code reusability and batch processing.	It cannot estimate the effort at all the different phase of SDLC. Its prediction is .68 which is quite good.
	Detailed COCOMO	Phase sensitive effort multipliers are each to determine the amount of effort required to complete each phase.	Lots of parameters involved in estimation time complexity is high. Its prediction is .70 which is good.
Non-Algorithmic Method	Analogy based Estimation	Experience and knowledge are used for actual projects	Attributes are required
	Expert Judgment	New technology, domain and architecture are the basis to estimate the cost	Experience of similar projects
	Top-Down	It requires very less detail about the project, moreover it is faster, simple and easier to use. Unlike other approaches it focuses on activities like integration, management etc	Low level problems are difficult to Identify
	Bottom-Up	This technique is more stable and error estimation is also performed	Time and system level activities are not considered

continues on following page

Many developmental approaches have been used for software effort estimation but, most of them were conventional software methods and therefore, failed to produce accurate results when it comes to web or mobile effort estimation. Several web specific effort estimation methods were also developed by researchers from the past few years, but, their results are still questionable. Due to their inaccuracy,

Table 12. Continued

Type	Approach	Advantages	Disadvantages
Machine learning Methods	Linear Regression	statistical models	Relationships between dependent and independent variables
	Support Vector Machine	Flexibility, Robustness, Unique solutions	computation is expensive, binary classifier
	Neural Network	Powerful method, mathematical formula, eases to use. Consistent with unlike databases, power of reasoning	Large complexity of network structure. There is no guideline for designing, the performance depends on large training data
	K-Means	Fast Result, Easy to implement	Difficult to predict K-value, Global clusters
	Hierarchical cluster	Easy to decide the clusters	Time complexity, Not possible to undo the previous step
	Fuzzy	Training is not required, flexibility	Hard to use, maintaining the degree of meaningfulness is difficult
	Artificial neural network based estimation	Artificial Neural Network based estimation methods are consistent with unlike databases and they provide power of reasoning in estimation process	Large amount of training data is required No guidelines or instructions are provided for designing.

Source: Rajeswari K. and Beena.R., 2018; Tailor O., Saini J. and Rijwani P. 2014

the tradition of using conventional approaches is still continuing to remain effort estimation approaches for web or mobile effort estimation.

The existing literature highlights that the existing software effort estimation strategies are not adequate to produce accurate and effective estimates, therefore, advocates the need to develop a more customized and tailor-made model for effort estimation inline within changing development technology to ensure accurate and effective effort estimation at early stages of software development.

REFERENCES

Aggarwal, K. K., Singh, Y., Chandra, P., & Puri, M. (2005). Bayesian regularization in a neural network model to estimate lines of code using function points. *Journal of Computational Science*, *1*(4), 505–509. doi:10.3844/jcssp.2005.505.509

Albrecht, A. J. (1979). Measuring application development productivity. In *Proceedings of the joint SHARE, GUIDE and IBM application development symposium*. IBM Corporation.

Alves, R., Valente, P., & Numes, N. J. (2013). Improving Software Effort Estimation with Human-Centric Models: a comparison of UCP and iUCP accuracy. *Proceedings of the 5th ACM SIGCHI symposium on Engineering interactive computing systems, 287-296.* 10.1145/2494603.2480300

Anda, B., & Dreiem, H. (2001). Estimating software development effort based on use cases-experiences from industry. *Fourth International Conference on the UML,* 487–502. 10.1007/3-540-45441-1_35

Azzeh, M., Neagu, D., & Cowling, P. (2010). Fuzzy grey relational analysis for software effort estimation. *Empirical Software Engineering*, *15*(1), 60–90. doi:10.100710664-009-9113-0

Back, T., Hammel, U., & Schwefel, H. (1997). Evolutionary Computation: Comments on the History and Current State. *IEEE Transactions on Evolutionary Computation, 1*(1), 3–17. doi:10.1109/4235.585888

Banker, R. D., Chang, H., & Kemerer, C. (1994). Evidence on Economies of Scale in Software Development. *Information and Software Technology, 1994*(5), 275–282. doi:10.1016/0950-5849(94)90083-3

Bauer, F. (1968). Software engineering: A report on conference sponsored. NATO Science Committee.

Boehm, B. (1981). Software Development Cost Estimation Approaches-A Surey. *Annals of Software Engineering, 10*, 177-205.

Boehm, B., Abts, C., & Chulani, S. (2000). Software development cost estimation approaches: A survey. *Annals of Software Engineering*, *10*(1), 177–205. doi:10.1023/A:1018991717352

Boehm, B. W. (1981). *Software engineering economics* (Vol. 197). Englewood Cliffs, NJ: Prentice-Hall.

Boehm, B. W., Abts, C., Brown, A. W., Chulani, S., Clark, B. K., Horowitz, W., ... Steece, B. (2000). *Software Cost Estimation with COCOMO 11*. Prenctice Hall.

Briand, L., & Emam, K. (1998). COBRA: A Hybrid Method for Software Cost Estimation, Benchmarking, and Risk Assessment. *Proc. of the Intern. Conference on Software Engineering (ICSE'98)*, 390-399. 10.1109/ICSE.1998.671392

Briand, L. C., & Wieczorek, I. (2002). *Resource Estimation in Software Engineering. In Encyclopedia of Software Engineering* (Vol. 2, pp. 1160–1196). John Wiley & Sons.

Bruegge, B., & Dutoit, A. H. (2003). *Object-Oriented Software Engineering: Using UML, Patterns and Java* (2nd ed.). Prentice-Hall.

Burgess, C. J., & Martin, L. (2007). Can genetic programming improve software effort estimation? A comparative evaluation. *Information and Software Technology, 43*(14), 863–867. doi:10.1016/S0950-5849(01)00192-6

Burgess, C. J., & Martin, L. (2007). Can genetic programming improve software effort estimation? A comparative evaluation. *Information and Software Technology, 43*(14), 863–867. doi:10.1016/S0950-5849(01)00192-6

Costagliola, G., Di Martino, S., Ferrucci, F., Gravino, C., Tortora, G., & Vitiello, G. (2006). A COSMIC-FFP approach to predict web application development effort. *Journal of Web Engineering, 5*(2), 93–120.

Costagliola, G., Di Martino, S., Ferrucci, F., & Vitiello, G. (2006). A COSMIC-FFP approach to predict web application development effort. *Journal of Web Engineering, 5*(2), 93–120.

De Marco, L., Ferrucci, F., & Gravino, C. (2013). Approximate COSMIC size to early estimate Web application development effort. *Presented at the Software Engineering and Advanced Applications, 2013. SEAA 2013. 39th EUROMICRO Conference*, 349–356.

Donald, J. R. (1993). *SoftCost-OO Reference Manual*. Torrance, CA: Reifer Consultants, Inc.

Donald, R. J. (2000). Web Development estimating quick-to-market software. *Software IEEE, 17*(6), 57–64. doi:10.1109/52.895169

Eck, D., Brundick, B., & Fettig, T. (2009). Parametric estimating handbook. The International Society of Parametric Analysis (ISPA).

Emilia, M. (2012). Using Knowledge Elicitation to Improve Web Effort Estimation: Lessons from Six Industrial Case Studies. In *34th International Conference on Software Engineering (ICSE)*. IEEE.

Emilia, M., Mosley, N., & Steve, C. (2006). Web Effort Estimation. In Web Engineering. Springer.

Emilia, M., & Steve, C. (2000). Web Development Effort Estimation using Analogy. *Software Engineering Conference, 2000, Proceedings*.

Fenton, N. E., & Pfleeger, S. L. (1997). *Software Metrics: A Rigorous and Practical Approach*. International Thomson Computer Press.

Freund, R. J., & Wilson, W. J. (1998). *Regression Analysis: Statistical Modeling of a Response Variable*. San Diego, CA: Academic Press.

Frohnhoff, S., & Engels, G. (2008). Revised Use Case Point Method - Effort Estimation in Development Projects for Business. In *Proceedings of the CONQUEST 2008 - 11th International Conference on Quality Engineering in Software Technology*. Potsdam: Dpunkt Verlag.

Gray, A., & MacDonell, S. (1996). A Comparison of Techniques for Developing Predictive Models of Software Metrics. *Information and Software Technology, 39*, 1997.

Gray, A. R., & MacDonell, S. G. (1997). A comparison of techniques for developing predictive models of software metrics. *Information and Software Technology, 39*(6), 425–437. doi:10.1016/S0950-5849(96)00006-7

Gray, R., MacDonell, S. G., & Shepperd, M. J. (1999). Factors Systematically associated with errors in subjective estimates of software development effort: the stability of expert judgment. *Proceedings of the 6th IEEE Metrics Symposium*. 10.1109/METRIC.1999.809743

Heemstra, F. J. (1992). Software cost estimation. *Information and Software Technology, 34*(10), 627–639. doi:10.1016/0950-5849(92)90068-Z

ISO/IEC 19761:2011, *Software engineering -- COSMIC: a functional size measurement method*. International Organization for Standardization.

Jacky, K., & Ross, J. (2008). Automated Support for Software Cost Estimation using Web-CoBRA. In *15th Asia Pacific Software Engineering Conference*. IEEE Computer Society.

Jensen, F. V. (1996). *An introduction to Bayesian networks*. London: UCL Press.

Jørgensen, M. (2007). Forecasting of software development work effort: Evidence on expert judgement and formal models. *International Journal of Forecasting, 23*(3), 449–462. doi:10.1016/j.ijforecast.2007.05.008

Karner, G. (1993). Metrics for objector. University of Linköping.

Kemerer, C. F. (1987). An empirical validation of software cost estimation models. *Communications of the ACM*, *30*(5), 416–429. doi:10.1145/22899.22906

Kirmani, M. M., & Wahid, A. (2015). Revised Use Case Point (Re-UCP) Model for Software Effort Estimation. *International Journal of Advanced Computer Science and Applications*, *6*(3), 65–71.

Kumar, S., Krishna, B. A., & Satsangi, P. S. (1994). Fuzzy systems and neural networks in software engineering project management. *Journal of Applied Intelligence*, *4*(1), 31–52. doi:10.1007/BF00872054

Kusuma, B. M. (2014). Software Cost Estimation Techniques. *International Journal of Engineering Research in Management and Technology, 3*(4).

Leung, H., & Fan, Z. (2001). *Software Cost Estimation*. Academic Press.

Leung, H., & Fan, Z. (2002). Software Cost Estimation. In Handbook of Software Engineering and Knowledge Engineering. Hong Kong Polytechnic University. doi:10.1142/9789812389701_0014

Lynch, J. (2009). *Chaos manifesto*. The Standish Group. Retrieved from http://www.standishgroup.com/newsroom/chaos_2009.php

Mair, C., Gada, K., & And Martin, L. (2000). An investigation of machine learning based prediction. *Journal of Systems and Software*, *53*(1), 23–29. doi:10.1016/S0164-1212(00)00005-4

Martin. (1996). Effort Estimation Using Analogy. *Proceedings of ICSE-18*, 170-178.

Melanie, R., Ross, J., & Isabella, W. (2003). Cost Estimation for Web Applications. *Proceedings of the 25th International Conference on Software Engineering (ICSE'03)*.

Mendes, E., Counsell, S., & Mosley, N. (2002). Comparison of web size measures for predicting web design and authoring effort. *IEE Proceedings. Software*, *149*(3), 86–92. doi:10.1049/ip-sen:20020337

Mendes, E., & Mosley, N. (2008). Bayesian Network Models for Web Effort Prediction: A Comparative Study. *Transactions on Software Engineering*, *34*(6), 723–737. doi:10.1109/TSE.2008.64

Software. (n.d.). In *Merriam-Webster*. Retrieved from https://www.merriam-webster.com/dictionary/software

Mills, H. D. (2010). The management of software engineering, part 1: Concepts of software engineering. *IBM Systems Journal*, *19*(4), 414–420. doi:10.1147j.194.0414

Myrtveit, I., & Stensrud, E. (1999). A Controlled Experiment to Assess the Benefits of Estimating with Analogy and Regression Models. *IEEE Transactions on Software Engineering, 25*(4), 510–525.

Nassif, A. B., Ho, D., & Capretz, L. F. (2011). Regression model for software effort estimation based on the use case point method. *International Conference on Computer and Software Modelling, 14*, 106-110.

Ott, R. L., & Longnecker, M. (2010). *An Introduction to Statistical Methods and Data Analysis*. Belmont: Cengage Learning Inc.

Putnam, L. H. (1978). A General Empirical Solution to the Macro Software Sizing and Estimating Problem. *IEEE Transactions on Software Engineering, 4*(4), 345–361. doi:10.1109/TSE.1978.231521

Rajeswari, K., & Beena, R. (2018). A Critique On Software Cost Estimation. *International Journal of Pure and Applied Mathematics, 118*(20), 3851–3862.

Rollo, T. (2000). Sizing E-Commerce. *Proceedings of Australian Conference on Software Measurement*.

Ruhe, M. (2002). *The early and accurate effort estimation of web applications*. Kaiserslautern, Germany: University of Kaiserslautern.

Ruhe, M., Jeffery, R., & Wieczorek, I. (2003). Using web objects for estimation software development effort for web applications. Presented at *Ninth International Software Metrics Symposium (METRICS '03)*, Sydney, Australia. 10.1109/METRIC.2003.1232453

Schofield, C. (1998). *An empirical investigation into software estimation by analogy* (Unpublished doctoral dissertation). Department of Computing, Bournemouth University, Bournemouth, UK.

Shepherd, M., & Kadoda, M. (2001). Comparing Software prediction Techniques using Simulation. *IEEE Transactions on Software Engineering, 23*(11), 1014–1022. doi:10.1109/32.965341

Shepperd, M., & Schofield, C. (1997). Estimating software project effort using analogies. *IEEE Transactions on Software Engineering, 23*(11), 736–743. doi:10.1109/32.637387

Shepperd, M. J., & Kadoda, G. (2001). Using simulation to evaluate prediction technique. In *Proceedings of the IEEE 7th International Software Metrics Symposium* (pp. 349-358). IEEE.

Shepperd, M. J., Schofield, C., & Kitchenham, B. (1996). Effort estimation using analogy. *Proceedings of, ICSE-18*, 170–178.

Syed, M. S., & Abdul, W. (2017). Web Effort Estimation Using FP and WO: A Critical Study. *Proceedings of the 2nd International Conference on Computing Methodologies and Communication (ICCMC 2018)*.

Syed, M. S., & Abdul, W. (2017a). Web Complexity Factors: A Novel Approach for Predicting Size Measures for Web Application Development. *Proceedings of the International Conference on Inventive Computing and Informatics(ICICI 2017)*.

Syed, M. S., & Abdul, W. (2017b). Effort Estimation Techniques for Web Application Development: A Review. *International Journal of Advanced Research in Computer Science, 8*(9), 125-131.

Tailor, O., Saini, J., & Rijwani, P. (2014). Comparative Analysis of Software Cost and Effort Estimation Methods: A Review. *International Journal of Computer Science and Mobile Computing, 3*(4), 1364-1374.

Trendowiz, A., & Joffery, R. (2014). Case Based Reasoning. In *Software Project Effort Estimation*. Springer International Publishing.

Walkerden, F., & Jeffery, R. (1999). An empirical study of analogy-based software effort Estimation. *Empirical Software Engineering, 4*(2), 135-158.

KEY TERMS AND DEFINITIONS

Actual Effort: The actual extent of resources that are utilized to perform successful software development.

Effort Estimation: Process of calculating the budget required to develop a software application.

Effort Estimation Models: Different models that practitioners use to perform effort estimation for different software developments.

Estimated Effort: The approximate prediction of efforts projected by estimator to perform application development on time and within the budget.

Mobile Application: Similar to that of web application in certain parameters developed to run on handheld devices with understandable interface.

Software Application: Conventional or traditional software application developed to deliver a specific kind of functionality meant to be used within the boundary of a particular organization.

Software Development: Systematic approach followed in development industry to develop software products

Web Application: Type of software application developed to be accessed via web browser and meant to address the requirements or diverse people with non-geographical access restriction.

Chapter 4
Artefact Consistency Management in DevOps Practice:
A Survey

Dulani Meedeniya

iD https://orcid.org/0000-0002-4520-3819
University of Moratuwa, Sri Lanka

Iresha Rubasinghe
University of Moratuwa, Sri Lanka

Indika Perera
University of Moratuwa, Sri Lanka

ABSTRACT

DevOps practices preserve the continuous innovation in software development. The collaborative nature and stakeholder communication are keys in DevOps that lead to highly effective and quality software outcomes with customer satisfaction. The software artefacts involved in a DevOps practice must adapt to frequent changes due to continuous stakeholder feedback. Hence, it is challenging to artefact consistency throughout the software life cycle. Although artefact traceability preserves the consistency management with theoretical support, there are practical limitations in traceability visualisation, change impact analysis, and change propagation aspects. This chapter presents an analysis of existing studies focused on software artefact traceability for the suitability in DevOps. It also identifies leading limitations and possible future research directions to resolve for the benefit of researchers and software practitioners.

DOI: 10.4018/978-1-7998-1863-2.ch004

Copyright © 2020, IGI Global. Copying or distributing in print or electronic forms without written permission of IGI Global is prohibited.

INTRODUCTION

Software System

Overview of a Software System

A software system is a combination of several software elements that evolves through a particular software development process model. It is an interface that connects the user with application software and computer hardware. It is a combination of a set of design decisions that lead to system architecture, which is a blueprint for any software system (Arora, & Arora, 2016). The study of theoretical concepts related to software system development, technical aspects, budgeting, management and maintenance is known as software engineering (Sommerville, 2010). With the rapid improvements in technology and resources, the importance of software systems has become vital in everyday activities. For instance, different domains such as finance, transportation, agriculture, military, academics, healthcare, business rely on software systems (Chang, 2005) (Sommerville, 2010). In practice, the aim is to maximise the use of automated software systems to minimise manual workforce and to improve quality. Thus, several well-defined software process models and technologies have been used in software system development.

Software Artefacts

Software artefacts refer to the intermediate by-products used in different phases of software development. These elements include System Requirement Specification (SRS), design diagrams, architectural documents and quality attributes or the non-functional design reports, source code, test scripts, walkthroughs, inspections, bug reports, build logs, test reports, project plans and risk assessments among many (Sommerville, 2010). Each artefact has its life cycle during software evolution. The types of artefacts in a software project may vary depending on the adapted software process model and technologies. Thus, a software system is a result of a collection of elements that goes through changes affecting each other at different levels. There are relationships and dependencies between these software artefacts, and it is essential to manage these software artefacts to maintain adequate consistency during changes. The improper management and outdated artefacts can lead to inconsistencies, synchronisation issues and lack of trust by stakeholders (Cleland-Huang, Zisman, & Gotel, 2012).

Software Development Life Cycle

Software Development Life Cycle (SDLC) denotes the overall software development related activities from the start of a software project until the completion and evolution. As shown in Figure 1, SDLC is the collection of core activities typically a software project follows regardless of project type, scale or domain (Sommerville, 2010) (Langer, 2016). The initial step is software project planning. Refinement can be applied to this phase based on the factors such as project type, stakeholder and organisational guidelines. A feasibility study is performed at this stage to identify the technical, financial, resource feasibility for the system completion. Next, the software requirements gathered from customers are further analysed, revised and prioritise, which is known as requirements engineering (Dick, Hull, & Jackson, 2017). Then, the actual software system design representing the intended software product is designed using design tools, different diagrams and mock-ups. The design is crucial, especially for implementation, where the software is coded to produce a useful product. Software developers are responsible for implementation using programming languages, supporting tools and diverse coding environments within given guidelines. Depending on the followed software process model, the application is tested incrementally or sequentially (Arora, & Arora, 2016) and transformed into a bug-free software product. Next, the software product is deployed, so that the end user can experience the system with proper user guidance. The technological, ethical, environmental circumstances and newer user requirements mainly lead to software maintenance. Thus, with the evolving needs, the deployed product is revised during the software maintenance phase.

Evolution of Software Systems

At present, software systems consider as critical business assets. A software system change is inevitable and hence, must be updated continuously to maintain the assets. In such situations, software evolution is preferred over building completely new software systems due to the cost and time benefits (Rajlich, 2014). Often, software evolution occurs in a software system life cycle at a stage where it is in active operation due to new requirements. Software evolution mainly depends on the type of software being maintained and cooperated development processes, which continue the software system lifecycle. This is highly coupled with the components that are affected due to changes which allow the cost and impact of changes to be estimated (Pete, & Balasubramaniam, 2015). Alongside, user expectations increase with higher demand and hence, software systems continuously improve with advanced technical solutions. The process of creating software systems with improvements by software engineering principles and methods is called software system evolution (Sommerville,

Figure 1. Software development life cycle

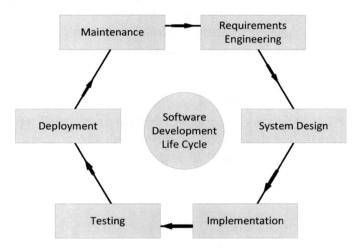

2010) (Mens, & Demeyer, 2008). It is a continuous effort to make software systems bug-free, efficient until the end user desires are fulfilled (Chang, 2005).

The improper or outdated software artefacts and their inconsistencies result in misleading the intermediate software system development processes due to the high coupling among elements. Hence, software development and maintenance become time-consuming with many issues such as higher cost and effort. Moreover, proper artefact management is essential in integrating artefacts continuously. The changes must propagate accurately in the integrations, which are challenging to be automated. However, software artefact consistency maintenance is essential with the rapid generation of information. Well-Defined traceability management among software artefacts is required to overcome the impact of evolutions. Further, improper traceability management may lead to product failures. Thus, traceability management strengthens the software maintainability and helps for system acceptance (Cleland-Huang et al., 2012).

Software Process

A software process is a collection of related activities in distinct phases that build an intended software product. The main stages of an SDLC include all the tasks that take place from the moment a problem is started to solve in terms of a software solution. However, the structure of phases varies, resulting in different types of software process models in practice. The plan-driven traditional Waterfall model consists of well-defined requirements and follows a sequential flow of data (Arora, & Arora, 2016). Evolutionary development handles immediate customer needs based on the refinement of initial development in an exploratory manner or using throwaway prototyping. Process iteration with the spiral model is another software process practice with incremental development (Sommerville, 2010). However, it is challenging to manage frequent artefact changes in these software process models.

Currently, Agile is the commercially leading software process model in generic software development in practice. Agile has an intimate and collaborative nature that secures ultimate customer satisfaction and balance in cost profit trade-off (Flora, & Chande, 2014). The Agile process mainly focuses on small rapid releases of software through the iterative and change-driven methodology. It is a non-linear and experimental process that accepts changes during software development (Rahman, Helms, Williams, & Parnin, 2015). However, the customer-centric informal behaviour in Agile often leads to chaotic complexities in large scale software project developments.

DEVOPS PRACTICE

Terminology in DevOps Practice

- **Development-Operations (DevOps):** DevOps is a practice that combines both 'Development' and 'Operations' work in a software development process (Bass et al., 2015) (Kim et al., 2016). DevOps is defined as a culture or a movement that highlights collaboration and communication between developers and operational team professionals in a software development environment. The goal of DevOps is to achieve automation and to improve software delivery with high frequency and quality.
- **Continuous Integration and Continuous Delivery (CICD):** DevOps practice emphasises the importance of having Continuous Integration and Continuous Delivery (CICD) during software development (Duvall, Matyas, & Glover, 2007). Continuous integration indicates the ability to allow software changes at any stage of the SDLC to any software artefact. Mainly, code-level changes in terms of new code additions, modifications and deletions consider as integrations. The faster software product releases are referred to by continuous delivery. Accordingly, Continuous Integration-Continuous Delivery pipeline accelerates quality software development in DevOps environments (Bass et al., 2015).

Software Development in DevOps Practice

Software development with DevOps (Development-Operations) practice has become a widely used approach in the industry. DevOps practice integrates both Agility and automation between development and operations teams to provide sufficient product efficiently. DevOps practice is highly coupled with the release cycle in Agile. It fills in the gap between the developer and operations team in a development environment to have consistency among stakeholder communication. It mainly facilitates CICD with frequent changes by applying Agile methods to operations with interactive stakeholders' feedback (Bass, Weber, & Zhu, 2015) (Kim, Debois, Willis, Humble, & Allspaw, 2016). Thus, it helps to achieve business goals by providing a high-quality product efficiently. Also, ensures customer satisfaction.

Consequently, software development in DevOps practice increases the productivity and influences the economies of scale. The main phases in DevOps include continuous building, testing, Continuous Integration (CI), delivery and monitoring that eventually minimise the defects in the operational level delivery. This process is supported by a compatible DevOps tool stack, as shown in Figure 2. For instance, the build automation tool Jenkins, software version controlling by GitHub, continuous delivery using Docker and project management with Trello are some of the support tools (Azeri, 2018).

DevOps Tool Stack

The CICD pipeline in a DevOps environment is supported by a set of tools such as Jenkins, Docker, Maven, Puppet, Travis, Ansible, Sonar and OpenStack support, as shown in Figure 2. The DevOps tool stack executes in a collaborative environment, although the tools are from different vendors. For instance, Jenkins is an open source build automation tool that supports continuous integration. Docker supports continuous deployment. Both Jenkins and Docker are integrable in the form of plugins. It is the main reason for their applicability in the CICD pipeline.

Jenkins used as a build automation server that monitors regular jobs execution. It generates a scenario where errors can be captured and enhance the capabilities to support the CICD pipeline. Figure 3 shows the basic workflow of building a software project on Jenkins automation server as a job. The Jenkins server performs tasks that invoke via a trigger (Hembrink, & Stenberg, 2013). The trigger can be a change in a linked version control system or a temporal trigger that builds in each of the fixed time intervals and display the results. For example, a build with Maven or Gradle includes the execution of pre-written shell scripts, tracking and storing the build outcomes and initialising integration tests. The configuration of Jenkins is simple through a web-based GUI and can deploy in large scale environment (Berg, 2015).

Figure 2. DevOps overview
Source: "QASource DevOps Experts," 2018

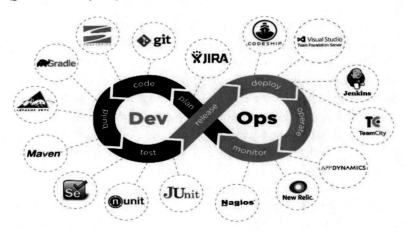

Docker is a general platform to build, ship, execute distributed applications and enhances the existence of microservices. Docker enables to hold and transport data accessible using containers or objects (Farcic, 2016). In practice, Docker containers are used to replace VMs for immutable deployments. Thus, the utilisation of Docker has reduced deployment efforts. Figure 4 illustrates the workflow of Docker. Docker file encapsulates the instructions required to build a source project with its dependencies based on environmental features. The execution of Docker file results in a Docker Image. It's a runtime instance represented using a Docker container. The execution of a Docker image supports continuous deployment ("Docker," 2018).

Moreover, Puppet (Farcic, 2016) and Travis ("Travis CI," 2018) are centralised configuration server in DevOps environments. Puppet supports to deploy microservices with less time and act as a platform to initiate system services, organize operating system-based packages. Travis supports to build and test open source software with the integration of GitHub repositories and enables team collaboration.

Furthermore, Project Management tools have a significant contribution to software development, especially in DevOps, where collaboration is essential. Thus, managing a large number of smaller teams, tracking software changes, tasks

Figure 3. Jenkins workflow

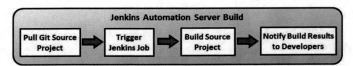

Figure 4. Docker workflow

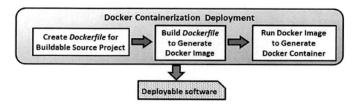

allocation among units are keep recorded using PM tools. Trello ("Trello," 2018) is a prominent, opensource, web-based PM application with API integration capabilities. It manages different tasks by assigning deadlines, priorities and progress among team members. Jira is another tool used by Agile teams for PM with tasks and issue tracking ("JIRA Software," 2018). Slack ("Slack," 2018) is a team collaboration tool, which stands for "Searchable Log of All Conversation and Knowledge". It is a cloud-based, proprietary tool with cross-platform capabilities that supports team communication using chat room features.

Challenges in DevOps Practice

Managing software artefact traceability in a DevOps environment is challenging due to many reasons. Generally, a DevOps environment consists of a large set of small teams. Hence, there can be issues in team collaboration. Mainly, the frequent code changes during continuous integration affect other artefacts in different impact levels (Bass et al., 2015). Thus, the artefact consistency management throughout CICD becomes challenging with the frequent changes of artefacts. Additionally, operational teams get overhead with the workload, while migrating from the traditional process and preserving the automation. DevOps tool stack related problems such as adopting new tools, maintaining their compatibility and interoperability and training the teams tend to be an overhead.

Further, adapting to the operational level in DevOps practice is challenging due to the lack of formalism compared to traditional software models. Thus, there is a need to address the challenges due to rapid artefact changes and team collaboration with multi-user accessibility. The development of these systems requires reliable traceability and consistent management for the correct functioning and maintenance of the product. Therefore, the requirement of having traceability support in a DevOps environment is significant than in a traditional software development environment.

Artefact Consistency Management

Overview of Software Traceability

Software artefact traceability is the process of tracking the behaviour of an artefact from the start of a software project until it evolves. It is also known by monitoring the life cycle of an artefact throughout a software project and maintaining the consistency among others. In the early stages, traceability has defined by considering the requirement artefact to revise them in the requirements engineering phase. Subsequently, traceability aspects have considered regardless of the artefact types and software process model categories (Sommerville, 2010). A professional body named 'Centre of Excellence for Software and Systems Traceability (CoEST)', has defined traceability as a way of interrelating artefacts with each other, to maintain links among them (Keenan et al., 2012). Technically, the connections between elements declare the traceability among them, which call as trace links or the traceability links. Further, a collection of all the traces corresponding to a software system is defined as a trace set (Cleland-Huang et al., 2012). Traceability matrix and traceability graph are the two most popular methods of representing traceability links (Marcus, Xie, & Poshyvanyk, 2005).

Terminology in Artefact Consistency Management

- **Traceability establishment:** Traceability management tracks the life cycle of a given artefact. Thus, it is essential to identify the behavioural aspects of an element such as how it evolves, what are the changes applied to it, how it impacts from the changes in other artefacts, etc. Traceability establishment is the process of creating links between artefacts, that have relationships or dependencies among them. These links enable to track elements both backward and forward (Cleland-Huang et al., 2012). Moreover, this trace-link creation helps to avoid any possible chaotic consequences in a DevOps environment, where artefacts are highly subjected to changes.
- **Change detection:** Artefacts in a software development process, often change to produce the intended software outcome (Sommerville, 2010). Particularly, in a DevOps environment, the CICD pipeline encourages frequent artefact changes. Higher the artefact changes, it is more important to identify the changes for better traceability management. Change detection is the process of determining the changes in artefacts during the SDLC.
- **Change Impact Analysis:** The artefact changes that occur during an ongoing software project may affect other artefacts. Change Impact Analysis (CIA) is the process of determining the consequences or the impact of an

artefact change in other parts of the software system (Sommerville, 2010). For instance, when a change is detected, the CIA identifies the impact of that change among other artefacts in the related trace paths. Since there are heterogeneous artefacts involved in a software project, the consequences of a single artefact change are not uniform on other artefacts. For instance, a change in a source code method name might affect corresponding test script and design diagram but may not affect requirements. Therefore, it is useful to identify affected artefacts and the severity level of the impact.

- **Consistency Checking:** As the impact of artefact changes can reflect on others differently, the artefacts tend to become unstable after a continuous integration process in a DevOps environment. Consistency checking ensures the stability among artefacts (Pete, & Balasubramaniam, 2015). The Inconsistent elements may not produce the expected software system (Walkinshaw, 2017).
- **Change Propagation:** Once the consequences of an artefact change are identified, reacting on those is known by change propagation. It is essential to manage any possible ripple-effects after changes to synchronise the artefacts. Hence, when a change impact is identified, the impacted elements should change accordingly (Li, Sun, Leung, & Zhang, 2013).
- **Project Management:** Project management is crucial during the SDLC in a DevOps environment where team-based communication and collaboration are high. Thus, it is essential to keep the teams and responsible stakeholders up-to-date about the status of the software projects (Sommerville, 2010) (Murray, 2016). The team members must be notified about their daily tasks, targets, deadlines and the clients and investors; likewise; outside parties must be informed about the project progress statuses. Additionally, the required artefact changes can be notified to the teams to follow up. Currently, these requirements achieve via many software tools which are a part of DevOps tools stack.

Importance of Traceability Management

In practice, it is expensive to manage consistency whenever artefact changes due to many relationships and dependencies. Although the number of artefacts is low, it requires more effort to maintain artefact relations. Hence, ensuring the correctness of trace-link relationship over time is essential in traceability management and is a multi-step activity (Mäder & Gotel, 2012) (Maro, Anjorin, Wohlrab, & Steghöfer, 2016). The proper identification of a feasible traceability management approach could minimise the cost and effort during the SDLC. Moreover, proper trace-link management is useful in software development to manage the artefact consistency and directs towards the intended software product. Traceability among artefacts helps to track the changes occurred such as new requirement additions, modifications and any artefact deletion (Sommerville, 2010) (Cleland-Huang et al., 2012). The importance is higher when there are frequent artefact changes due to rapid software evolution (Mens, & Demeyer, 2008).

The Process of Traceability Management

In a software development project, identification of the relationships and dependencies between artefacts is essential to maintain the consistency among elements throughout the SDLC. Figure 5 shows the main phases in the traceability management process. Traceability establishment process creates links between artefacts based on their dependencies. This process can be automated with the use of natural language processing techniques and refine with expert knowledge. These links need to be updated continuously based on artefact changes. Thus, artefact change detection is required to capture the changes in artefacts due to addition, modification and deletion. Once an element is changed, that can cause consequences on linked artefacts in different levels and severities. Identifying those effects of an artefact change on other elements is known by change impact analysis, which should be modelled considering artefact categories and relationship types among them. Consequently, some artefact changes may require propagating to linked artefacts to update traceability relations. Change propagation refers to the ripple effect of a change impact. Traceability visualisation is vital to analyse the overall traceability connectivity and filter-out the dependencies of a given artefact. Accordingly, consistency management refers to transforming the traceabilities back into a stable state after change detection, CIA and change propagation (Meedeniya, Rubasinghe & Perera, 2019).

Traceability Management Techniques And Tools

Traceability Management Approaches

Several techniques and approaches are used to establish and manage software artefact trace links (De Lucia, Oliveto, & Tortora, 2008) (Winkler, & von Pilgrim, 2010). Rule-based traceability approach is a popular method that uses a set of rules to create trace-links. These rules are defined for the artefact semantics, relationships, grammatical features of textual artefacts and their synonyms (Cleland-Huang et al., 2012). This approach is mainly practical for small to medium level scopes.

Hypertext-based traceability is another method that uses mark-up specification languages such as XML, XMI, HTML and JavaML to render and trace among different artefact types. This method has mainly applied only with requirements

Figure 5. Traceability management process

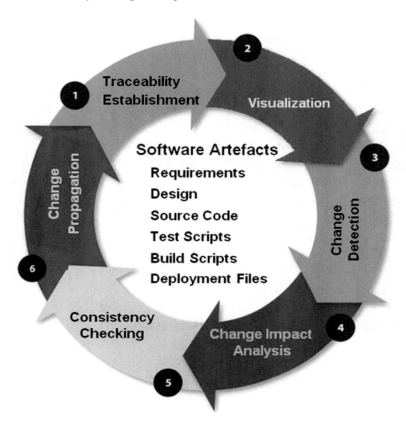

and source code artefacts and lacks the applicability to other heterogeneous artefact types (Mäder, & Gotel, 2012) (Cleland-Huang et al., 2012). In contrast, event-based traceability is dynamic and synchronises continuously with the environment, since events are the key to trigger and manage traceability (Mäder, Gotel, Kuschke, & Philippow, 2008). Event-based traceability approaches have automation capability due to the use of the publish-subscriber method. However, this approach has issues in achieving scalability along with dynamicity.

Other less significant traceability approaches include constraint-based, goal-centric, transformation-based, probabilistic and model-driven traceability. In summary, constraint-based traceability is beneficial in traceability maintenance (Fockel, Holtmann, & Meyer, 2012). But it requires to have a set of constraints defined for traceability links, which may become difficult for a broader application. Transformation-based consists of incremental transformations such as graph transformations (Riebisch, Bode, Farooq, & Lehnert, 2011). The template-based models are used in model-driven traceability applications (Javed, & Zdun, 2014). Model-driven and transformation-based both are mostly applicable for model-driven development software systems. The goal-centric traceability is applied to non-functional requirements tracing with no broad applications (Galvão, & Goknil, 2007). Probabilistic traceability is suitable to handle traceability consisting uncertainties since it is associated with probabilistic models like Bayes' theorem though depends on assumption declarations. These are often domain dependent such as for model-driven development projects. However, these approaches can be used as a combination such that event-based can be associated with predefined rules as well.

Among these, some of the approaches apply to a specific type of artefacts. For instance, the rule-based and hypertext-based traceability support techniques are mainly used to establish relationships in requirements and source code artefacts (Mäder, & Gotel, 2012) (Cleland-Huang et al., 2012). Event-based and constraint-based methodologies, along with publish-subscribe mechanisms, are used for traceability maintenance. However, these methods have scalability issues when the project scale increases (Galvão, & Goknil, 2007). Thus, a generic traceability solution is still hard to obtain using these techniques.

Tool Support for Tractability Management

One of the approaches for maintaining traceability is tool-based approaches, where a specific tool is used for tracing purpose of an artefact. The tool support for artefact traceability and continuous integration is an evolving area with the use of existing and novel techniques. The representation and visualisation of the identified traceability results is a challenge for proper artefact management. Table 1 summarises the advantages and limitations of some of the existing traceability management tools.

Although there are different traceability tools, the majority have addressed only requirements or source code artefact. IBM DOORS ("IBM-Rational DOORS," 2017), RequisitePro ("Rational RequisitePro," 2017), Cradle ("3SL," 2018), ReqView ("ReqView," 2017) and recently released YAKINDU ("YAKINDU Traceability," 2019) are some prominent requirements traceability tools. IBM DOORS is a multi-platform requirement management tool. It facilitates traceability support for requirements artefact with annotations, graphical views and analytical features. This tool is widely used in the software industry for the requirement and project management ("IBM-Rational DOORS," 2017). Another similar tool by IBM is RequisitePro for requirements management and use case writing ("Rational RequisitePro," 2017). However, in practice, IBM DOORS is leading ahead of RequisitePro due to extensive customer support with quick bug fixes, updates and features. Cradle is a proprietary requirement artefact management tool. It supports document management, project management with information assurance for Agile environments. Document version

Table 1. Tool support for traceability management

Tool	Usefulness	Limitations
TraceME (Bavota et al., 2012)	Visualise artefact trace-links using traceability dependency graphs.	It is limited to Eclipse IDE as a plugin. Research-level tool.
ADAMS Re-Trace (De Lucia et al., 2008)	Support heterogeneous artefact traceability management and recovery.	It is limited to Eclipse IDE as a plugin.
IBM Jazz (Calefato, Gendarmi, & Lanubile, 2009)	Support collaborative integration of data and tasks in design and source code level.	It is limited to Eclipse IDE as a plugin. Interface complexity.
Caliber-RM (Borland, 2006)	Allow stakeholder collaboration with versioning. Support impact identification and visualisation of requirements.	Proprietary. Limited for requirements artefacts. Platform dependent with Windows OS.
Cradle ("3SL," 2018)	Designed for Agile development. Scalable and multi-user accessible.	It is a proprietary tool. It is limited for requirements and lacks the CIA.
IBM DOORS ("IBM-Rational DOORS," 2017)	Support cross-platform traceability from requirement to design level. Support CIA, visualisation and versioning.	It is limited for requirements artefact. It is a proprietary tool.
RequisitePro ("Rational RequisitePro," 2017)	A collaborative requirements management tool that supports use case generation.	It is limited for requirements artefact and lacks tool maintenance support in updates. It is a proprietary tool.
YAKINDU ("YAKINDU Traceability," 2019)	Support tool integration with the considered artefacts. Visualise query and generate traceability coverage and CIA results.	It is limited for requirements artefact. It is a proprietary and patent-pending tool.
TraceMaintainer tool (Mäder et al., 2008)	A rule-based tool for post-requirements management with UML models.	Research-level tool.
Palantír (Sarma, Redmiles, & Van Der Hoek, 2012)	Support change detection and CIA with continuous coordination. Provides graphical representation.	Capture change data at the file level and user notification of conflicts at the code entity level.
ReqView ("ReqView," 2017)	Present structured requirements in a tabular way and visualise in a traceability matrix.	It is limited for requirements artefact. It is a proprietary tool.
SAT-Analyser ("SAT-Analyser," 2019)	Traceability support for different artefacts for all phases of SDLC with compatibility for CIs. Support change detection using XML comparison, CIA using network analysis, change propagation, visualisation using traceability graphs and validation.	Research-level tool. Limited with natural language processing for requirement extraction. Based on UML design and Java programming language related artefacts.

management with traceability, visualisation and coverage analysis are features that make it remarkable in practice ("3SL," 2018).

Another well-established proprietary tool is ReqView for requirement traceability for structural requirements given in tabular format ("ReqView," 2017). YAKINDU is a proprietary tool that has addressed Agility adequately with trace visualisations, configuration features and coverage analysis report generation ("YAKINDU Traceability," 2019). The tool RETRO is more towards a case study and focuses on requirements artefact (Hayes et al., 2007). TraceMaintainer tool (Mäder et al., 2008) provides traceability support to both requirements and UML designs. The tool TraceME has addressed all the main artefact types and stands as an Eclipse plugin (Bavota et al., 2012). ADAMS Re-Trace is another Eclipse plugin that has considered the main types of artefacts and has used the LSI as the IR technique (De Lucia et al., 2008). Many tools remain integrative with an IDE such as Eclipse IDE rather than being an independent tool. That can become a limitation when integrating with DevOps tools stack.

Further, SAT-Analyser ("SAT-Analyser," 2019), Software Artefacts Traceability Analyzer, provides the tool support to manage traceability management. Currently, its focus artefacts are the textual description for requirements, UML class diagrams for design, Java source code for implementation, JUnit test cases for testing and Maven build scripts for configuration. There is a possibility to extend their approach for different other artefacts. This approach has covered all the main phases in the traceability management process. Further, SAT-Analyser tool is featured with web-based multi-user accessibility to allow DevOps teams to use the tool actively along with DevOps tools stack to support the CICD process.

Related Studies On Traceability Management

Information Retrieval Related Work

In the traceability establishment process, information retrieval plays a vital role, as the accuracy of the trace-link creation depends on the extracted artefacts. The Vector Space Model (VSM) is one of the IR techniques that treat queries and elements, especially documents as vectors. It assumes the terms are always independent of each other and uses a similarity-based methodology to rank them. On the contrary, Latent Semantic Indexing (LSI) is an IR approach that is useful to address the documents having the same semantic information (Lucia, Fasano, Oliveto, & Tortora, 2007). It focuses on complete user queries instead of individual word translations during information retrieval. Term Frequency-Inverse Document Frequency (TF-IDF) is another statistic measure useful to identify the strength of a word. Most ranking functions are composed of this in queries (De Lucia et al., 2008). Moreover, most of the IR based techniques such as VSM, LSI and TF-IDF have shown high performances in the trace-link establishment (Marcus et al., 2005) (Hayes et al., 2007). Nevertheless, these techniques have compatibility and scalability issues and lack automated tool-support. Table 2 states some of the IR techniques used in traceability related tools.

Artefact Consistency Management Studies

Software artefact consistency management has addressed in different levels of scope in the literature. Among several related studies, this section considers recent studies that have discussed significantly one or many phases in artefact consistency management as the research space. Table 3 summarises a set of literature with the considered features and techniques. In an earlier work (Lucia et al., 2007), information retrieval techniques such as VSM, LSI have shown an essential task for traceability, change detection and consistency management. This work has addressed heterogeneous artefacts with semi-automation in traceability recovery. Another study has described the use of an event-based methodology for traceability maintenance and CIA (Sarma et al., 2012). Although it has a useful notification system for change propagation, the automation capabilities are lacking. A rule-based traceability approach for several artefacts using multi-level dependency modelling is presented in (Lehnert, Farooq, & Riebisch, 2013).

Table 2. Summary of IR techniques used in traceability tools

Tool	Artefacts	Information retrieval technique			
		VSM	TF-IDF	LSI	Other
TraceME (Bavota et al., 2012)	All	X			
RETRO (Hayes et al., 2007)	Requirements, design, test	X	X	X	
ReqAnalyst (Lormans, & van Deursen, 2009)	Requirements			X	Query-View
ADAMS Re-Trace (Oliveto, 2008)(De Lucia et al., 2008)	All			X	
TraceTool (Mischler, & Monperrus, 2014)	SRS		X	X	
Traceclipse (Klock, Gethers, Dit, & Poshyvanyk, 2011)	Source code	X			
TraceViz (Chang, Hung, & Newman, 2012)	Multimedia			X	
TraceMaintainer tool (Mäder et al., 2008)	Requirements, UML structural design models				Rule-based

Table 3. Summary of traceability management related studies

Related work	Traceability establishment	Change detection	Change impact analysis	Consistency management	Change propagation
Application of information retrieval for traceability recovery (Lucia et al., 2007)	Information retrieval	VSM.	Rule-based	LSI	-
Heterogeneous artefact traceability management (Lehnert et al., 2013)	Rule-based	-	Rule-based	Multi-perspective	Dependent links
Feature-based software evolution (Passos et al., 2013)	Feature-based	Feature-based	Feature dependencies	-	-
Change detection for parallel source code (Sarma et al., 2012)	Event-based	-	Event-based	Manually	Notification
Traceability management for continuous integrations (Rubasinghe et al., 2018a)	Rule-based with string comparison	Versioning. XML comparison.	Rule-based with network analysis.	Automatic	Graph traversal. Updates and notification

Although the CIA has shown high accuracy, there is limited support in dynamic UML. The study by Passos et al. (Passos et al., 2013) has focused on the artefacts up to development phase. However their approach is restricted to feature-oriented software projects. It computes the dependencies among features in the software project for the CIA. The approach presented by (Rubasinghe, Meedeniya, & Perera, 2018a), consists of continuous integration tasks and collaborates with DevOps tool stack. Moreover, the main phases of the tool SAT-Analyzer, which is proposed by the authors include trace-link creation, visualisation, validation, scheduling algorithms, versioning, XML-based artefact change detection, weighting scheme-based CIA model for artefact impact computation, graph-based change propagation and project management to maintain the artefact consistency. It has mainly occupied a rule-based approach for traceability and CIA, while graph traversal for change propagation.

Related Studies on Change Impact Analysis

Several studies have addressed software artefact Change Impact Analysis (CIA). The main aim of the CIA is to determine the consequences of an artefact modification in other related elements (Sommerville, 2010)(Lehnert, 2015). Traceability is a supportive technique in the identification of affected artefacts and is a key notion in the software maintenance process. For instance, in areas such as Model-Driven Engineering (MDE), before changing a metamodel, it is crucial to measure the impact of the changes among the artefacts to understand whether the evolution is sustainable or not. Table 4 summarises some of the related work on the CIA according to their scope of artefacts.

Table 4. Scope comparison of related studies based on change impact analysis

Related work	Artefact level				
	Requirements	Design	Code	Test case	Build Script
Traceability for CIA (Ibrahim et al., 2005)	X	X	X	X	
Goal-oriented requirement traceability CIA (Lee et al., 2010)	X				
Requirement CIA using meta-models (Goknil et al., 2014)	X				
CIA towards software re-use and maintenance (Lehnert, 2015)		X	X	X	
Software artefact traceability recovery (Zhang et al., 2016)	X	X	X		
Requirements traceability for CIA (Duarte et al., 2016)	X				
Requirement CIA on software architecture (Goknil et al., 2016)	X	X			
Requirement traceability visualization (Rodrigues et al., 2016)	X				
CIA for software artefact maintenance (Shahid, & Ibrahim, 2016)	X			X	
Text similarity-based CIA for UML models (Kchaou et al., 2017)		X			
Rule-based artefact traceability (Lehnert et al., 2013)		X	X	X	
Traceability in DevOps practice (Rubasinghe et al., 2018b)	X	X	X	X	X

A probabilistic CIA approach with gall graphs has presented in (Ibrahim, Idris, Munro, & Deraman, 2005) for heterogeneous artefacts. The use of formal semantics for requirements CIA is significant in the study (Goknil, Kurtev, van den Berg, & Spijkerman, 2014). In contrast, Lee et al. (Lee, Deng, Lee, & Lee, 2010) have used graph theory for CIA in requirements artefact. A rule-based CAI solution for design, code and test case artefacts is discussed in (Lehnert, 2015) with a tool named EMFTrace. The work (Zhang, Wan, & Jin, 2016) has presented a traceability recovery approach for requirements to code artefacts. A traceability knowledge body named TraceBoK by classifying requirements artefact has presented by Duarte et al. (Duarte, Duarte, & Thiry, 2016). The work by (Goknil, Kurtev, & van den Berg, 2016) has extended a tool named TRIC to demonstrate their CIA approach that has used formal semantics for requirements and architecture artefacts.

Traceability visualisation with different techniques like Sunburst and tree, matrix, graphs and traceability evaluation has mainly considered in (Rodrigues, Lencastre, & Filho, 2016) only for requirements artefact. A tool named HYCAT has presented in (Shahid, & Ibrahim, 2016) as a CIA solution for requirements artefact using traceability matrix. The work by (Kchaou, Bouassida, & Ben-Abdallah, 2017) has shown a higher accuracy level for their information retrieval-based CIA approach that has focused on design artefacts such as UML sequence and class diagrams. The recent work (Rubasinghe, Meedeniya, & Perera, 2018b) has addressed traceability management of different software artefacts covering the entire SDLC. The weighting scheme based on a mathematical model has used for CIA in SAT-Analyzer. It has used the eigenvector centrality measure that captures the level of importance in each artefact among others. A rule-based scenario has adapted for graph traversal paths, and user alteration is used to improve the accuracy.

Related Studies on Traceability Visualisation

Several visualisation methods are available in the literature to analyse the trace-link relationships and the impact of changes in the artefacts. Lists are one of the earliest forms of visualisation method. It has the least advantages in modern demands. Their applicability is limited for a single dimension with smaller data capacity, and data needs to be stored sequentially. Traceability matrix is primarily introduced for requirement artefacts to state the relationships between the requirements and test cases. In general, the traceability matrix is a tabular format that holds a two-dimensional structure. It is used to determine all the relationships between two sets of artefacts types (Sommerville, 2010). All the captured requirements are listed and map each with test cases. Thus, the traceability matrix confirms whether all requirements given by clients are fulfilled or not. In practice, the quality assurance persons are responsible for handling typical traceability matrix documents.

A tabular form of visualisation represents by cross-references having a list of links for each artefact (Chen, Hosking, & Grundy, 2012). However, this technique is not widely addressed or applied in traceability related visualisation. In contrast, tree-map provides a two-dimensional hierarchical tree structure for data visualisation. It gives more capacity for data to be expressed and used for computing purposes. The data are represented hierarchically in the shape of nested rectangles such that a rectangle denotes each tree branch. Thus, this is an optimal visualisation method that takes maximum usage of space with utilisation. Different sizes and colours are highly used in the approach to illustrate the dimension of data. There exist tiling algorithms to decide on those parameters.

Another widely used visualisation technique is traceability graph that denotes a node-link structure as a graph (Kugele, & Antkowiak, 2016). Usually, a traceability graph is a directed graph that shows which is depending on which node. One significant advantage in traceability graphs is the applicability of well-established graph theories and graph analysis methods such as network analysis. Although different colours, sizes and shapes can be used in this approach, overcoming scalability and visual clutter issues are still challenging. Comparatively, traceability graph is rich in scalability over other techniques. Further, Sunburst and Netmap is a customised visualisation method with a radial structure with no broader recognition (Filho, & Lencastre, 2012).

Related studies have used several visualisation techniques to represent traceability results as given in Table 5. Most of the traceability visualisation techniques have slightly considered model driven features. Thus, there is a limitation of supporting a range of software types (Kugele, & Antkowiak, 2016). Many studies have addressed issues such as visual clutter and scalability (Merten, Jüppner, & Delater, 2011) (Filho, & Lencastre, 2012) and integrated with a specific IDE. However, most of the studies have not addressed different types of software artefacts. They have considered a few types of artefacts, such as requirements or source code. Hence, there is a potential need for a generic software artefact visualisation methodology. The traceability visualisation in SAT-Analyzer (Rubasinghe, Meedeniya, & Perera, 2018b), is developed in three views, Gephi-based informative, Python-based analytical and JavaScript-based interactive. Traceability visualisation is enhanced in three variations to overcome scalability issues and to fasten decision making since time is critical in a more collaborative DevOps environment.

DISCUSSION

General Features in Software Traceability Management

This chapter mainly explores the associated techniques and tools to achieve software artefact traceability in a DevOps environment to assist researchers and software practitioners. The addressed parameters include recent and highly cited related studies on traceability establishment, visualisation, change detection, CIA, consistency checking and change propagation. We have discussed the required aspects to secure traceability in a collaborative DevOps environment in an analytical point of view. Traceability establishment, traceability visualisation, CICD pipeline in DevOps, artefact change detection in CI activities, corresponding CIA, consistency checking, change propagation and project management have described with the support of related works. Furthermore, the literature on traceability validation, CIA validation and evaluation techniques, have not emphasised within the scope of this chapter.

As disused in the chapter, the current research space includes traceability solutions in both research-level and industry-level tools, which apply to traditional software development environments is one common observation. They include features to safely cope with artefact traceability when the change frequency is low. Moreover, traceability visualisation is another satisfactorily addressed aspect in research space with minor limitations. Further, there are rapidly evolving DevOps related tools that get added to DevOps tools stack to enrich the collaborative nature.

Table 5. Comparison of related work on traceability visualisation techniques

Related work	Visualisation technique						
	List	Traceability matrix	Cross-reference	Treemap	Traceability graph	Sunburst / Netmap	Other
Requirements traceability visualization (Merten et al., 2011)	√					√	
Traceability visualization of source code and documentation (Chen et al., 2012)		√	√				
Integration of multiple traceability visualizations (Rodrigues et al., 2016)		√		√	√	√	
Customised traceability visualization (Zhou, Huo, Huang, & Xu, 2008)							hyperbolic tree
Scalable requirements traceability visualization (Filho, & Lencastre, 2012)		√		√		√	
Requirements traceability visualization (Kugele, & Antkowiak, 2016)					√		metaphor-based
Traceability visualization for DevOps (Rubasinghe, Meedeniya, & Perera, 2018b)					√		

Limitations in Software Traceability Management

The existing software traceability related solutions have several limitations in supporting DevOps environments. Majority of the related studies have addressed a few types of artefacts only (Dekhtyar, Poly, Obispo, & Hayes, 2018). For instance, many studies have addressed only requirement and source code artefacts. Only, few studies have considered artefacts covering the phases in the entire SDLC (Rubasinghe, Meedeniya, & Perera, 2018b); however, those studies also have not addressed all the possible software artefacts with a generalised approach. Moreover, artefact change detection is addressed mainly for source code changes in the current industry practice.

One of the main limitations in the present context of software traceability is the lack of automated tool support to engage in the CICD pipeline collaboratively with DevOps tools stack, with impressive performances and technique support. Some related traceability tools are specific to a given Integrated Development Environment (IDE) such as Eclipse. Most are not compatible with existing DevOps tools stack (Bavota et al., 2012). Thus, the automation of traceability establishment is hard in a DevOps environment. Hence, the support of traceability with continuous integration is essential throughout the SDLC as it is not preserved in the current practices to its fullest (Chang, 2005). Additionally, the traceability representation with visual clutter is an issue in related studies. It limits better decision-making capabilities with the increase of project scale.

Challenges in Software Traceability Management

The software industry is still hesitating to adapt software traceability in practice due to several challenges. It is challenging to build a general framework that supports traceability management with a wide range of customizability. Additionally, traceability does not provide tangible direct advantages to software development. Therefore, there is a need for a tool that supports all the artefact types and development environments in managing traceability. On the other hand, DevOps practices support collaboration between the many functions engaged in the current software development processes. Hence, a technically feasible approach to manage software artefact traceability and impact analysis in a DevOps environment is essential for software application development. The current software industry is still reluctant to adopt traceability aspects into the settings due to the initial cost, time and effort. Also, ensuring the accuracy of traceability is another challenge that leads software practitioners to re-think in applying traceability in software projects. However, artefact traceability management supports to deliver a quality product with customer satisfaction. Hence, there is a requirement of having proper software traceability validation and evaluation techniques to avoid traceability management being an overhead.

Future Research Directions in Software Traceability Management

The existing challenges motivate the research on software artefact traceability management with well-defined approaches to integrate with DevOps practice. Also, it is significant to manage artefact consistency efficiently and accurately during software development to support CICD nature. Moreover, manual traceability management is impractical with frequent artefact changes and project scalability due to the necessary effort and possible flaws. Thus, there is a demand for automated support tools to manage traceability in DevOps practice.

As future research directions, the most vital aspect to be focused on is to provide traceability among various heterogeneous artefact types such that requirement, design diagrams, source codes in different programming languages, test scripts and configuration files representing all the major phases in an SDLC. Next, it is equally essential to building an approach for continuous artefact change management, which is the main difference in DevOps over traditional software process models. The traceability among artefacts must be synchronised during artefact change integrations. Therefore, it is important to have a solution methodology for artefact change detection, measure the impact of changes over different artefact types and change propagation without being restricted only on source code artefact. Also, traceability visualisation and validation are useful research directions having performance a key quality attribute to avoid traceability management being an overhead. Moreover, it is ideal for providing the solutions in a DevOps tools stack compatibly manner to preserve the collaborative team-based nature in DevOps. Finally, a generalised artefact consistency management framework to support the DevOps environment is still a trending research area.

CONCLUSION

Software systems in every domain become highly complex and competitive. It requires the ability to perform in high reliability to sustain without being replaced by a newer software system. The development of these systems requires reliable traceability and consistency management for the correct functioning and maintenance of the product. Agile software development has become a widely used approach due to its highly collaborative and cost-effective nature. It comprises of practices such as DevOps, continuous integration and continuous delivery. DevOps reduce the gap between development and the operations, whereas the continuous integration referrers frequent merging of developer working copies. The resulting rapid changes of artefacts are required to trace for preserving the maintainability in DevOps. Hence, traceability management is essential in DevOps practice for artefact consistency maintenance during continuous changes. Existing related work on software traceability are more focused on requirements to code level artefact types that limit their applicability for a DevOps environment with frequent artefact changes. Therefore, the need of a broaden traceability management approach to be compatible with heterogeneity, and continuous artefact integrations along with DevOps tools stack has identified in this chapter.

This chapter has explored existing approaches to establish and maintain traceability links between all stages of software development in DevOps practice. The survey includes the studies on detecting the changes in trace links between software artefacts, analysing the impact caused by the changes, visualise the consequences of a change and provide traceability support for the continuous integration nature in a collaborative environment. Moreover, this chapter has evaluated related tools and techniques that support software artefact traceability management in DevOps practice. Finally, this chapter has listed the main limitations and challenges in artefact consistency management and suggested some recommendations for future research directions.

ACKNOWLEDGMENT

This research was supported by the University of Moratuwa, Sri Lanka [Senate Research Committee Grant SRC/ST/2019/07].

REFERENCES

Arora, R., & Arora, N. (2016). Analysis of SDLC Models. *International Journal of Current Engineering and Technology*, 6(1), 268–272.

Azeri, I. (2018). *What Is CI/CD?* Retrieved May 28, 2018, from https://dzone.com/articles/what-is-cicd

Bass, L. J., Weber, I. M., & Zhu, L. (2015). *DevOps : A Software Architect's Perspective* (1st ed.). Addison-Wesley Professional.

Bavota, G., Colangelo, L., De Lucia, A., Fusco, S., Oliveto, R., & Panichella, A. (2012). TraceME: Traceability Management in Eclipse. In *28th IEEE International Conference on Software Maintenance (ICSM)*. (pp. 642–645). IEEE. 10.1109/ICSM.2012.6405343

Berg, A. M. (2015). *Jenkins Continuous Integration Cookbook* (2nd ed.). Packt Publishing.

Borland. (2006). *Borland ® CaliberRM TM*. Author.

Calefato, F., Gendarmi, D., & Lanubile, F. (2009). Embedding social networking information into jazz to foster group awareness within distributed teams. *2nd International Workshop on Social Software Engineering and Applications (SoSEA)*, 23–28. 10.1145/1595836.1595842

Chang, S. K. (2005). *Handbook of Software Engineering And Knowledge Engineering: Recent Advances. World Scientific Publishing*. World Scientific Publishing. doi:10.1142/9789812775245

Chang, Y. J., Hung, P. Y., & Newman, M. (2012). TraceViz: "brushing" for location based services. 14th International Conference on Human-Computer Interaction with Mobile Devices and Services Companion, 219–220. New York, USA. doi:10.1145/2371664.2371717

Chen, X., Hosking, J., & Grundy, J. (2012). Visualizing traceability links between source code and documentation. In *Symposium on Visual Languages and Human-Centric Computing (VL/HCC)*. (pp. 119–126). IEEE. doi.org/10.1109/VLHCC.2012.6344496

Cleland-Huang, J., Zisman, A., & Gotel, O. (2012). *Software and Systems Traceability. Software and Systems Traceability* (1st ed.). London: Springer-Verlag. doi:10.1007/978-1-4471-2239-5

De Lucia, A., Oliveto, R., & Tortora, G. (2008). Adams re-trace: traceability link recovery via latent semantic indexing. In *13th International Conference on Software Engineering (ICSE '08)* (pp. 839–842). New York: ACM. 10.1145/1368088.1368216

Dekhtyar, A., Poly, C., Obispo, S. L., & Hayes, J. H. (2018). Automating Requirements Traceability: Two Decades of Learning from KDD. doi.org/ doi:10.1109/D4RE.2018.00009

Dick, J., Hull, E., & Jackson, K. (2017). *Requirements Engineering* (4th ed.). Springer International Publishing Switzerland. doi:10.1007/978-3-319-61073-3

Docker. (2018). Retrieved August 28, 2018, from https://docs.docker.com

Duarte, A. M. D., Duarte, D., & Thiry, M. (2016). TraceBoK: Toward a Software Requirements Traceability Body of Knowledge. In *24th International Requirements Engineering Conference (RE)*. (pp. 236–245). IEEE. 10.1109/RE.2016.32

Duvall, P. M., Matyas, S., & Glover, A. (2007). *Continuous Integration: Improving Software Quality and Reducing Risk. Addison-Wesley Professional* (1st ed.). Addison-Wesley Professional.

Farcic, V. (2016). *The DevOps 2.0 Toolkit: Automating the Continuous Deployment Pipeline with Containerized Microservices* (1st ed.). CreateSpace Independent Publishing Platform.

Filho, G. A. de A. C., & Lencastre, M. (2012). Towards a Traceability Visualisation Tool. In 8th International Conference on the Quality of Information and Communications Technology. (pp. 221–223). IEEE. 10.1109/QUATIC.2012.60

Flora, H. K., & Chande, S. V. (2014). A Systematic Study on Agile Software Development Methodologies and Practices. *International Journal of Computer Science and Information Technologies.*, 5(3), 3626–3637.

Fockel, M., Holtmann, J., & Meyer, J. (2012). Semi-automatic establishment and maintenance of valid traceability in automotive development processes. In *2nd International Workshop on Software Engineering for Embedded Systems (SEES)* (pp. 37–43). IEEE. 10.1109/SEES.2012.6225489

Galvão, I., & Goknil, A. (2007). Survey of traceability approaches in model-driven engineering. In *International Enterprise Distributed Object Computing Workshop*. (pp. 313–324). IEEE. 10.1109/EDOC.2007.42

Goknil, A., Kurtev, I., & van den Berg, K. (2016). *A Rule-Based Change Impact Analysis Approach in Software Architecture for Requirements Changes*. Eprint ArXiv:1608.02757

Goknil, A., Kurtev, I., van den Berg, K., & Spijkerman, W. (2014). Change impact analysis for requirements: A metamodeling approach. *Information and Software Technology*, *56*(8), 950–972. doi:10.1016/j.infsof.2014.03.002

Hayes, J. H., Dekhtyar, A., Sundaram, S. K., Holbrook, E. A., Vadlamudi, S., & April, A. (2007). REquirements TRacing On target (RETRO): Improving software maintenance through traceability recovery. *Innovations in Systems and Software Engineering*, *3*(3), 193–202. doi:10.100711334-007-0024-1

Hembrink, J., & Stenberg, P. G. (2013). Continuous integration with Jenkins. *Coaching of Programming Teams (EDA 270)*, 1–8.

IBM-Rational DOORS. (2017). Retrieved October 14, 2017, from https://www.ibm.com/us-en/marketplace/rational-doors

Ibrahim, S., Idris, N. B., Munro, M., & Deraman, A. (2005). Integrating Software Traceability for Change Impact Analysis. *Integrating Software Traceability for Change Impact Analysis*, *2*(4), 301–308.

JIRA Software. (2018). Retrieved October 2, 2018, from https://www.atlassian.com/software/jira

Kchaou, D., Bouassida, N., & Ben-Abdallah, H. (2017). UML models change impact analysis using a text similarity technique. *IET Software*, *11*(1), 27–37. doi:10.1049/iet-sen.2015.0113

Keenan, E., Czauderna, A., Leach, G., Cleland-Huang, J., Shin, Y., & Moritz, E., … Hearn, D. (2012). TraceLab: An experimental workbench for equipping researchers to innovate, synthesize, and comparatively evaluate traceability solutions. In *34th International Conference on Software Engineering (ICSE)* (pp. 1375–1378). Zurich, Switzerland: IEEE. 10.1109/ICSE.2012.6227244

Kim, G., Debois, P., Willis, J., Humble, J., & Allspaw, J. (2016). *The DevOps Handbook* (1st ed.). IT Revolution Press.

Klock, S., Gethers, M., Dit, B., & Poshyvanyk, D. (2011). Traceclipse: an eclipse plug-in for traceability link recovery and management. *6th International Workshop on Traceability in Emerging Forms of Software Engineering*, 24–30. 10.1145/1987856.1987862

Kugele, S., & Antkowiak, D. (2016). Visualization of Trace Links and Change Impact Analysis. In *24th International Requirements Engineering Conference Workshops (REW)* (pp. 165–169). Beijing, China: IEEE. 10.1109/REW.2016.039

Langer, A. M. (2016). *Guide to Software Development* (2nd ed.). London: Springer-Verlag London; doi:10.1007/978-1-4471-6799-0

Lee, W. T., Deng, W. Y., Lee, J., & Lee, S. J. (2010). Change impact analysis with a goal-driven traceability-based approach. *International Journal of Intelligent Systems*, *25*(8), 878–908. doi:10.1002/int.20443

Lehnert, S. (2015). *Multiperspective Change Impact Analysis to Support Software Maintenance and Reengineering*. The University of Hamburg.

Lehnert, S., Farooq, Q. U. A., & Riebisch, M. (2013). Rule-based impact analysis for heterogeneous software artifacts. In *European Conference on Software Maintenance and Reengineering, (CSMR)*. (pp. 209–218). Genova, Italy: IEEE. 10.1109/CSMR.2013.30

Li, B., Sun, X., Leung, H., & Zhang, S. (2013). A survey of code-based change impact analysis techniques. *Software Testing, Verification & Reliability*, *23*(8), 613–646. doi:10.1002tvr.1475

Lormans, M., & van Deursen, A. (2009). Reconstructing Requirements Traceability in Design and Test Using Latent Semantic Indexing. Technical Report Series (TUD-SERG-2007-007). Delft University of Technology, Software Engineering Research Group.

Lucia, A. De, Fasano, F., Oliveto, R., & Tortora, G. (2007). Recovering traceability links in software artifact management systems using information retrieval methods. ACM Transactions on Software Engineering and Methodology, 16(4), 13:1-13:50. doi:10.1145/1276933.1276934

Mäder, P., & Gotel, O. (2012). Towards automated traceability maintenance. *Journal of Systems and Software*, *85*(10), 2205–2227. doi:10.1016/j.jss.2011.10.023 PMID:23471308

Mäder, P., Gotel, O., Kuschke, T., & Philippow, I. (2008). traceMaintainer - Automated Traceability Maintenance. In *16th IEEE International Requirements Engineering Conference* (pp. 329–330). Catalunya, Spain: IEEE. 10.1109/RE.2008.25

Marcus, A., Xie, X., & Poshyvanyk, D. (2005). When and how to visualize traceability links? In *3rd International Workshop on Traceability in Emerging Forms of Software Engineering (TEFSE '05)* (pp. 56–61). New York: ACM. 10.1145/1107656.1107669

Maro, S., Anjorin, A., Wohlrab, R., & Steghöfer, J. P. (2016). Traceability maintenance: factors and guidelines. In *31st IEEE/ACM International Conference on Automated Software Engineering (ASE 2016)* (pp. 414–425). New York: ACM. 10.1145/2970276.2970314

Meedeniya, D. A., Rubasinghe, I. D., & Perera, I. (2019). Software Artefacts Consistency Management towards Continuous Integration: A Roadmap. *International Journal of Advanced Computer Science and Applications*, *10*(4), 100–110. doi:10.14569/IJACSA.2019.0100411

Mens, T., & Demeyer, S. (2008). *Software Evolution* (1st ed.). Berlin: Springer-Verlag Berlin Heidelberg. doi:10.1007/978-3-540-76440-3

Merten, T., Jüppner, D., & Delater, A. (2011). Improved representation of traceability links in requirements engineering knowledge using Sunburst and Netmap visualizations. In *4th International Workshop on Managing Requirements Knowledge, MaRK'11* (pp. 17–21). Trento, Italy: IEEE. 10.1109/MARK.2011.6046557

Mischler, A., & Monperrus, M. (2014). *An Approach for Discovering Traceability Links between Regulatory Documents and Source Code Through User-Interface Labels*. Eprint ArXiv:1403.2639

Murray, A. P. (2016). *The Complete Software Project Manager: Mastering Technology from Planning to Launch and Beyond*. Wiley.

Oliveto, R. (2008). Traceability Management meets Information Retrieval Methods - Strengths and Limitations. In *12th European Conference on Software Maintenance and Reengineering* (pp. 302–305). Athens, Greece: IEEE. 10.1109/CSMR.2008.4493332

Passos, L., Apel, S., Kästner, C., Czarnecki, K., Wasowski, A., & Guo, J. (2013). Feature Oriented Software Evolution. In *7th International Workshop on Variability Modelling of Software-intensive Systems-VaMoS '13* (p. 17:1-17:8). Pisa, Italy: ACM. 10.1145/2430502.2430526

Pete, I., & Balasubramaniam, D. (2015). Handling the differential evolution of software artefacts: A framework for consistency management. In *IEEE 22nd International Conference on Software Analysis, Evolution, and Reengineering (SANER)* (pp. 599–600). IEEE. 10.1109/SANER.2015.7081889

QASource DevOps Experts. (2018). Retrieved August 28, 2018, from https://www.qasource.com/devops#!devops-expertise

Rahman, A. A. U., Helms, E., Williams, L., & Parnin, C. (2015). Synthesizing Continuous Deployment Practices Used in Software Development. In *Agile Conference* (pp. 1–10). IEEE. 10.1109/Agile.2015.12

Rational RequisitePro. (2017). Retrieved July 5, 2017, from https://www.oit.va.gov/Services/TRM/ToolPage.aspx?tid=41

ReqView. (2017). Retrieved May 7, 2018, from https://www.reqview.com/

Riebisch, M., Bode, S., Farooq, Q. U. A., & Lehnert, S. (2011). Towards comprehensive modelling by inter-model links using an integrating repository. In *18th IEEE International Conference and Workshops on Engineering of Computer-Based Systems, ECBS 2011* (pp. 284–291). IEEE. 10.1109/ECBS.2011.32

Rodrigues, A., Lencastre, M., & Filho, G. A. de A. C. (2016). Multi-VisioTrace: Traceability Visualization Tool. In *10th International Conference on the Quality of Information and Communications Technology (QUATIC)* (pp. 61–66). Lisbon, Portugal: IEEE. 10.1109/QUATIC.2016.019

Rubasinghe, I. D., Meedeniya, D. A., & Perera, G. I. U. S. (2018a). Traceability Management with Impact Analysis in DevOps based Software Development. 7th international conference on advances in computing, communications and informatics (ICACCI), 1956-1962. 10.1109/ICACCI.2018.8554399

Rubasinghe, I. D., Meedeniya, D. A., & Perera, G. I. U. S. (2018b). Automated Inter-artefact Traceability Establishment for DevOps Practice. In *17th IEEE/ACIS International Conference on Computer and Information Science, (ICIS 2018)* (pp. 211-216). IEEE. 10.1109/ICIS.2018.8466414

Sarma, A., Redmiles, D. F., & Van Der Hoek, A. (2012). Palantír: Early detection of development conflicts arising from parallel code changes. *IEEE Transactions on Software Engineering*, 38(4), 889–908. doi:10.1109/TSE.2011.64

SAT-Analyser. (2019). Retrieved April 10, 2019, from https://sites.google.com/cse.mrt.ac.lk/sat-analyser

Shahid, M., & Ibrahim, S. (2016). Change impact analysis with a software traceability approach to support software maintenance. In *13th International Bhurban Conference on Applied Sciences and Technology (IBCAST)*. (pp. 391–396). IEEE. 10.1109/IBCAST.2016.7429908

3. SL. (2018). *Cradle Overview*. Retrieved July 6, 2017, from https://www.threesl.com/cradle/

Slack. (2018). Retrieved October 2, 2018, from https://slack.com

Sommerville, I. (2010). *Software Engineering* (10th ed.). New York: Addison-Wesley Professional.

Travis, C. I. (2018). Retrieved July 5, 2017, from https://travis-ci.org/

Trello. (2018). Retrieved October 2, 2018, from https://trello.com/

Walkinshaw, N. (2017). *Software Quality Assuarance* (1st ed.). Springer International Publishing. doi:10.1007/978-3-319-64822-4

Winkler, S., & von Pilgrim, J. (2010). A survey of traceability in requirements engineering and model-driven development. *Software & Systems Modeling*, 9(4), 529–565. doi:10.100710270-009-0145-0

Yakindu Traceability. (2019). Retrieved January 25, 2019, from https://www.itemis.com/en/yakindu/traceability/

Zhang, Y., Wan, C., & Jin, B. (2016). An empirical study on recovering requirement-to-code links. In *17th IEEE/ACIS International Conference on Software Engineering, Artificial Intelligence, Networking and Parallel/Distributed Computing (SNPD)*. (pp. 121–126). Shanghai, China: IEEE. 10.1109/SNPD.2016.7515889

Zhou, X., Huo, Z., Huang, Y., & Xu, J. (2008). Facilitating software traceability understanding with ENVISION. In *International Computer Software and Applications Conference* (pp. 295–302). IEEE. 10.1109/COMPSAC.2008.36

ADDITIONAL READING

Antoniol, G., Cleland-Huang, J., Hayes, J. H., & Vierhauser, M. (2017). Grand Challenges of Traceability: The Next Ten Years. arXiv preprint arXiv:1710.03129, 2017

Cleland-Huang, J., Gotel, O. C. Z., Hayes, J. H., Mäder, P., & Zisman, A. (2014). Software traceability: trends and future directions. In *Future of Software Engineering (FOSE 2014)* (pp. 55–69). New York, USA: ACM; doi:10.1145/2593882.2593891

Galvão, I., & Goknil, A. (2007). Survey of traceability approaches in model-driven engineering. In *IEEE International Enterprise Distributed Object Computing Workshop (EDOC)*. (pp. 313–324). IEEE. 10.1109/EDOC.2007.42

Javed, M. A., & Zdun, U. (2014). A systematic literature review of traceability approaches between software architecture and source code. In *18th International Conference on Evaluation and Assessment in Software Engineering (EASE '14)*. (pp. 1–10). New York, USA: ACM. 10.1145/2601248.2601278

Jiménez, M., Castaneda, L., Villegas, N. M., Tamura, G., Müller, H. A., & Wigglesworth, J. (2019). DevOps Round-Trip Engineering: Traceability from Dev to Ops and Back Again. In: Bruel J.M., Mazzara M., Meyer B. (eds) Software Engineering Aspects of Continuous Development and New Paradigms of Software Production and Deployment. DevOps 2018. (73-88) 11350. Springer, Cham. doi:10.1007/978-3-030-06019-0_6

Meedeniya, D. A., Rubasinghe, I. D., & Perera, I. (2019). Traceability Establishment and Visualization of Software Artefacts in DevOps Practice: A Survey. *International Journal of Advanced Computer Science and Applications*, *10*(7), 66–76. doi:10.14569/IJACSA.2019.0100711

Rath, M., Rendall, J., Guo, J. L. C., Cleland-Huang, J., & Mäder, P. (2018). Traceability in the wild: automatically augmenting incomplete trace links. In *40th International Conference on Software Engineering (ICSE '18)*. (834-845). New York, NY, USA. 10.1145/3180155.3180207

KEY TERMS AND DEFINITIONS

Change Set: A set of artefacts that are affected due to artefact additions, modifications, or deletions.

CIA: Change impact analysis.

CICD: A practice of continuous integration continuous delivery pipeline in a DevOps environment.

DevOps: Development-operations.

IDE: Integrated development environment.

Industry-Level: Commercial software development companies.

IR: Information retrieval.

Ontology: A collection of pre-defined words and their synonyms.

PM: Project management.

SDLC: Software development life cycle.

Chapter 5
Tool Support for Software Artefact Traceability in DevOps Practice:
SAT–Analyser

Iresha Rubasinghe
University of Moratuwa, Sri Lanka

Dulani Meedeniya
(iD) https://orcid.org/0000-0002-4520-3819
University of Moratuwa, Sri Lanka

Indika Perera
University of Moratuwa, Sri Lanka

ABSTRACT

Software development in DevOps practice is a widely used approach to cope with the demand for frequent artefact changes. These changes require a well-defined method to manage artefact consistency to ease the continuous integration process. This chapter proposes a traceability management approach for the artefact types in the main phases of the software process including requirements, design, source code, testing, and configuration. This chapter addresses traceability management, including trace link creation, change detection, impact analysis, change propagation, validation, and visualisation. This chapter presents a tool named SAT-Analyser that is applicable for any software development method and designed for continuous integration, multi-user collaboration, and DevOps tool stack compatibility. The SAT-Analyser is assessed using case studies and shown an impact analysis accuracy of 0.93 of F-measure. Further, the feedback by DevOps practitioners has shown the suitability and innovativeness of the proposed approach.

DOI: 10.4018/978-1-7998-1863-2.ch005

Copyright © 2020, IGI Global. Copying or distributing in print or electronic forms without written permission of IGI Global is prohibited.

INTRODUCTION

A software system is a combination of several software artefacts that evolves through a software development process model. Software artefacts refer to the intermediate by-products used in different phases of the SDLC such as SRS documents, design diagrams, architectural documents and quality attributes or the non-functional design reports, source code, test scripts, walkthroughs, inspections, bug reports, build logs, test reports, project plans, risk assessments (Sommerville, 2010). It is essential to manage the relationships and dependencies among artefacts to maintain adequate consistency towards the completion of the software product. The improper management and outdated elements can lead to inconsistency among artefacts, synchronisation issues and lack of trust for the system by stakeholders. Therefore, software artefact traceability is required to follow the artefact life cycle during the software development process.

DevOps is a recently emerged software development practice that increases the collaboration among developers and operations teams. It is required to manage the consistency among the software artefacts throughout the SDLC phases and project teams, with the nature of frequent artefact changes. Traceability supports to track the artefact changes, their transformations and relationships in both forward and backwards directions. Traceability management is a multi-step process and should ensure the correctness and performance (Maro, Anjorin, Wohlrab, & Steghöfer, 2016) (Mäder & Gotel, 2012). However, traceability in practice is popular due to the high cost and effort required to manage the artefacts relationships and maintain consistency during changes. Also, there is a lack of automated and platform independent tool support in traceability management. Thus, automated traceability management and consistency maintenance that covers a variety of artefacts in software development are essential.

This chapter addresses traceability and artefact consistency management in DevOps practice. We propose an approach for software artefact traceability management and a prototype tool 'Software Artefact Traceability Analyser' (SAT-Analyser) as the proof-of-work. This study considers different software artefact types representing the main activities in a software process. These artefacts include requirements in natural language text, UML class design diagram, Java source code, JUnit test scripts and build-scripts configuration files. The methodology consists of several modules to manage traceability through the trace-link establishment, change detection, change impact analysis (CIA), change propagation, visualisation, validation and integration with the DevOps tool stack. The applicability of the tool is evaluated using case-study based analyses and a usability study among DevOps practitioners. Thus, the proposed approach attempts to fulfil the research hindrance in traceability support in DevOps practice.

RELATED WORK

The artefact traceability acts as the pillars for artefact change management (De Lucia, Fasano, & Oliveto, 2008). As considered in several related studies, the traceability establishment process establishes the inter-relationships and intra-relationships by linking each artefact based on their dependencies. The main task associated with traceability management includes artefact pre-processing, trace-line creation, change detection, CIA, change propagation and consistency checking to support continuous integration in DevOps practice (Rubasinghe, Meedeniya, & Perera, 2017).

Some recent studies in the context of traceability have focused on their appropriateness to Agility and DevOps. An approach for requirement artefact traceability and CIA for Agile environments is presented in (Carniel, & Pegoraro, 2018). They have proposed a meta-model that maps dependencies among user stories, tasks and manages requirement evolution with the CIA based on a set of assumptions. However, its usability in practise is yet to be achieved as a complete tool.

The study (Maro, Steghöfer, & Staron, 2018) has discussed the current challenges and appropriate solutions in traceability related to automotive domain. They have shown that the existing related solutions are inapplicable to the automotive field in practice due to limitations in characteristics and higher complexity. However, the implemented traceability tool for arbitrary artefacts lacks full automation capabilities. A continuous integration framework for traceability in DevOps named TORNADO is proposed in (Jiménez et al., 2019). They have introduced a bidirectional solution that eliminates the gap between developers and operations team tasks by automatically updating deployment and configuration specifications when a change occurs. Their approach has evaluated with a proof-of-concept and has shown an acceptable level of feasibility.

Most of the existing traceability management tools are platform dependent. For instance, Caliber-RM tool supports only Windows environment ("Borland ® CaliberRM TM," 2003). TraceMaintainer is an independent tool that works with any CASE tools in any heterogeneous environment. However, it is limited for the support towards the requirements and design artefacts (Mäder et al., 2008). LDRA-TBmanager is a tool that has addressed the elements related to testing activities in SDLC, and it supports the applications developed using any programming language ("LDRA - Requirements Traceability," 2018). An agile based tool Echo presented in (Lee et al., 2003), has addressed requirements and design artefacts. TraceME (Bavota et al., 2012) and ArchEvol (Nistor, 2005) are integrative tools with the Eclipse IDE as a plugin.

Moreover, it is complex to track the issues in distributed systems due to the decentralised nature where many components are in different locations or cloud platforms. Therefore, distributed tracing is a solution to detect performance issues, track user requests across complex systems. Several industry-level tracing tools designed for distributed systems are available in the literature. Some of the opensource tools for distributed tracing systems with graphical user interfaces are Zipkin by Twitter, Jaeger by Uber technologies and Appdash by Sourcegraph ("opensource. com," 2019).

Accordingly, it is observable that the IR methods have involved in requirement traceability, whereas event-based and rule-based approaches have used in change detection, CIA and change propagation. Although there are several tools and techniques related to traceability management, there exist associated limitations. Many related studies have certain boundaries such as being addressing only a few artefact types, not focusing on complete SDLC, lack of support towards continuous integration and lack of automation.

The lack of automated tool support that covers all types of software artefacts in the SDLC is a limitation in overall consistency management (Mäder et al., 2008) (Lee et al., 2003)(Meedeniya, Rubasinghe & Perera, 2019). The mostly addressed elements in traceability management are requirements, design and source code artefacts. Many related studies have not addressed the artefacts in later stages of SDLC such as test scripts, configuration files and deployment files. Moreover, the change detection and CIA related works are even limited only for source code artefact (Acharya & Robinson, 2011). Some of the tools depend on a given IDE such as Eclipse (Bavota et al., 2012)(Nistor, 2005) or a platform or operating system ("Borland ® CaliberRM TM," 2003). Thus, the independent tool level traceability solutions are less compared to other rapidly evolving software related tools like DevOps tools stack. Scalability is another main issue in many relevant studies, that limits traceability management when the system is complex or large-scale. Similarly, visual clutter is another limitation in visualising traceability aspects (Holten, 2006). Accordingly, the existing studies lack the traceability management to cope with continuous integrations for the entire SDLC. Thus, there is a requirement of having a generic traceability management tool with extensible features.

SAT-ANALYSER DESIGN CONSIDERATIONS

This study designs an approach for artefact traceability management and implements as a prototype tool called Software Artefact Traceability Analyser (SAT-Analyser). The main goal is to achieve heterogeneous artefact traceability in a software process, applicable to DevOps practice. Thus, this chapter addresses traceability among different artefact types, impact analysis of changes, change propagation, consistency management, interactive visualisation, validation, comply with CICD principles, integrable with DevOps tools stack and collaborative with DevOps teams. Mainly, we have defined a mathematical derivative weighting scheme for the CIA process.

Figure 1 shows the abstract workflow of SAT-Analyser tool. The input artefacts include textual requirements, design in UML class diagram, source code in Java, unit test in JUnit and build script in Maven pom.xml. The data pre-processor transforms each artefact type into an intermediate XML format, generates traces, visualises and analyses them. Then the continuous integration process consists of a scheduler to initiate the change detection process when a deployment request is triggered. The method detects artefact changes based on their XML versions using version control. After that, identify the impact and propagates the changes accordingly. Finally, updates changed artefact and notify deployer via a PM tool by bringing the system into a consistent state. Figure 2 shows a detailed system workflow. The data elements include Java grammar, JSON parser, artefact elements, an XML writer, WordNet, dictionary ontology, thresholds, Neo4j graph database and Gephi graph platform. The notations IN, V1/2/3, CP, CIA, CD, CM denote inputs, versions, change propagation, change impact analysis, change detection and consistency management, respectively.

The layered architecture of SAT-Analyser is shown in Figure 3 with the presentation layer, business logic and data access layer. The design is an extension of our previous work with added Jenkins server integration and deployment features (Rubasinghe, Meedeniya, & Perera, 2018b).

The presentation layer handles the tool's inputs and outputs. The business logic layer contains modules to pre-process data, establish trace-links and support the continuous integration process. The pre-processor extracts data from the row artefacts and converts to an XML format. The traceability generator creates trace links between elements based on the identified relationships. The continuous integration module consists of processes that detect changes, analyse the impact, propagate the change impact and manage the artefact consistency. During the continuous deployment, the pre-processor obtains the latest source code and build script artefacts via the Jenkins automation server. The data access layer provides the data management required by the business logic layer. Ontologies, WordNet for artefact identification, XML representations for traceability management and visualisation support data include in the data access layer. The presentation layer visualises the results with informative, analytical and interactive graph views and provides notification back to Docker Deployer. Then the delivery manager deploys the software.

Figure 1. SAT-Analyser abstract workflow

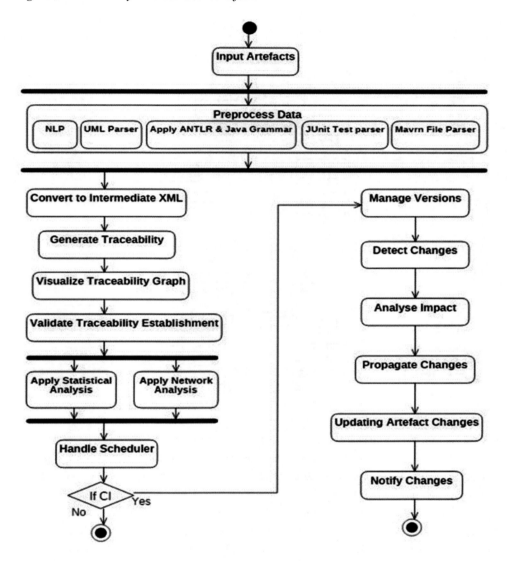

DATA PRE-PROCESSING OF SAT-ANALYSER TOOL

Generally, the textual contents in artefacts provide descriptive details about their informal semantics and data pre-processing helps to extract the required data from the raw data. Requirements can be processed using Natural Language Processing (NLP) tasks such as tokenisation, text normalisation, morphological analysis, anaphora analysis, and stemming (MacDonell, Min, & Connor, 2005)(Cleland-Huang et al.,

Figure 2. SAT-Analyser detailed workflow

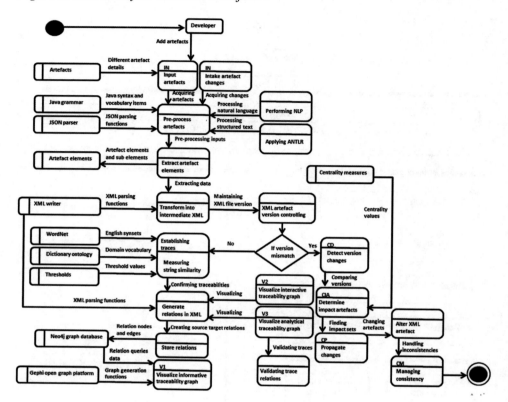

2012) (Arunthavanathan et al., 2016). If the textual contents of artefacts are similar, then they are conceptually related and creates the trace links. Other elements pre-process with file readers, UML parsers and programming language specific parsers (Ibrahim & Ahmad, 2010).

SAT-Analyser considers requirements, design, source code, unit test script and builds script artefacts. We have taken requirement in document (.docs) or text format (.txt), design diagrams in metadata-JSON file format (.mdj) following UML notation, source codes in Java programming language (.java), unit test artefact in JUnit script files (.java) and Maven build script pom file (.xml). The NLP module with Stanford CoreNLP extracts artefact elements such as classes, methods, attributes and relationships from the requirements. The NLP module consists of sub-modules such as Part-of-Speech (POS) tagger, parser, Named Entity Recognizer (NER) and Anaphora analysis. Initially, the NLP module tokenises the pronouns of a given requirement, and Anaphora analysis identifies the coreferences in given sentences before extracting the artefact elements. Consequently, nouns are extracted to detect

Figure 3. Architectural view of SAT-Analyser

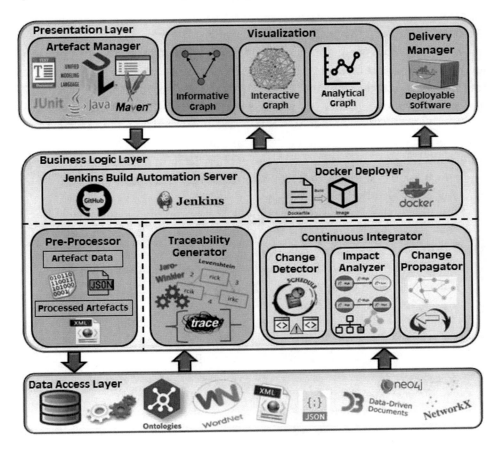

artefact elements. A parse tree is generated using Stanford CoreNLP to obtain a detailed granularity of sentences by using POS tagging.

Accordingly, the classes, methods, attributes and relations extract as the main elements. This study has used pre-defined rules to distinguish classes and attributes from the noun set. For instance, if a verb phrase is following a noun, that noun is extracted as class names. If a noun or adjective is not following a verb phrase, then those are obtained as attributes. Methods derived from the noun phrases associated with class names. Relationship identification is defined to identify the association and generalisation type of relationships. Then, the morphological analysis is performed to convert the contents into a root form for redundancy elimination purpose. Afterwards, stemming analysis and redundant elimination are used to retrieve a unique set of data related to the requirements of the system.

We used UML design tools that supports JSON (.mdj), XMI (.xmi) and UML (.uml) formats. It is used to extract data via a JSON reader since JSON format has used to store the design and class diagram concepts. Two pre-defined dictionaries are integrated with this parsing module to fine-tune the data extraction by eliminating non-realistic extractions in class diagrams. Moreover, a parser is used to pre-process source code artefacts from the project workspace. The tool ANTLR is used to generate lexers, tokens and listener classes for Java. Thus, an abstract syntax tree of a source code file is generated by ANTLR and processed using the Java grammar. The source code data are extracted by traversing the syntax trees using the tree walker integrated with ANTLR to identify class declarations, methods, attributes, generalisation and association relationships. Moreover, they are designed to store in a temporary Neo4j database.

Algorithm 1 shows the data extraction process from the input artefacts.

Algorithm 1 Data pre-processing

Require: Software artefacts (requirements, design, source code)
Ensure: associating input data to a project

1. **input:** artefact a
2. if (a== requirements)$\rightarrow$ a_req = NLP_module(a)
3. if (a== design)$\rightarrow$ a_uml = UML_parser(a)
4. If (a== source code)$\rightarrow$ a_src= SRC_parser(a)
5. If (a== unit test)$\rightarrow$ a_ut= UT_parser(a)
6. If (a== build script)$\rightarrow$ a_bs= BS_parser(a)
7. a_{xml} = Convert_to_XML(a)
8. If (all 5 a_{xml} exists)
9. Build the project structure module
10. Make folder structure
11. Initiate graph files
12. Else
13. Notify failure
14. **output:** new artefact management project

Based on the artefact type, the parser is selected. For instance, the artefacts requirement, design, source code, JUnit test script, build script are forwarded to process via NLP_module, UML_parser, SRC_parser, UT_parser, BS_parser algorithm, respectively. Then the extracted artefact data converts to a common format using XML writers using Convert_to_XML algorithm. A new project creates when all artefacts related XML files are available. Thus, Algorithm 1 gives the steps related to the creation of a new project.

Algorithm 2 shows the NLP based pre-processing of the requirements artefacts written in the English language in the .txt or the .doc file formats. Initially, the tokenisation is performed to segment the statements into words and sentences, and anaphora analysis is used for coreference identification to identify pronouns and re-organise the requirement statements. Then, the data extraction is performed to determine the names of classes, methods, attributes and relationships. A rule-based approach is designed for each element such as class rules, method rules, attribute rules and relationship rules. Once the artefacts are collected, the morphological analysis with stemming analysis is conducted to transform the extracted requirements elements into a further base form by eliminating redundancies due to plurality. Consequently, it outputs the pre-processed requirements elements.

Algorithm 2 NLP_module
 Require: Software artefacts: requirements in natural language
 Ensure: pre-process requirements artefact data
  1. **input:** requirements artefact a
  2. while (a)
  3. tokanisation
  4. Anaphora analysis
  5. Data extraction
  6. Return classes, methods and attributes
  7. if (classes, methods, attributes exists)
  8. morphological analysis
  9. Stemming analysis
  10. Redundant elimination
  11. **output:** pre-processed requirements artefact

Algorithm 3 shows the pre-processing of the design artefacts. UML class diagrams designed using StarUML and Modelio tools are input as the design artefacts, as they contain the class diagram details in JSON or the model-based formats which eases the processing. Thus, StarUML and Modelio readers are used to extract the encoded information in a class diagram, including class names, methods and attributes.

Algorithm 3 UML_parser
 Require: Software artefacts: design in UML class diagram
 Ensure: pre-process design artefact data
  1. **input:** design artefact a
  2. if (a== uml class file)
  3. process via StarUML reader OR Process via Modelio reader
  4. Data extraction

5.   Return classes, methods and attributes
6.   **output:** pre-processed design artefact

The pre-processing of Java source code artefacts is shown in Algorithm 4. The Another Tool for Language Recognition (ANTLR) is used to generate Java grammar-based syntax trees, to traverse the tree using its tree walker and to make use of the listeners for tracking. Hence, the class declarations, methods, attributes are extracted with the aid of the above mentioned ANTLR capabilities. The extracted source code artefacts are stored temporarily in a Neo4j graph database. Algorithm 5 states the pre-processing of unit test artefact given in JUnit test scripts. ANTLR tool is used to generate Java grammar from the input JUnit test scripts. The extracted unit test artefacts are stored as the output of this algorithm in a Neo4j graph database. The pre-processing of build script artefact in Maven dependency file as a pom.xml file is given in Algorithm 6. The Maven build script pom.xml files are in a .xml tag structure. Thus, the XML data extraction is performed directly on pom.xml file to extract build script (project) name and dependency plugins names. Then, the Neo4j graph database stores the extracted build script artefacts.

Algorithm 4 SRC_parser

    Require: Software artefacts: source code in Java programming language
    Ensure: pre-process source code artefact data

1.   **input:** source code artefact a
2.   if (a== java source files)
3.   process via ANTLR & Java grammar
4.   Data extraction
5.   Return object-oriented classes, methods and attributes
6.   Store in Neo4j DB
7.   **output:** pre-processed source code artefact

Algorithm 5 UT_parser

    Require: Software artefacts: unit test in JUnit test scripts
    Ensure: pre-process unit test artefact data

1.   **input:** unit test artefact a
2.   if (a== JUnit test script)
3.   process via ANother Tool for Language Recognition (ANTLR)
4.   Process via Java and JUnit grammar
5.   Data extraction
6.   Return JUnit classes, methods and attributes
7.   Store in Neo4j DB
8.   **output:** pre-processed unit test artefact

Algorithm 6 BS_parser

    Require: Software artefacts: build script in Maven dependency pom.xml

    Ensure: pre-process build script artefact data

        1.   **input:** build script artefact a

        2.   if (a== build script file)

        3.   process using XML data extraction

        4.   Return build script name, plugin dependency names

        5.   Store in Neo4j DB

        6.   **output:** pre-processed build script artefact

The artefact processing modules write the pre-processed and extracted artefact data in XML format using XML writers separately. The XML format is selected as the common conversion format as XML structures help to build complex graphs with readability over others. A new traceability project is created if the XML formats of all artefact are available. The extracted pre-processed elements are processed through the Convert_to_XML algorithm to convert the data into a common format using XML writers, as shown in Algorithm 7. The input to this algorithm is designed to be the pre-processed artefact elements. Hence, all pre-processed artefact element data are written using XML writers. The outcome of this algorithm is a separate XML file for each artefact type that contains relevant, extracted artefact data.

Algorithm 7 Convert_to_XML

    Require: pre-processed artefact data

    Ensure: Convert pre-processed software artefact to a common format

        1.   **input:** pre-processed artefact a

        2.   if (a== requirements OR design OR source code OR unit test OR build script)

        3.   XML writer (pre-processed classes, methods, plugins, attributes)

        4.   Return a.xml

        5.   **output:** XML conversion of an artefact

TRACEABILITY LINK ESTABLISHMENT PROCESS

The traceability links between the elements and sub-elements are created using the pre-processed and extracted data. WordNet and self-generated dictionary are used to map the traces, and calculate the similarity among artefacts, respectively, to manage trace-links. Levenshtein algorithm is used to calculate the similarity among two strings at a time, where the strings represent the extracted artefacts and output the 'edit distance value', that are stored in WordNet. Thus, the similarity among the two words is signifies based on the minimum edit operations needed to convert from a given string to another string. The edit operations include the addition of a character into a string, removal of a character from a word and replacing a character. A threshold value is defined as 0.85 for the similarity calculation based on the edit distances. Thus, the artefacts that exceed the defined threshold are defined as having a higher similarity and map together. The self-generated dictionary fine-tunes the performance of the matching artefacts. Trace-link generation uses the threshold-based mapping that refers to the relationship building process.

In previous work, a semantic network has created for word matching through the build relationship module of this traceability link generation component of the SAT-Analyser (Arunthavanathan et al., 2016). The distance between the nodes in the semantic network is measured to identify the matching percentage and keeps track of the artefact element words. For instance, the network shown in Figure 4 is created by considering the words Bank, Library, Online, Offline, etc. Thus, each word is stored with its relevant similar words and properties. The properties include name-value pairs, a word's parent class data. An API provided by the Apache Jena Library is used to build the ontology model.

This study uses the Resource Description Framework (RDF) as a data format that accurately describes a metadata model and supports data merging and interchanging features. RDF represents in different formats such as JSON and XML. Figure 5 shows the artefact specific XML file conversions based on a pre-defined XML model. The XML artefact models separately generate for all supported types of software artefacts namely, requirements, UML class diagrams, Java code, JUnit test files and Maven build script. Accordingly, the relationships among artefact elements are stored and modified based on the detected changes, CIA and change propagation results during the software development.

Figure 4. Semantic network for words

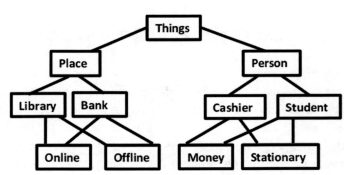

Figure 5. Pre-defined relationship XML model

```
<Relations>
    <Relation id="...">
            <SourceNode>... </SourceNode>
            <TargetNode>...</TargetNode>
    </Relation>
    <Relation id="...">
        ...
    </Relation>
</Relations>
```

Traceability Link Visualisation

The visualisation component in SAT-Analyser represents the traceability links using graph-based techniques. Figure 6 shows the three views: an informative view based on Neo4j with Gephi, analytical view using Python NetworkX and interactive view based on JavaScript D3.js, for better data analysis and decision making. The informative view provides multiple static filtered views and more information about a given node. For instance, a filtered view of a given requirement artefact shows only the methods, fields and relationships associated with it. The interactive view support features such as drag, hover and browse nodes. It shows the direct links and CIA values of a node. The analytical view is used for the validation process.

The modular view of the visualisation component is shown in Figure 7. The inner modules manage intra-relations of the artefact types. Thus the relationship management is defined for each artefact. The Neo4j graph database stores the finalised relation nodes. Additionally, the relations are stored in JSON format for interactive visualisations.

Software Artefact Change Detection

Change is always inevitable and necessary to handle the consistently to reduce the cost irrespective of the software development model (Chawathe, Rajaraman, Garcia-Molina, & Widom, 1996). Figure 8 shows the structure of the change detection component of SAT-Analyser tool. The artefacts changes can occur in any type, and

Figure 6. Visualisation views

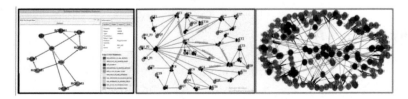

Figure 7. Visualisation module

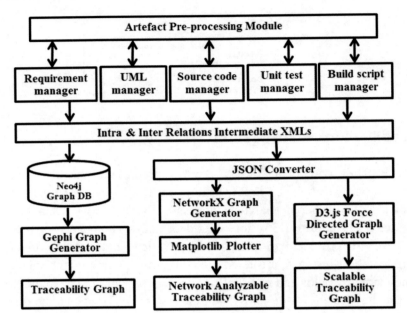

the consistency should manage during the continuous integration process. An artefact integration may contain either element additions, alterations or removals. Whenever a new artefact input is received, the tool generates the intermediate XML format, extract the needed elements. The XML version recorder adds the version suffix to the newly created XML file based on the previously generated version suffixes. Then the changes are detected by comparing the new intermediate XML files and the corresponding artefact type of the previous XML version.

A scheduler module is designed based on an executor framework to initiate the detection of artefact changes. Figure 9 shows the component diagram of the scheduler. The scheduled thread pool defines the number of tasks and threads. The CI trigger object denotes the functionality of the continuous integration artefact fetching. The scheduled executor service component handles the periodical behaviour of the scheduler. A fixed delay is set as the scheduler frequency to invoke CI Trigger via the thread. The executor service component contains the executor framework that holds the runnable interfaces corresponding to threads.

Change Impact Analysis

Change impact analysis (CIA) can be initiated through change detection as they are a sequence of activities in this problem domain. Figure 10 shows the iterative process

Figure 8. Change detection component

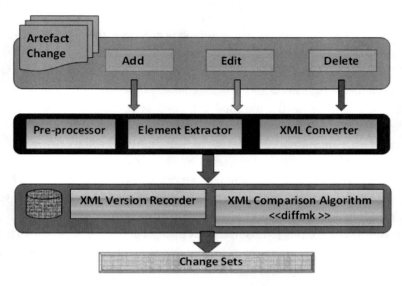

Figure 9. Scheduler workflow

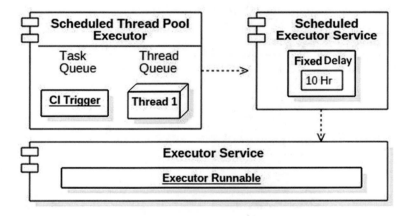

of CIA (Li, Sun, Leung, & Zhang, 2013). The process determines the impact of an artefact modification, computes the Estimated Impact Set (EIS) and changes the Actual Impact List (AIS) accordingly. The elements of the AIS differs based on the execution procedure of a given change. CIA can be performed before a change for better understandability, impact prediction and cost estimations. Consequently, the CIA performs after the execution of a modification to get the ripple effect of the modification to propagate the changes.

The changed artefacts set obtained from the change detector, and the trace links from the traceability generator are input to the CIA module in SAT-Analyser tool. Impact Generator handles the weighted scheme for the artefacts. The weight calculator assigns a weight to each node and edge using their Eigenvector centrality value (Rubasinghe et al., 2018b). Influence factor calculator provides a two-level influence factor for each node and edge. We have calculated the change impact using a rule-based algorithm with a minimal cost and complexity. CIA rules are defined by considering the practical dependency scenarios by avoiding calculation overhead and proceed with high impact artefacts to increase the performance. Impact Analyser shows the results as change impact sets and their respective values. The decision manager triggers the impacted set to change propagator to navigate the changes.

SAT-Analyser displays the automatically identified CIA results correspond to the change types addition, modification and deletion. Additionally, this view allows manual user modifications to ensure correctness. The final altered CIA results are considered to propagate the changes further to graph manager for visualisation and relations manager to update the artefacts. More details of this process are explained in the case-study evaluation section, as shown in Figure 23.

Figure 10. Change impact analysis process (Source: Li et al., 2013)

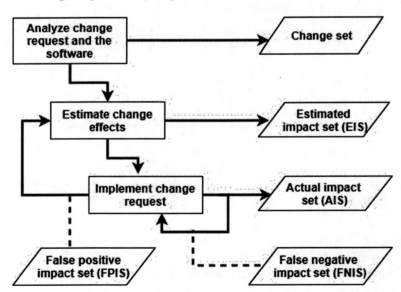

Change Propagation

The interactive view of the changes propagated relation graph is shown in Figure 11. The modified node and impacted nodes are shown in a larger node size, while the deleted and the impacted nodes are removed from the graph views. Additionally, the influence factor values of edges are shown on the edges, and influential factor of nodes can be seen by hovering on a node. Moreover, the neighbourhood is highlighted when a node is double-clicked. In parallel, the notifications are triggered to inform the change propagation to the teams. Accordingly, relevant project teams update their responsible raw artefacts. Then the relations manager is triggered, and the artefact XML files of the changes propagated artefact types are updated. However, in SAT-Analyser, if the change is the type of addition, then all artefacts' XML files and the Relations.xml file are re-generated during that traceability re-establishment.

Consistency Management

The consistency management module follows a rule-based approach, and the workflow is shown in Figure 12. The process uses the version history to manage consistency during continuous integration. It monitors the version directory structure and rolls back in an unsuccessful integration attempt. During the change detection, the artefact XML comparator ensures the consistency of inputs to the change detector component and the outcome is handled in a separate directory structure by the consistency

Figure 11. Change propagated interactive graph view ("SAT-Analyser," 2018)

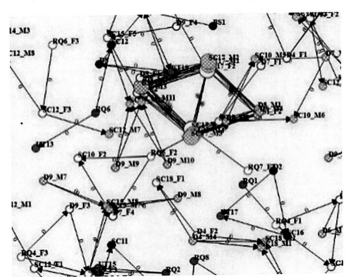

manager. The artefact stabiliser module executes during the CIA process for the stability of the current version, by transferring non-altered artefact types XML files from the previous version to the current version.

SAT-Analyser notifies the change propagation results to DevOps teams by integrating with the Trello project management tool ("Trello," 2018). Trello is selected due to its open source availability and popularity. We have used Trello Java API to integrate with SAT-Analyser. For each change propagation confirmation, a newer card is created automatically in a dedicated list in the Trello board. The Trello card name is generated with the given change propagated traceability project name with the date and time for unique identification, as shown in Figure 13. The CIA results that lead to change propagation are embedded in each card description. Once, the change propagation is confirmed, the Trello board is loaded in the browser with the new card instance, as shown in Figure 14. Accordingly, the teams are notified of the artefact changes and requested to alter the corresponding affected artefacts.

Figure 12. Consistency management workflow

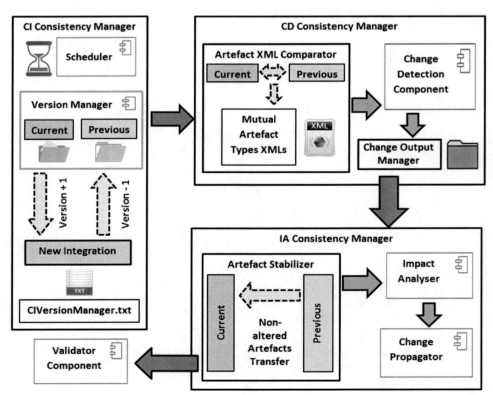

Figure 13. Trello change propagation card instance

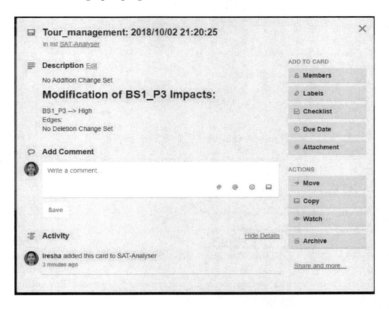

Figure 14. Trello board with change propagation notification

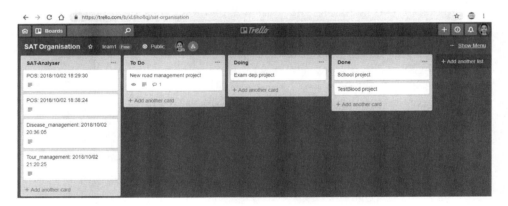

Figure 15 shows the web-based GUI of the tool, developed using AjaxSwing platform. It transforms Java Swing to HTML at run time and uses the open-source Java Servlet container Apache Tomcat server. Thus, SAT-Analyser is featured with cross-browser compatibility such that the team members can access the tool in real-time using their client device browsers connected with the server. User session timeouts, update intervals, auto-refreshing are defined to enable dynamic multi-user accessibility.

Figure 15. Multi-user accessible SAT-Analyser web version

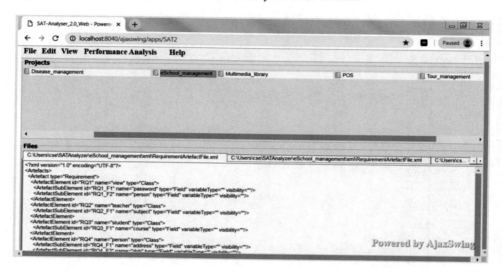

Traceability Validation

Traceability establishment and CIA methodology proposed in SAT-Analyser is evaluated using two methods. The statistical method is based on precision, recall and F-measure (Hattori, Guerrero, Figueiredo, Brunet, & Dam, 2008), is used to measure the accuracy of the artefact extraction process for trace link creation. The network analysis method uses centrality measures of each node of the traceability graph (Rubasinghe, Meedeniya, & Perera, 2018a). We have considered artefact-level centrality measures such as degree, betweenness, closeness and Eigenvector centrality. The validation module is developed using Python NetworkX libraries that support network graph analysis with Java-based GUIs, Python Matplotlib and JavaScript D3.js based graph visualisation extensions. Also, the tool measures performance in terms of time and resource allocation. The process is explained using a case study.

CASE STUDY: TOUR MANAGEMENT

Artefact Change Types

SAT-Analyser tool is supported with 17 artefact change types as follows covering the entire SDLC. C1: Add a main requirement, C2: Add a moderate importance requirement, C3: Add a low importance requirement, C4: Modify a requirement, C5: Delete a requirement, C6: Add a design component, C7: Modify a design component, C8: Delete a design component, C9: Add a source code artefact, C10: Modify a source code artefact, C11: Delete a source code artefact, C12: Add a unit-test artefact, C13: Modify a unit-test case, C14: Delete a unit-test artefact, C15: Add a configuration artefact, C16: Modify a configuration artefact, C17: Delete a configuration artefact.

Experiment Setup

This study has used a tour management software solution to assess the proposed method. Figure 16 shows a part of the requirements, which input as original artefacts. The tour company provides a set of trips, where users select a tour and confirm by a payment ("SAT-Analyser", 2018). Figure 17 shows the corresponding design artefact, UML class diagram, of the tour management system. Among the classes, there is an inheritance relationship between the guide, driver and manager with employee class. An aggregation relationship between town and route classes, a composition between tour and route classes exist in the design with other association relationships. The other artefacts related to the source code, test scripts and build scripts are given in the SAT-Analyser tool web portal ("SAT-Analyser," 2018).

Once the original artefacts are input, SAT-Analyser applies the data pre-processing to identify the main artefact elements as listed in Figure 18. The tool generates a unique identifier for each artefact, where the sub-elements attributes (fields), plugins and methods denoted using _F, _P and _M, respectively. Further, Table 1 summarises the manual artefact identification and categorisation by the experts, that can be used for the evaluation process of the tool, and this will be not used in practice.

Traceability Establishment Process

A part of the tool generated traceability relations XML structure is shown in Figure 19. For instance, a relation between RQ1: Route to D6: Manager is listed as a directed link from Route to Manager, since Manager assigns a route to each tour. Figure 20 shows a section of the corresponding traceability graph that shows the relationships between artefacts with an interactive view.

Figure 16. Case-study description

In a tour management system, there are three types of employees, namely manger, driver and guide. An employee must record the employee code, name, address and a contact number. A tour is identified by a unique tour ID and a date. The manager reserves a tour for a passenger. This is one of the main requirements of the system. When a passenger registers for a tour, he/ she provide the name, address, contact number, birth date, gender and preferences. Another main task of the manager is that manager assigns route to a tour. A route has a route length, tour duration and town names. Moreover, manager assigns a driver for each tour. Additionally, when a passenger makes the payment for a tour, the manager creates bill to the passenger. A bill consists of the date, passengers count and tour ID. Furthermore, a guide elaborates each tour for the passengers during a tour. Further, a route has one or more towns. For each route, a town records its overnight stay details.

Figure 17. Case study design diagram

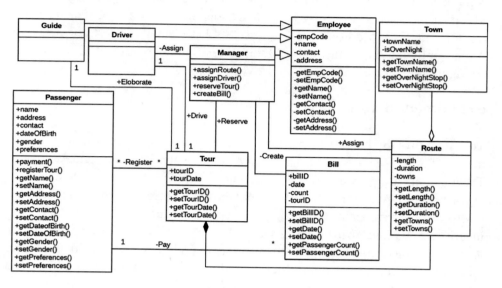

Figure 18. Artefact summary

Table 1. Artefact categorisation

Artefact type	Low	Medium	High
Requirement	RQ1, RQ3	RQ2, RQ6, RQ8	RQ4, RQ5, RQ7
Design	D2, D4	D1, D3, D5, D6	D7, D8, D9
Source Code	S7, S9	S2, S3, S4, S5	S1, S6, S8
Test Script	UT7, UT9, UT10	UT2, UT3, UT4, UT5	UT1, UT6, UT8, UT9
Configuration files	-	-	BS1

Figure 19. Relations.xml instance

```
<Relation id="155">
    <SourceNode>RQ2_F2</SourceNode>
    <RelationPath>ReqFieldToUMLOperation</RelationPath>
    <TargetNode>D9_M11</TargetNode>
</Relation>
<Relation id="156">
    <SourceNode>RQ1</SourceNode>
    <RelationPath>ReqClassToUMLClass</RelationPath>
    <TargetNode>D6</TargetNode>
</Relation>
```

Figure 20. Traceability visualisation graph

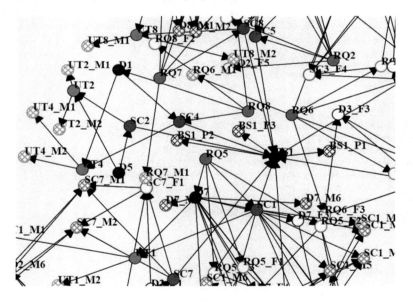

Figure 21 shows the centrality measures for the network analysis-based traceability validation. This case study consists of single build script artefact, that link with each source code class artefact. The network analysis validates these relationships, by showing the highest betweenness and closeness centrality values for the build script (BS1), considering the nodes in the network graph. Moreover, one of the maximum eigenvector centralities is held by the node SC6_M4 that denotes the method setPreferences () in the Tour class, which is a major artefact in this case study.

Figure 21. Network analysis summary

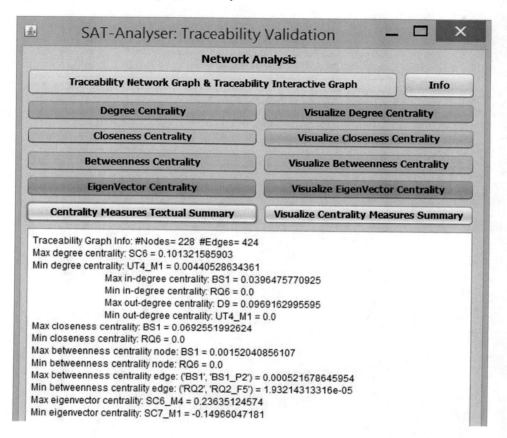

Continuous Integration Process

The tool is tested with five types of changes as follows. C2: Add a moderate importance requirement, C5: Delete a requirement, C6: Add a design component, C13: Modify a unit-test artefact and C17: Delete a configuration artefact. Figure 22 shows the tool generated change detection results. Consequently, the changes have identified correctly and listed the affected artefact element, sub-element ID and name. Accordingly, the CIA results are shown in Figure 23. For example, consider the type C13: modified unit test artefact. The corresponding artefact UT5: ManagerTest has impacted on its two child nodes UT5_M1: setUpClass method and UT5_M2:tearDownClass method, which has a lower impact value. The propagated changes are re-visualised, and Figure 24 shows a part of the traceability graph. For example, the newly added D9_M15 is represented in the graph while BS1_P2 has removed and earlier BS1_P3 has become BS1_P2 by making the IDs consistent.

Figure 22. Change detection window

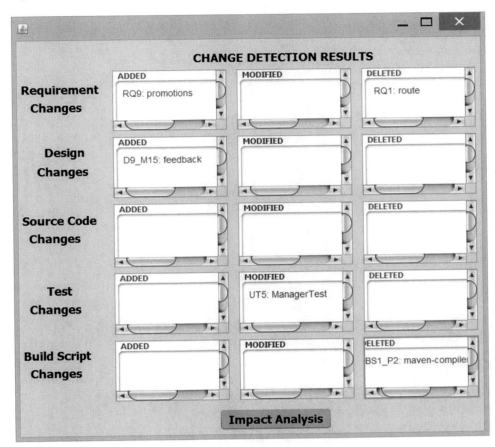

Performance Analysis

The CIA accuracy based on the statistical measures is shown in Figure 25. The tool identifies the impact related to modification and deletion change types. However, there are five missing impact items in the addition change type since the corresponding artefacts are not modified according to the added changes. Thus, the addition of RQ9 must impact on the design (D), source code (SC) and a UT item, while the addition of D9_M15 must impact on an SC sub-element and may impact on a UT item. Accordingly, the CIA process recall is obtained as 0.86, F-measure as 0.93 and precision as 1.0. Moreover, artefacts with more links have a high CPU consumption.

Figure 23. Change impact analysis window

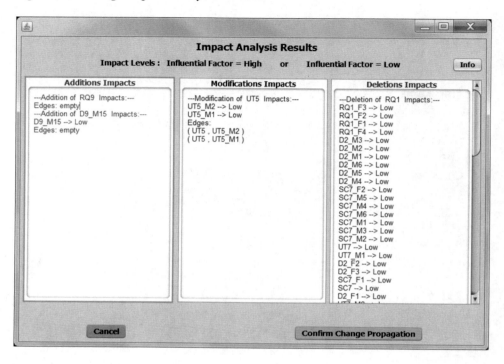

Figure 24. Change propagation instance

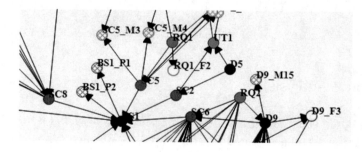

This study has assessed the usability of the tool using a survey of 20 DevOps practitioners. As a part of the questionnaire, they have asked to select the most relevant words that best describe the SAT-Analyser based on their perspective. Figure 26 shows the tag cloud that denotes user feedback. The most emphasised terms for the tool are Traceability, Supportive and Improvable, which derive a high level of user satisfaction about SAT-Analyser indicating a future direction to improve the usability beyond a prototype-level with more HCI aspects.

Figure 25. CIA statistical analysis results

Figure 26. SAT-Analyser usability tag cloud

DISCUSSION

Comparison with Existing Studies

This study has proposed a methodology for software artefact traceability management and developed in SAT-Analyser tool. We have maintained the artefact consistency through change detection, CIA, change propagation that supports CICD pipeline in a DevOps environment, where Agile principles are practically applied deviating from traditional software development processes. The feature selection of the proposed SAT-Analyser tool is based on an initial survey conducted among DevOps practitioners. We considered the requirements in natural language as it is the industry practice. UML class diagrams are selected because the code base is dependent on the class diagram. Unit testing is selected that checks the individual functions for errors. Considering the continuous integration tasks, we have set up the scheduler with different options such that automated fixed intervals, dynamic and manual triggers to invoke change detection to avoid the overhead and reduce the cost. In practice, change detection is defined mainly for source code changes and no proper tools to automated detectors are used for other artefact changes.

SAT-Analyser detects changes in all artefact types not being limited to the source code. We also gave prominence to source code changes, since it is the most affected artefact type. Also, the design architecture supports extensible features that allow incorporating the remaining sub artefacts.

According to the initial survey, 66.7% of the DevOps participants accepted that traceability handling might be useful, while rest is unaware of the concept of traceability. Thus, we have represented trace-link relationships using graph-based interactive and analytical visualisation. Many analytical approaches for CIA process have been conducted on graphs using related theories and mathematical models. 33.3% of the participants reported that they do not use any impact analysis for changes and rest is having a vague idea about CIA methods due to lack of knowledge. They have mentioned the factors such as time and effort consumption limit the use of CIA in practice. This study has defined a novel dependency-based CIA with a mathematical weighting scheme using EVC considering the influential factor of an artefact. In practice, change propagation methods are automatically deployed to the Jenkins server and executed based on pre-defined protocols and policies. Change propagation is crucial for decision making, and hence, traceability graphs are re-visualised for every change propagation.

In industry practice, continuous integration is supported by tools such as Jenkins, CodeDeploy, CodePipeline, Puppet, Jira, TravisCI, and TeamCity. SAT-Analyser has integrated with Jenkins, Docker for deployment activities and GitHub repository for its open source capabilities. Additionally, SAT-Analyser is integrated with the project management tool Trello, as it provides Agile Kanban boards, thus support the CICD pipeline. Moreover, we have shown the applicability of the proposed method for different project scales and domains, using case study-based evaluation. Table 2 summarises the current industry perspectives in DevOps environments for traceability related features over the SAT-Analyser. In industry practice, only the change detection and CI are addressed in tool level using Jenkins and GitHub source code handling without considering the other artefact types.

Table 2. Traceability management in a DevOps practice vs SAT-Analyser tool

Feature	Industry practice	SAT-Analyser Tool
Traceability creation and visualisation	No proper tools.	Trace link creation using string similarity method. Traceability graph-based visualisation.
Change detection	No proper tools to auto-detect changes of every artefact. Use monitoring tools to detect failures in Jenkins for source code building.	Detect changes for every artefact integration using XML comparison.
Impact analysis	Manually decide the range of affected artefacts in the code level. No proper CIA method due to time and effort concerns.	Calculate the level of impact for every change using Eigenvector centrality.
Change propagation	Automatically deploy to the Jenkins server. Use pre-defined rules for source code management.	Propagate changes according to impacts and re-visualise in a traceability graph.
Continuous integration	Use Jenkins as a solution for source code integration with build automation.	Change detection process consists of a scheduler. The tool integrates with Jenkins, GitHub code repository and Trello project collaboration.

Moreover, Table 3 shows SAT-Analyser features over existing traceability management tools. The main limitations in existing tools such as lack of heterogeneous artefact support, change detection, CIA, change propagation, IDE independency are successfully addressed in the SAT-Analyser prototype tool.

The approach we designed and developed as SAT-Analyser tool supports traceability management of software projects in both traditional and Agile based process. It is intended to facilitate requirements in a DevOps environment with CICD concepts that support artefact changes and collaborative behaviour. In traditional software development, the frequency of artefact changes is minimal due to the sequential nature, where the artefact changes are not accepted at a later stage of SDLC. Thus, in general, software development, the traceability and impact analysis process is required only at the beginning and end of the process. Hence, the requirement of incorporating the CI features with scheduling and versioning included in this research work would be lesser significant in traditional methods, while the traceability model would be equally important as for DevOps. Therefore, the frequency of change detection, their impact analysis, change propagation, visualisation, team collaboration and validation features included in this research work are uniquely useful and supports continuous integration in DevOps practice.

Table 3. Existing traceability management tools vs SAT-Analyser

Tools / Features	Trace ME (Bavota et al., 2012)	IBM DOORS ("IBM-Rational DOORS," 2017)	LDRA-TBmanager ("LDRA," 2018)	Arch Evol (Nistor, 2005)	SAT-Analyser
Consider different artefact types	√		√		√
Visualise traceability		√		√	√
Validation methods					√
Continuous integration tasks		√	√	√	√
Detect artefact changes					√
Analyse the impact of a change	√	√			√
Propagate the change impact					√
Consistency checking		√			√
Project management		√			√
Integrate with DevOps tools stack					√
Independent of a specific IDE					√
Tool performance analysis					√

Thus, these features of SAT-Analyser are actively supported for the usage of CICD pipeline in a DevOps environment, since any artefacts change can happen at any stage of SDLC.

Future Research Directions

DevOps practices ease the Agile processes and maximise productivity with software evolution. Thus, there exists a large DevOps tool stack, that introduces new tools and updates existing tools with advanced features. These tools should be compatible and integrable to enable collaborative nature, which is a crucial aspect of DevOps. SAT-Analyser fits into the DevOps tool stack by addressing the heterogeneous artefact traceability that has not been sufficiently focused by existing tools.

This study can be extended in many directions. The supported artefact types can be extended with more sub artefact categories such as support for different programming languages as the DevOps tools stack is dynamic with latest technologies. Performance and accuracy of the traceability creation can be enriched with advanced NLP features and information retrieval techniques. The CIA model based on Eigenvector centrality values can be improved to better identification of the influential value of a node or a link. Moreover, SAT-Analyser can be extended as a software quality assessment tool that assesses the quality of the design and code. This would be a significant future improvement to facilitate traceability support regardless of project scale. Traceability visualisation with better scalability is another promising future work. Integrating the three visualisation variations provided in SAT-Analyser together would be useful. Additionally, the usability aspects of the tool can be improved into an industry-level DevOps supportive tool by integrating Human-Computer Interaction (HCI) concepts for user friendliness along with refined performance parameters.

In another perspective, traceability can be applied for distributed systems with the excessive use of microservices. Generally, adopting microservices is advantageous in Agile development as it increases agility, team independence and system flexibility (Jones, 2019). However, it can be challenging to manage the routing with better user experience, when many microservices run on different servers continuously. Microservices can eventually increase the inter-dependencies within a system, which affect the service routing and management. Hence, traceability for microservices based systems enables to secure the agility with team independence. Additionally, this helps to route among microservices, since traceability creates awareness about system relationships and dependencies. Hence, the proposed approach can be extended with the support for more artefacts types that are commonly associated in distributed computing, microservices architecture and cloud services.

Further, traceability can be applied for security scanning in open source management ("WIPO," 2019). Several security risks and vulnerabilities are associated with the open source tools, software solutions and updates. For instance, the tool Blackduck is one such open source management tool that helps to track the components in source code and to avoid security, license and policies related risks ("Blackduck," 2019). Thus, the use of traceability approach in the context of security scanning, when changing the base operating system or release of new software features, is another possible future research direction.

CONCLUSION

At present, software systems have become complex and competitive, requiring the ability to perform in high reliability to sustain, without being replaced by a new software system. The software development process embraces Agile principles and transforming into DevOps practices by supporting continuous integration concepts. The DevOps reduces the gap between development and the operations, whereas the continuous integration referrers frequent merging of developer working copies enables high ROI. The development of these systems requires reliable traceability and consistent management for the correct functioning and maintenance of the product.

This chapter addressed traceability management of software artefacts with a change impact analysis model to maintain the artefact consistency during the continuous integrations in DevOps practice. Mainly, we have considered the requirement, design diagram, source code, unit test and build script artefact types, covering each stage in SDLC. A proof-of-work prototype tool, SAT-Analyser is implemented based on the proposed methodology. The traceability establishment process is based on string comparison and NLP based information retrieval methods. The traceability visualisation is supported with Gephi-based informative view, Python-based analytical and JavaScript-based interactive graph network. These views help for efficient decision making in a DevOps environment. This approach consists of a scheduler, change detector, change impact analyser, change propagator, consistency manager, collaboration components to support the continuous integration nature in DevOps practice.

Further, SAT-Analyser tool integrates with DevOps tool stack and provides multi-user accessibility with a web-based solution. Thus, the DevOps teams can use the tool actively with DevOps tools stack. In current DevOps practice, traceability management and validation have identified as essential to manage artefact consistency, where a higher number of tools stack in active use. The proposed approach is evaluated using case studies based on real software projects on different scales and user acceptance test among DevOps practitioners. The results have signified the usefulness of the research outcome for the software engineering domain as migration from theoretical principles to practice.

ACKNOWLEDGMENT

This research was supported by the University of Moratuwa, Sri Lanka [Senate Research Committee Grant SRC/ST/2019/07].

REFERENCES

Acharya, M., & Robinson, B. (2011). Practical change impact analysis based on static program slicing for industrial software systems. In *Proceedings of the 33rd international conference on Software engineering (ICSE '11)*. (p. 746). New York: ACM Press. 10.1145/1985793.1985898

Arunthavanathan, A., Shanmugathasan, S., Ratnavel, S., Thiyagarajah, V., Perera, I., Meedeniya, D., & Balasubramaniam, D. (2016). Support for Traceability Management of Software Artefacts using Natural Language Processing. In *Proceedings of the Moratuwa Engineering Research Conference (MERCon)*. (pp. 18–23). IEEE. 10.1109/ MERCon.2016.7480109

Bavota, G., Colangelo, L., De Lucia, A., Fusco, S., Oliveto, R., & Panichella, A. (2012). TraceME: Traceability Management in Eclipse. In *Proceedings of the 28th IEEE International Conference on Software Maintenance (ICSM)* (pp. 642–645). IEEE. 10.1109/ICSM.2012.6405343

Blackduck. (2019). Retrieved May 14, 2019, from https://www.blackducksoftware. com

Borland ® CaliberRM ™. (2003). Retrieved from http://www.danysoft.com/free/ CyV_Cal.pdf

Carniel, C. A., & Pegoraro, R. A. (2018). Metamodel for Requirements Traceability and Impact Analysis on Agile Methods. In Agile Methods. WBMA 2017. Communications in Computer and Information Science (vol. 802, pp. 105-117). Springer. doi:10.1007/978-3-319-73673-0_9

Chawathe, S. S., Rajaraman, A., Garcia-Molina, H., & Widom, J. (1996). Change detection in hierarchically structured information. *SIGMOD Record, 25*(2), 493–504. doi:10.1145/235968.233366

Cleland-Huang, J., Chang, C. K., & Christensen, M. (2003). Event-based traceability for managing evolutionary change. *IEEE Transactions on Software Engineering, 29*(9), 796–810. doi:10.1109/TSE.2003.1232285

Cleland-Huang, J., Zisman, A., & Gotel, O. (2012). *Software and Systems Traceability. Software and Systems Traceability* (1st ed.). Springer-Verlag London; doi:10.1007/978-1-4471-2239-5

De Lucia, A., Fasano, F., & Oliveto, R. (2008). Traceability management for impact analysis. In *Proceedings of the Frontiers of Software Maintenance, FoSM 2008* (pp. 21–30). IEEE. 10.1109/FOSM.2008.4659245

Hattori, L., Guerrero, D., Figueiredo, J., Brunet, J., & Dam, J. (2008). On the Precision and Accuracy of Impact Analysis Techniques. In *Proceedings of the 7th IEEE/ACIS International Conference on Computer and Information Science (ICIS 2008)*. (pp. 513–518). IEEE. 10.1109/ICIS.2008.104

Holten, D. (2006). Hierarchical Edge Bundles: Visualisation of Adjacency Relations in Hierarchical Data. *IEEE Transactions on Visualization and Computer Graphics*, *12*(5), 741–748. doi:10.1109/TVCG.2006.147 PMID:17080795

IBM-Rational DOORS. (2017). Retrieved October 14, 2017, from https://www.ibm.com/us-en/marketplace/rational-doors

Ibrahim, M., & Ahmad, R. (2010). Class Diagram Extraction from Textual Requirements Using Natural Language Processing (NLP) Techniques. In *Proceedings of the 2nd International Conference on Computer Research and Development*. (pp. 200–204). IEEE. 10.1109/ICCRD.2010.71

Jiménez, M., Castaneda, L., Villegas, N. M., Tamura, G., Müller, H. A., & Wigglesworth, J. (2019). DevOps Round-Trip Engineering: Traceability from Dev to Ops and Back Again. In Software Engineering Aspects of Continuous Development and New Paradigms of Software Production and Deployment. DEVOPS 2018 (pp. 73-88). Springer. doi:10.1007/978-3-030-06019-0_6

Jones, M. (2019). Microservices Architecture in the Real World. *TechEvents.online. RedisConf19*. Retrieved May 20, 2019, from https://www.techevents.online

LDRA - Requirements Traceability. (2018). Retrieved July 5, 2017, from http://www.ldra.com/en/software-quality-test-tools/group/by-software-life-cycle/requirements-traceability

Lee, C., Guadagno, L., & Jia, X. (2003). An agile approach to capturing requirements and traceability. *Proceedings of the 2nd International Workshop on Traceability in Emerging Forms of Software Engineering*, 1–7.

Li, B., Sun, X., Leung, H., & Zhang, S. (2013). A survey of code-based change impact analysis techniques. *Software Testing, Verification & Reliability*, *23*(8), 613–646. doi:10.1002tvr.1475

MacDonell, S. G., Min, K., & Connor, A. M. (2005). Autonomous requirements specification processing using natural language processing. In *Proceedings of the 14th International Conference on Intelligent and Adaptive Systems and Software Engineering (IASSE '05)*. (pp. 266–270). Toronto, Canada: ISCA.

Mäder, P., & Gotel, O. (2012). Towards automated traceability maintenance. *Journal of Systems and Software*, *85*(10), 2205–2227. doi:10.1016/j.jss.2011.10.023 PMID:23471308

Mäder, P., Gotel, O., Kuschke, T., & Philippow, I. (2008). traceMaintainer - Automated Traceability Maintenance. In *Proceedings of the 16th International Requirements Engineering (RE '08).* (pp. 329–330). IEEE 10.1109/RE.2008.25

Maro, S., Anjorin, A., Wohlrab, R., & Steghöfer, J. P. (2016). Traceability maintenance: factors and guidelines. In *Proceedings of the 31st IEEE/ACM International Conference on Automated Software Engineering.* (pp. 414–425). New York: ACM. 10.1145/2970276.2970314

Maro, S., Steghöfer, J., & Staron, M. (2018). Software traceability in the automotive domain: Challenges and solutions. *Journal of Systems and Software*, *141*, 85–110. doi:10.1016/j.jss.2018.03.060

Meedeniya, D. A., Rubasinghe, I. D., & Perera, I. (2019). Traceability Establishment and Visualization of Software Artefacts in DevOps Practice: A Survey. *International Journal of Advanced Computer Science and Applications*, *10*(7), 66–76. doi:10.14569/IJACSA.2019.0100711

Nistor, E. C., Erenkrantz, J. R., Hendrickson, S. A., & van der Hoek, A. (2005). ArchEvol. In *Proceedings of the 12th international workshop on Software configuration management (SCM '05).* (pp. 99–111). New York: ACM Press. 10.1145/1109128.1109136

opensource.com. (2019). Retrieved May 15, 2019, from https://opensource.com/article/18/9/distributed-tracing-tools

Rubasinghe, I. D., Meedeniya, D. A., & Perera, I. (2017). Towards Traceability Management in Continuous Integration with SAT-Analyzer. In *Proceedings of the 3rd International Conference on Communication and Information Processing (ICCIP 2017)* (pp. 77-81). ACM. 10.1145/3162957.3162985

Rubasinghe, I. D., Meedeniya, D. A., & Perera, I. (2018a). Automated Inter-artefact Traceability Establishment for DevOps Practice. In *Proceedings of the 2018 IEEE/ACIS 17th International Conference on Computer and Information Science (ICIS 2018)* (pp. 211–216). Singapore: IEEE. 10.1109/ICIS.2018.8466414

Rubasinghe, I. D., Meedeniya, D. A., & Perera, I. (2018b). Traceability Management with Impact Analysis in DevOps based Software Development. In *Proceedings of the International Conference on Advances in Computing, Communications and Informatics (ICACCI).* (pp. 1956–1962). Bangalore, India: IEEE. 10.1109/ICACCI.2018.8554399

SAT-Analyser. (2018). Retrieved November 10, 2018, from https://sites.google.com/cse.mrt.ac.lk/sat-analyser/case-studies

Sommerville, I. (2010). *Software Engineering* (10th ed.). New York: Addison-Wesley Professional.

Trello. (2018). Retrieved October 2, 2018, from https://trello.com

WIPO. (2019). Retrieved May 15, 2019, from https://patentscope.wipo.int/search/en/detail.jsf?docId=US226141321

ADDITIONAL READING

Antoniol, G., Cleland-Huang, J., Hayes, J. H., & Vierhauser, M. (2017). Grand Challenges of Traceability: The Next Ten Years. arXiv preprint arXiv:1710.03129, 2017

Chen, X., Hosking, J., Grundy, J., & Amor, R. (2018). DCTracVis: A system retrieving and visualizing traceability links between source code and documentation. *Automated Software Engineering*, *25*(4), 703–741. doi:10.100710515-018-0243-8

Lomotey, R. K., Pry, J., & Sriramoju, S. (2017). Wearable IoT data stream traceability in a distributed health information system. *Pervasive and Mobile Computing*, *40*, 692–707. doi:10.1016/j.pmcj.2017.06.020

Meedeniya, D. A., Rubasinghe, I. D., & Perera, I. (2019). Software Artefacts Consistency Management towards Continuous Integration: A Roadmap. *International Journal of Advanced Computer Science and Applications*, *10*(4), 100–110. doi:10.14569/IJACSA.2019.0100411

Mills, C. (2017). Towards the automatic classification of traceability links. In *Proceedings of the 32nd IEEE/ACM International Conference on Automated Software Engineering-ASE 2017*. (pp. 1018–1021). IEEE. 10.1109/ASE.2017.8115723

Murshed, S. M. M. (2016). An investigation of software vulnerabilities in open source software projects using data from publicly-available online sources. Columbia University Computer Science Technical Reports, CUCS-007-16.

Pete, I., & Balasubramaniam, D. (2015). Handling the differential evolution of software artefacts: A framework for consistency management. In *Proceedings of the IEEE 22nd International Conference on Software Analysis, Evolution, and Reengineering (SANER)*. (pp. 599–600). IEEE. 10.1109/SANER.2015.7081889

Rath, M., Rendall, J., Guo, J. L. C., Cleland-Huang, J., & Mäder, P. (2018). Traceability in the wild: automatically augmenting incomplete trace links. In *Proceedings of the 40th International Conference on Software Engineering (ICSE '18).* (834-845). New York, NY, USA. 10.1145/3180155.3180207

Rubasinghe, I. D., Meedeniya, D. A., & Perera, I. (2018). Software Artefact Traceability Analyser : A Case-Study on POS System. In *Proceedings of the 6th International Conference on Communications and Broadband Networking (ICCBN 2018).* (pp. 1–5). Singapore: ACM. 10.1145/3193092.3193094

Santana, M., Sampaio, A., Andrade, M., & Rosa, N. S. (2019). Transparent tracing of microservice-based applications. In *Proceedings of the 34th ACM/SIGAPP Symposium on Applied Computing (SAC '19).* (pp. 1252–1259). New York, NY, USA: ACM. 10.1145/3297280.3297403

KEY TERMS AND DEFINITIONS

Change Set: A set of artefacts that are affected due to artefact additions, modifications, or deletions.

Cross-Browser: Different types of web browsers.

Graph-Based: Use graph as the visualisation method.

Industry-Level: Commercial software development companies.

Ontology: A collection of pre-defined words and their synonyms.

Proof-of-Work: A prototype solution to demonstrate the theoretical contribution.

Rule-Based: A set of defined rules based on constraints.

Chapter 6
Continuous Deployment Transitions at Scale

Laurie Williams
North Carolina State University, USA

Kent Beck
Facebook, USA

Jeffrey Creasey
LexisNexis, USA

Andrew Glover
Netflix, USA

James Holman
SAS Institute Inc., USA

Jez Humble
*DevOps Research and Assessment
LLC, USA*

David McLaughlin
Twitter, USA

John Thomas Micco
VMWare, USA

Brendan Murphy
Microsoft, UK

Jason A. Cox
The Walt Disney Company, USA

Vishnu Pendyala
Cisco Systems Inc., USA

Steven Place
IBM, USA

Zachary T. Pritchard
Slack, USA

Chuck Rossi
Facebook, USA

Tony Savor
Facebook, USA

Michael Stumm
University of Toronto, Canada

Chris Parnin
North Carolina State University, USA

ABSTRACT

Predictable, rapid, and data-driven feature rollout; lightning-fast; and automated fix deployment are some of the benefits most large software organizations worldwide are striving for. In the process, they are transitioning toward the use of continuous deployment practices. Continuous deployment enables companies to make hundreds

DOI: 10.4018/978-1-7998-1863-2.ch006

Copyright © 2020, IGI Global. Copying or distributing in print or electronic forms without written permission of IGI Global is prohibited.

or thousands of software changes to live computing infrastructure every day while maintaining service to millions of customers. Such ultra-fast changes create a new reality in software development. Over the past four years, the Continuous Deployment Summit, hosted at Facebook, Netflix, Google, and Twitter has been held. Representatives from companies like Cisco, Facebook, Google, IBM, Microsoft, Netflix, and Twitter have shared the triumphs and struggles of their transition to continuous deployment practices—each year the companies press on, getting ever faster. In this chapter, the authors share the common strategies and practices used by continuous deployment pioneers and adopted by newcomers as they transition and use continuous deployment practices at scale.

INTRODUCTION

Continuous deployment is a software engineering process where incremental software changes are automatically tested and deployed to production environments without manual steps in the deployment pipeline (Rahman et al. 2015). Continuous deployment enables companies, such as Facebook (Savor et al. 2016), to make hundreds or thousands of software changes to live computing infrastructure every day, while maintaining service to millions of customers. Such ultra-fast changes create a new reality in software development.

Over the past four years, we have held the Continuous Deployment Summit, hosted at Facebook (Parnin et al. 2017) (2015), Netflix (2016), Google (2017), and Twitter (2018). For three years from 2015 to 2017, representatives from eleven companies, Cisco, Disney, Facebook, Google, IBM, LexisNexis, Microsoft, Netflix, SAS, Slack, and Twitter, have shared the triumphs and struggles of their transition to continuous deployment practices—each year the companies press on, getting ever faster. In this paper, we share the common strategies and practices used by continuous deployment pioneers and adopted by newcomers as they transition and use continuous deployment practices at scale. Every company is still making this journey toward continuous deployment.

PERSISTENT AND INCREMENTAL PRACTICE ADOPTION

As Einstein advises, "Persistence is the most powerful force on earth, it can move mountains." The uniting factor among all the Summit companies was the persistent movement toward becoming more efficient, improving customer satisfaction and business results and increasing release frequency through the incremental adoption of continuous deployment practices. Each year, the Summit companies demonstrated measurable increases in the adoption of the practices.

Some of the Summit companies, such as Google, Facebook, and Netflix, were "born" using continuous deployment practices. Older companies, such as Microsoft, IBM, Cisco, and SAS, have large legacy products in their portfolio that were "born and raised" with a waterfall-type software development process. Disney supports a wide range of software products—from websites to safety-critical software that runs theme-park rides. These older companies could have decided continuous deployment was not appropriate for some of their products. Instead, these giants took demonstrable steps each year to "turn their ship around."

Each company found its unique way to bring about continuous change. Disney attributes its success with the use of continuous deployment practices to their company's values established by Walt Disney himself: Curiosity, Confidence, Courage, and Constancy. The developers are curious to see if the practices could help them with their business results; they are confident in their abilities, systems, and checks so they dare to make changes. Constancy helps them continue to incrementally adopt more practices. Microsoft has a range of product types from Yammer and Bing, which use continuous deployment practices similar to those of Google, Facebook, and Netflix; to its monolithic software, such as Microsoft Exchange and Windows operating system. Inspired by continuous deployment practices, Microsoft Exchange now deploys to beta customers using a ring deployment model, where a release is deployed to a new ring level every week, finally reaching beta customers in the sixth week—if no problems are detected. Finally, Facebook has applied this principle to changing their release process for all developers in the company.

MOBILE FIRST

Summit companies recognize that worldwide growth in the use of mobile applications exceeds that of web and other cloud-based applications. This growth trend motivated Facebook CEO, Zuckerberg, to announce a "Mobile First!" strategy in 2012, which directed new development to occur first for mobile applications before developing for the other platforms. Mobile First! strategy is followed by other Summit companies, such as Google. However, the frequency of updates of mobile software has traditionally lagged that of web applications for many reasons. Mobile versions can only be released through the Apple and Google app stores that control the frequency of releases and impose constraints on development. Users may not auto-install updates and can decide when and if to upgrade; conceivably every release of a mobile app that ever existed could be installed across their user base.

The need to support and test hundreds of Android hardware variants increases the computational cost complexity and speed of the verification process, thereby further slowing down deployment. Finally, quality requirements are higher for mobile apps as there are more limited options for taking remedial action through deploying a new version when a defect is detected, compared with web- and cloud-based apps.

Chuck Rossi, the director of release engineering at Facebook, delivered the keynote at the 2017 Summit. At Facebook, mobile applications are used by over a billion people each day (Rossi et al. 2016). Rossi shared that over a period of four years, Facebook has decreased the deployment speed from 6 weeks to 4 weeks to 2 weeks to 1 week. Mobile applications are deployed more frequently to its internal users during a one-week stabilization phase that occurs the week after development is complete to conduct "dogfood" testing. Summit companies also use tools, such as the Gatekeeper tool, and feature flags in the code to dynamically control from the cloud the features that users see in an app. Even though the customer installations of new versions of the app will occur periodically, the companies can still control the incremental rollout of new individual features across their user base and can disable problematic changes in the advent of unexpected behavior without requiring customers to update their apps.

DEVELOPER PRODUCTIVITY METRICS (LOOK WITHIN)

Companies are increasingly looking inward at their productivity, to evolve practices or improve tool infrastructure for developers. These opportunities offer a much richer source of information beyond simple metrics, such as lines of code produced, and are more deeply tied to customer behavior.

At Google, searching for internal libraries is a common task and deeply integrated into developer tooling and culture. Given that many possible library choices may exist, one determining factor may be signals (Trockman 2018), information cues that indicate attributes, such as quality, that may bias a developer towards one particular library. Google has recently integrated metrics that serve as signals into project dashboards. For example, the metrics include pre-submit speed (i.e. time to run tests before committing to a repository), release frequency (hypothesizing that projects with higher frequency are healthier), green builds/week (builds with fewer failures), and number of post-release patches (how error-prone is the code). A project with good project health metrics (called PH-levels) can be perceived as more reliable and thus might be more likely to be adopted. Developers are encouraged to strive for healthy PH-levels. However, some metrics are considered controversial for certain teams, who want to opt-in/opt-out of certain metrics. Despite these challenges, PH-levels can help maintain a shared sense of productivity.

Finally, participants cautioned about direct interpretations of developer productivity metrics. Some participants at the Summit argued that simply increasing release frequency (say, 8 weeks to 4 weeks) does not necessarily improve developer productivity. Instead, the increased frequency forces upgrades in tooling and automation, which in turn reduces errors and inefficiencies in the process. In another example, a common low-hanging fruit that an organization may target for optimization is increasing the speed of tooling. However, Microsoft provided several cases where tools were made faster, but observed no tangible benefit in productivity gains: Instead, developers simply changed when they ran the tool (from night-time to day-time). Ultimately, the participants recommended instead of simply striving to hit or game metrics, organizations should target desirable changes in developer behavior.

TOOLS EMBODY CULTURE

Creating a shared sense of culture and maintaining architectural integrity in a large organization can be difficult; especially when the number of developers can be counted in the thousands and with teams operating in small independent units. Traditionally, many software organizations have relied on centralized architecture teams to help manage standards (Parsons 2005). However, an alternative paradigm has emerged, where architectural principles can be enforced through strong investments in tooling.

At the Summit, companies shared various ways in which tooling played a central role in creating a shared engineering culture. Perhaps the most illustrative example is the introduction of chaos engineering at Netflix. At Netflix, developers mostly work in small teams that support a single feature or microservice. Given Netflix's anti-process culture and lack of centralized architectural teams but high interdependence of microservices, there needed to be some way to communicate and enforce architectural principles across the whole organization. Chaos engineering (Basiri et al. 2016), is the practice of introducing small changes or unexpected events into production environments to analyze how these changes or events could impact the behavior of the system. For example, by introducing a chaos monkey, a tool that randomly turned off AWS instances during working hours, the tool could help enforce architectural principles of maintaining stateless and resilient microservices.

Enforcing cultural changes through tools can result in adoption barriers. For example, Microsoft wanted to introduce stronger coding practices that could reduce potential security problems. In one instance, trying to turn-on compiler errors for uninitialized variables (a potential security concern) as a general policy resulted in a large pushback from many development teams. While understanding the security implications, many developers often viewed these compiler findings as false positives and did not want them turned on as errors for their projects. To combat a similar problem at Google, the static analysis tool, Tricorder (Sadowski et al. 2015), allows developers to give feedback on any finding (e.g., "Does not work in IE8"). Further teams can opt-out of specific types of findings or even opt-in specialized findings. If a finding is found not to be useful 10% of the time, the tool findings may eventually be disabled across the company.

Tooling allows developers to share common workflows across the company and even between companies. Some companies, such as Google and Facebook, invest in their web-based IDE. By having all developers share the same interfaces for developing code, the companies can ensure that all developers share the same workflow for processes such as code review, code search, and reviewing findings from static analysis tools. At the Summit, the participants noted the increasing importance of partnership and investment of tooling across multiple companies and open source communities. Open-source tools, such as Spinnaker (which supports specifying and customizing deployment workflows), have been developed in partnership between Netflix and companies such as Microsoft, Google, and Pivotal. Some parameters and decisions can be highly variable between teams and products: How long is a canary experiment; at what step do you sign-off on a deploy; how does your particular service handle state? Scale differences between companies and communities introduce a complication. For example, at Twitter, upstream open source patches often end up breaking Twitter's production environment because the open source community operates at a much lower scale. Despite these challenges, companies cite numerous benefits, such as attracting talent and improving tool value. As one participant stated: "It makes sense to work together when you're the only two companies in the world that face the same issue."

TESTING AND RELEASE IN PRACTICE

Operating continuous deployment pipelines at scale requires numerous shifts in technology and practices. Traditional problems are amplified, while new problems and pain points emerge. At Google, the demand for continuous integration (CI) services double each year, with over 4.5 million tests being run daily—if not properly optimized, this demand would require more servers to run than Google's primary product itself: search.

At the Summit, companies discussed numerous pain points related to testing and shared various strategies that could help address them. One of the most common pain points expressed was flaky tests, that is, tests that intermittently fail due to random factors, such as resource availability (Luo et al. 2014). At Google, an internal analysis of failing tests found that 84% of the time a failure is due to a flaky test.

Several strategies were discussed to combat flaky tests. Companies have started calculating the flakiness of tests or try to tag flaky tests based on historical data. At Google, tests are kept below 1–5% flakiness or are quarantined. At Facebook, the current practice is to simply delete flaky tests without mitigation. Several companies reported reliability issues of running tests in Jenkins due to resource exhaustion or inconsistent state of the workspace. To improve the reliability of running tests in Jenkins, IBM and Netflix are moving towards running tests in containers. Finally, participants at the Summit discussed the goal of moving toward predicting failing builds and the presence of flaky tests. For example, if the dependency chain between a changed source file and a failing unit test is more than ten hops away, it is likely to be a flaky test.

Companies also discussed various issues and strategies for deploying releases into production. At LexisNexis, releases occur every three weeks during off-hours. Each release requires manual coordination and blessing of released features—a customized Gantt chart is used to coordinate the order of flips for new versions of shared services. Once everything is in place, manual testers verify the release; meanwhile, developers of each service/module are on standby to patch any problems. At Disney, release management was more frequent, with three release windows per week. However, developers did not have full autonomy for making release decisions; a highly centralized process is used and overseen by executives for no/go decisions on each release. Meanwhile, Netflix remained at the head of the pack with 4000 deployments a day.

HOLDING ONTO SCHEMAS

For some companies, the biggest barrier to full continuous deployment adoption is a lack of an effective strategy for deploying schema changes to relational databases (or their usage at all). For example, in many database engines, a simple operation such as renaming a column in a table would require locking all rows and thus prevent any new data from being stored, while the rename operation took place. Major schema changes could effectively shutdown an application for many hours (de Jong et al. 2017).

This challenge was especially apparent in companies that supported legacy applications. For example, IBM used to take a month to migrate a system to a new version at a customer's site. The primary challenge was coordinating code and database changes with on-premises instances. Eventually, IBM shortened the process to one hour. For LexisNexis, a 200-year-old company with software components that are over 15 years old, deploying database changes remains one of the most challenging aspects of continuous deployment. For every deployment to production, the deployment process is often on hold for several hours as they wait for the DBA to clear the release. In addition to schema changes, other issues can make deployment with databases problematic.

For SAS, dumping and restoring databases to accommodate schema changes can take hours. At Microsoft, database rollbacks are avoided at all costs, especially if the failure rate is low. Companies that have built continuous deployment-ready architectures often discard relational databases entirely or develop new storage technologies that can handle schema changes. For example, Netflix uses a key-value based store, Cassandra, and microservice architecture. Any changes to a database are handled by managing access to versioned calls at the service layer. Graph databases, such as Facebook's social graph, avoid these locking issues entirely by being able to add new nodes and edges, then removing old edges and nodes when done without any downtime. Still, even the most advanced architectures cannot escape issues related to schema changes. At Facebook, changes to the schema for storing messages and photos required a year-long migration to a more efficient schema.

INTENTIONAL FEATURE EXPERIMENTATION

Companies have, for decades, used telemetry to capture usage of their software to identify quality issues or to help improve deployed features. Since the inception of the Lean Startup (Ries 2011) practice, Internet-based and other companies have been using data obtained via feature experimentation instrumentation to make data-driven decisions on whether a new feature or algorithm should "pivot or persevere" in the released product. Specifically, companies are removing features from their code if these features do not have a positive impact on their customers. Five of the Summit companies have evolved their continuous deployment processes to include feature experimentation.

To enable experimentation, feature toggles may be implemented in the software to create multiple experiences for different customers. Feature toggles are essentially conditional blocks – if/else statements that can be used to enable or disable a feature selectively (Schermann, Cito, & Leitner, 2018). For example, when Facebook released Live video, they realized an individual live video could receive up to 2500 comments per second. Facebook built experiments to evaluate multiple algorithms for filtering and ranking comments to choose the algorithm that performs best at elevating comments with high engagement. Data scientists work with the development team to design experiments, develop hypotheses, collect metrics, and analyze collected data. The paper documenting the 2015 Continuous Deployment Summit contained the adage, "Every feature is an experiment." (Parnin et al. 2017) However in later summits, the reality of the experiment complexity and the sheer amount of data needed to be collected has made Summit companies more intentional in their choice of when to run an

experiment. For example, Google is cautious of experiments that may have implications to ad revenue, so typically small, incremental experiments are run. Naively, companies with large user bases may initially believe they would obtain feedback on a new feature rapidly, such as in hours or a small number of days. However, users behave differently throughout the day, on different days of the week, and at different times of the month. Representative experiments on stable features take longer than expected. Microsoft has analyzed 21,220 experiments applied in Bing (Kevic et al. 2017). Their results indicate that an experiment runs an average of 42 days before a "pivot or persevere" decision is made. As discussed above, feature rollout to mobile customers are delayed relative to online customers, making mobile experiments slower and more technically challenging. Summit companies did not use feature experimentation for bug fixes, infrastructure changes, or architecture changes.

SHAMELESS RETROSPECTIVES

Retrospectives are meetings in which a team inspects and adapts their methods and teamwork after completing a unit of work. Retrospectives enable learning, act as a catalyst for change, and generate action (Derby and Larsen 2006)—as long as the environment for retrospective discussion is safe. Allow shame and blame to enter the retrospective, and these benefits are obliterated. Shame crushes our tolerance

Figure 1. Cycle of shame

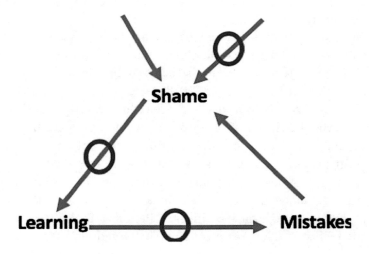

for vulnerability, thereby killing engagement, innovation, creativity, productivity, information flow, and trust (Brown 2012).

In the 2016 Summit, Kent Beck who was at Facebook at the time, delivered a keynote about the role of shame in software development as depicted by the Cycle of Shame (Figure 1). The Cycle of Shame uses the notation of influence diagrams (Weinberg 1992). With influence diagrams, a regularly directed arrow indicates that more of the source activity tends to create more of the destination activity (i.e. an amplifier), such as more mistakes generate more shame. A directed arrow with a circle over it indicates that more of a source activity tends to create less of the destination activity (i.e. an inhibitor), such as more shame drives less learning. Starting from the regular arrow into Shame in Figure 1, more shame drives less learning which drives more mistakes which drives more shame. Conversely, starting from the arrow with the circle, less shame drives more learning which drives fewer mistakes which drives less shame.

Within the context of the Cycle of Shame, Beck remarked positively about how little shame there was in the engineering culture at Facebook. An engineer can freely share the details about a mistake that he or she has made, owning the mistake—and most importantly not blaming anyone else for the mistake. The engineer shares the consequences of the mistake, details the remedial action, and provides suggestions for how that type of mistake could be avoided in the future. In sharing this information, the engineer does not feel shame, benefiting his or her learning and that of the team members. The practice of shameless retrospectives resonated with Summit companies as an essential component of the continuous process improvement needed while adopting continuous deployment practices, which are often disruptive changes to the organization.

LEVERAGING CULTURE AND PRACTICES TO ENHANCE SECURITY

Alongside continuous deployment practices, organizations are increasingly adopting software security practices. However, from a frequency of adoption perspectives, firms most often adopt software security practices for reasons, including responding to a security event, detecting vulnerabilities, and preventing vulnerabilities (Williams et al. 2018). Integrating software security practices in a continuous deployment environment is challenging because teams must integrate these practices at speed, perhaps in an environment that chooses speed over deliberate, methodical approaches to testing, security, and quality (McGraw 2017).

Many of the Summit companies have their software security group "silo'ed" into a separate organization, as is also common in most non-Summit companies.

Some of the smaller organizations, such as Twitter and Slack, have stronger partnerships between the developers and their software security group, moving towards a DevSecOps model, in which the security silo is broken down. At Slack, teams often use Trello for collaborative, team-based project management. Based upon the perceived risk of a new feature or product, their security team puts cards on the team's Trello board to signify the software security practice or reviews that are needed to take place before the release. At both Slack and Twitter, the security group partners with the development team starting with the requirements and design phases. The philosophy of the security groups is that rather than taking the role of fishing for security vulnerabilities when development is complete, the role of the security team is to "teach the development team to fish" whereby the development team specifies, designs, and implements secure products. All Summit teams desire better automated security tools that could detect both architecture/design- and code-level vulnerabilities with fewer false positives, a call for security researchers and tool vendors.

Continuous deployment practices can enhance the security of a product. The use of feature toggles is prevalent by Summit companies to support dark launches and feature experiments. Dark launches release new features into production surreptitiously, without any real users noticing them (Schermann, Cito, & Leitner, 2018). The system still duplicates the user requests to evaluate the new features in the clandestine releases. Summit companies, such as Twitter, use feature toggles to prevent features with security and/or privacy implications from being accessible to external users until the security team has conducted their checks. Using this procedure, developers can still continuously integrate code to these important features, but a separate security/privacy process can take place before the public launch. Teams instrument their code and constantly monitor the behavior of users to enable feature experimentation. This same instrumentation and monitoring can be used to detect anomalous behavior by attackers. Finally, organizations can use their normal process to rapidly deploy security fixes that will more likely be installed by customers. In the middle of 2016, security researchers found critical vulnerabilities in both Chrysler and Tesla automobiles. Tesla was able to deploy their fix over the air, while Chrysler sent USB sticks to its customers due to the lack of a better deployment process.

CONCLUSION

The eleven companies that participated in the annual summit, reveal their commitment toward adopting software development practices that move them closer to continuous deployment. All the companies at the Summit have experience applying continuous deployment practices and are aware of the challenges in applying these practices. At one end of the spectrum, the adoption may be challenging yet feasible for deploying hundreds or thousands of times of day, supporting feature experiments that can drive data-driven decisions. On the other end of the spectrum, legacy products may be deployed multiple times per year rather than once per year with a corporate strategy shifting toward more cloud-based solutions that can be deployed more frequently. Regardless of where they are on the spectrum, the Summit companies share a bond of a commitment to continuous process improvement and sharing technical solutions, approaches, and use of tools.

ACKNOWLEDGMENT

One of the authors who now works at VMWare had worked at Google during the time of the Summits. Google has reviewed and approved the contents of this paper.

REFERENCES

Basiri, A., Behnam, N., De Rooij, R., Hochstein, L., Kosewski, L., Reynolds, J., & Rosenthal, C. (2016). Chaos engineering. *IEEE Software*, *33*(3), 35–41. doi:10.1109/MS.2016.60

Brown, B. (2012). *3 Ways To Kill Your Company's Idea-Stifling Shame Culture*. Fast Company.

de Jong, M., van Deursen, A., & Cleve, A. (2017, May). Zero-downtime SQL database schema evolution for continuous deployment. In *2017 IEEE/ACM 39th International Conference on Software Engineering: Software Engineering in Practice Track (ICSE-SEIP)* (pp. 143-152). IEEE. 10.1109/ICSE-SEIP.2017.5

Derby, E., Larsen, D., & Schwaber, K. (2006). *Agile retrospectives: Making good teams great*. Pragmatic Bookshelf.

Kevic, K., Murphy, B., Williams, L., & Beckmann, J. (2017, May). Characterizing experimentation in continuous deployment: a case study on bing. In *Proceedings of the 39th International Conference on Software Engineering: Software Engineering in Practice Track* (pp. 123-132). IEEE Press. 10.1109/ICSE-SEIP.2017.19

Luo, Q., Hariri, F., Eloussi, L., & Marinov, D. (2014, November). An empirical analysis of flaky tests. In *Proceedings of the 22nd ACM SIGSOFT International Symposium on Foundations of Software Engineering* (pp. 643-653). ACM.

McGraw, G. (2017). Six Tech Trends Impacting Software Security. *Computer*, *50*(5), 100–102. doi:10.1109/MC.2017.143

Parnin, C., Helms, E., Atlee, C., Boughton, H., Ghattas, M., Glover, A., ... Stumm, M. (2017). The top 10 adages in continuous deployment. *IEEE Software*, *34*(3), 86–95. doi:10.1109/MS.2017.86

Parsons, R. I. (2005). Enterprise architects join the team. *IEEE Software*, *22*(5), 16–17. doi:10.1109/MS.2005.119

Rahman, A. A. U., Helms, E., Williams, L., & Parnin, C. (2015, August). Synthesizing continuous deployment practices used in software development. In 2015 Agile Conference (pp. 1-10). IEEE. doi:10.1109/Agile.2015.12

Savor, T., Douglas, M., Gentili, M., Williams, L., Beck, K., & Stumm, M. (2016, May). Continuous deployment at Facebook and OANDA. In *2016 IEEE/ACM 38th International Conference on Software Engineering Companion (ICSE-C)* (pp. 21-30). IEEE. 10.1145/2889160.2889223

Schermann, G., Cito, J., & Leitner, P. (2018). Continuous experimentation: Challenges, implementation techniques, and current research. *IEEE Software*, *35*(2), 26–31. doi:10.1109/MS.2018.111094748

Trockman, A., Zhou, S., Kästner, C., & Vasilescu, B. (2018, May). Adding sparkle to social coding: an empirical study of repository badges in the npm ecosystem. In *Proceedings of the 40th International Conference on Software Engineering* (pp. 511-522). ACM.

Weinberg, G. (1992). *Systems Thinking, Quality Software Management* (1st ed.). New York: Dorset House.

Williams, L., McGraw, G., & Migues, S. (2018). Engineering Security Vulnerability Prevention, Detection, and Response. *IEEE Software*, *35*(5), 76–80. doi:10.1109/MS.2018.290110854

ADDITIONAL READING

Arachchi, S. A. I. B. S., & Perera, I. (2018, May). Continuous Integration and Continuous Delivery Pipeline Automation for Agile Software Project Management. In 2018 Moratuwa Engineering Research Conference (MERCon) (pp. 156-161). IEEE. doi:10.1109/MERCon.2018.8421965

Laukkanen, E., Paasivaara, M., Itkonen, J., & Lassenius, C. (2018). Comparison of release engineering practices in a large mature company and a startup. *Empirical Software Engineering*, *23*(6), 3535–3577. doi:10.100710664-018-9616-7

Mahdavi-Hezaveh, R., Dremann, J., & Williams, L. (2019). Feature Toggle Driven Development: Practices usedby Practitioners. *arXiv preprint arXiv:1907.06157*.

Ravichandran, A., Taylor, K., & Waterhouse, P. (2016). *DevOps for Digital Leaders*. doi:10.1007/978-1-4842-1842-6

Schermann, G., Cito, J., Leitner, P., & Gall, H. C. (2016, May). Towards quality gates in continuous delivery and deployment. In *2016 IEEE 24th international conference on program comprehension (ICPC)* (pp. 1-4). IEEE. 10.1109/ICPC.2016.7503737

Schermann, G., Cito, J., Leitner, P., Zdun, U., & Gall, H. (2016). *An empirical study on principles and practices of continuous delivery and deployment (No. e1889v1)*. PeerJ Preprints.

Shahin, M., Zahedi, M., Babar, M. A., & Zhu, L. (2019). An empirical study of architecting for continuous delivery and deployment. *Empirical Software Engineering*, *24*(3), 1061–1108. doi:10.100710664-018-9651-4

Chapter 7
Data in DevOps and Its Importance in Code Analytics

Girish Babu
Cisco Systems Inc., Canada

Charitra Kamalaksh Patil
MNP LLP, Canada

ABSTRACT

Robust DevOps plays a huge role in the health and sanity of software. The metadata generated during DevOps need to be harnessed for deriving useful insights on the health of the software. This area of work can be classified as code analytics and comprises of the following (but not limited to): 1. commit history from the source code management system (SCM); 2. the engineers that worked on the commit; 3. the reviewers on the commit; 4. the extent of build (if applicable) and test validation prior to the commit, the types of failures found in iterative processes, and the fixes done; 5. test extent of test coverage on the commit; 6. any static profiling on the code in the commit; 7. the size and complexity of the commit; 8. many more. This chapter articulates many ways the above information can be used for effective software development.

INTRODUCTION

Robust DevOps plays a huge role in the health and sanity of software and the metadata generated during this activity need to be harnessed for deriving useful insights. This area of work can be classified as *Code Analytics* and comprises of the following (but not limited to) –

DOI: 10.4018/978-1-7998-1863-2.ch007

Copyright © 2020, IGI Global. Copying or distributing in print or electronic forms without written permission of IGI Global is prohibited.

1. Commit history from the Source Code Management system (SCM)
2. The engineers that worked on the commit
3. The reviewers on the commit
4. The extent of build (if applicable) & test validation prior to the commit, the types of failures found in iterative processes & the fixes done
5. Test extent of test coverage on the commit
6. Any static profiling on the code in the commit
7. The size and complexity of the commit

The proposed chapter introduces the various attributes that are available during DevOps, means to use them effectively and their application in source code analytics that can help produce good quality software at increasing velocity. Each section also gives a pictorial view of the role played by each metadata and how they can be represented visually for effective insights.

Section 1 describes how commit history can be used to derive BugSpots/BugCache (Rahman, et al, 2011). The techniques in this paper are extended to give a 'phase-containment' view to bugs / commits which is used in Cisco systems by the author.

Section 2 dwells into the code review practices and the meta data that is available during this activity and its application for sound peer reviews in the development life cycle. An effective illustration around this is described in the papers *Search-Based Peer Reviewers Recommendation in Modern Code Review* (Ouni, et al, 2016) and *A Large-Scale Study on Source Code Reviewer Recommendation* (Lipcˇak & Rossi, 2018).

Section 3 forays into code coverage measures from various test cycles and its potential use in determining efficacy of the test activities, a paper in this area of note is *Examining the Effectiveness of Testing Coverage Tools: An Empirical Study* (Alemerien & Magel, 2014).

Section 4 goes into static analysis and static profiling of software, which is one of the earliest indicators of quality and stability of software. This uses recommendations described in the papers *Structured Testing: A Testing Methodology Using the Cyclomatic Complexity Metric* (Watson & McCabe, 1996) and *The Correlation among Software Complexity Metrics with Case Study* (Dr. Tashtoush, et al, 2014).

Section 5 leverages the study on cyclomatic complexity analysis (Watson & Mccabe, 1996) to expand its use in code analytics.

Section 6 ventures into the DevOps workflow itself and why it is relevant to interject many of the earlier insights right into the CI/CD (Continuous Integration / Continuous Delivery) pipeline. It also circles around the first five sections and how they contribute to meta data necessary for code analytics.

FUNDAMENTALS

Commit History

From the underlying SCM, deriving the commit history is extremely important to mine the behaviour of code. The ability to find *HotSpots* based on frequency & count of commits will yield considerable insights on areas of constant churn. It'll also help identify engineers who are struggling or experts with certain areas.

Often underappreciated and under-utilized is the importance of information that is available in the Source Code management (SCM) and defect / ticket tracking systems. Typically, the following information (but not limited to) is useful from these systems –

1. Nature of change (i.e. – bug fix, feature development, feature extension, code clean-up)
2. Priority of change (i.e. – High, Medium, Low)
3. Requestor (i.e. – Internal testing found, Customer reported)
4. Nature of issue (i.e. – security defect, usability defect, configuration, documentation)
5. Change agent (i.e. – engineer making the change)
6. Time *of* change (i.e. – the date & time when it was done)
7. Time *to* change (i.e. – effort needed to understand and make the changes)
8. Applicability (i.e. – the product / service where it is needed)

From the underlying SCM, deriving the above information & more is extremely important to mine the behaviour of code. You can use the above details to derive the following (and many more) insights –.

BugSpots / HotSpots

A number of enterprises with rapidly expanding code bases and large legacy software are using techniques to find high churn areas that are servicing defects. An oft-quoted source is the research paper on BugCache (Rahman, et al, 2011).

The technique described in the paper and extended / made popular in enterprises like Alphabet Inc. (http://google-engtools.blogspot.com/2011/12/bug-prediction-at-google.html) and Cisco Systems helps teams identify areas that need attention for *hardening*. One popular use of this data is to drill down to function level, perform detailed complexity analysis (defined later in this chapter) and rework or rewrite that specific area.

The ability to find *HotSpots* based on frequency & count of commits will yield considerable insights on areas of constant churn, especially affecting high value customers of your software. Using *nature of change* of commits, helps slice and dice HotSpots and allows you to look at them in a phase-contained manner.

The figure 1 articulates ability to understand how *HotSpot progression* occurs in a software module, allowing teams to prioritize which areas need attention closer to a customer release.

In many cases, *HotSpots* also help identify *change agents* or engineers who are struggling with certain modules or experts in those specific areas that can help better them. An interesting dimension to this is if a really good engineer shows up in the list, the root cause could potentially be bad or incomplete code reviews. A method to determine if the (lack of) expertise of change agents is a cause for *HotSpots* is to establish patterns around the size of code (a popular measure is lines and the complexity of code) contributed during feature development and post that phase. If the amount of code (size and complexity measure) is higher in post development phases, relative to other engineers working on that software, then this should warrant a closer look into the activities of that engineer.

An interesting dimension in *HotSpot* analysis is to look at the **Applicability** of changes. i.e. – which customer facing services are churning the most. This is a relevant and critical factor in library or infra or core modules that are shared across

Figure 1. Sample hotspots view

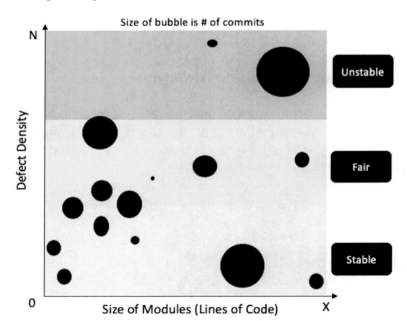

different customer services or products. Knowing stability of software relative to services or products helps teams prioritize and harden (aspect of solidifying the performance and stability) software that they own.

Defect Density

A popular measure of *actual* software quality is defect density, more precisely the number of defects per thousand lines of code – commonly attributed as Defect per KLOC.

Slicing defect density by software modules is a quick way to classify stability of software modules by size, and to understand where resource investments are needed for quick improvement.

'Phase Contained' Defect Density

An effective way to also look at defect density is to make the view phase contained (i.e. slicing the view across different phases of time or attributes). Additionally, this is impactful to always look at this measure relative to the churn on code (change in lines of code – added / modified / deleted).

Figure 3 is an example of this view.

A quick observation in the above is *module A* having an expected growth in defect density relative to the lines of code added into the module. On the other hand, *module B* is having higher growth in defect density while the module size has remained stable or dormant. This would give insights to the owners to invest in stabilizing *module B*.

Determination of Expert Code Reviewers

Peer review of code is an oft ignored or underplayed area, and in most organizations is deemed to be just another part of the process that is rushed. However, the value of it when done diligently, and especially by experts is considerably high. Some

Figure 2. Defect density snippet

```
Dd = (Nd * 1000)/ Nloc
where Dd -> defect density
Nd -> Number of defects in the module
Nloc -> Number of lines of actual code (without
comments, blanks, empty lines) in the module
```

Figure 3. Sample phase contained defect density

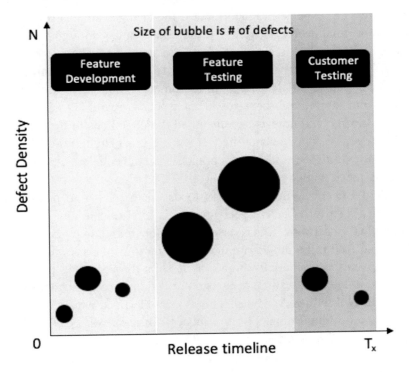

of the studies done in Cisco Systems around this area show that a lot of customer reported issues would have been caught by early reviews; and to this end, using the frequency of activities by engineers (either committing code to an area or contributing to the code review process) to determine experts and recommend for code review is important. The cost of finding a potential issue or bug during peer reviews is lowest. Additionally, peer reviews help find flaws in implementation, in terms of missed or misunderstood requirements, very early in the product lifecycle.

Code Peer Reviews are an extremely critical step in the software development process. Various studies have shown that early and effective reviews tend to catch over 70% of field defects (defects found after they have shipped to customers), and to achieve this, identifying the right experts to review is necessary.

Before articulating the means and reasons for determination of expert reviewers, following are few key reasons for peer code reviews –

- **Feature Parity**: For new features, does the current implementation cater to the requirements. This determination is best done by an expert who understands the need, goes over source code and is able to translate that into a matrix of complete & incomplete scenarios. For defect fixes on existing features, peer reviewers are expected to determine if the changes are catering to the spirit of the original needs, as well as if the new changes done to fix the reported defect are complete in exercising both the old and new behaviors.

- **Unit Testing Effectiveness**: For the newly implemented features, reviewers are best placed to determine if (automated) unit tests are exercising a maximum number of scenarios. This aspect is really key since developers tend to focus on unit tests exercising all the code lines in the execution path that they have added or modified. However, it is extremely important to also determine if all the 'loops' and 'branches' in the code are also tested – think if-else, for or while loops, etc.

- **Logical Errors**: While reviewers focus on the first two points above, an obvious need for effective peer reviews is to eliminate any obvious logical errors in the software. This is the earliest stage of finding potential defects and is considered to be the least expensive. Any logical errors that slip through tend to cost exponentially higher as it slips through each phase (like unit testing, integration testing, pre-customer validation and customer use).

- **Coding Guidelines & Styles**: This is an underrated aspect of peer reviews yet has a profound impact on the success for a software development team. Defining or following coding guidelines and styles is extremely important to ensure software is not highly complex or badly written (in terms of code maintenance for the future). Software developed without proper formats in terms of comments, readability and logical nomenclature (like variable names, temporary loop elements, etc.) largely is difficult to maintain as it grows in size and is generally an area that tends to figure high in HotSpot evaluations.

- **Understanding Code Base**: Code review as a practice for reading existing code is generally an effective way for engineers to understand and build expertise, both in how that software works and in how to write effective software from other experts. This helps them learn technological and programming techniques for long term success.

- **Improves Estimation**: This is an obvious and apparent take on importance of peer reviews. Understanding software functionality and how effective software is written helps teams and individuals estimate time and risk for software effectively.

- **Improves Development**: Knowing that experts are going to look at the code written puts pressure on developers to be vigilant while writing software. This is another aspect of gamification brought to make software development effective.

- **Improves communication**: This is a facet of software and product development that ultimately plays a very large role in the success of a product or company. Peer reviews largely helps in improving the communication between team members, breaking any shackles that may exist. When this happens, teams tend to trust others more and generally tend to communicate on other aspects of the software lifecycle.

An important question at this juncture is – when should peer reviews be done in the software development lifecycle?

There are generally two points in the development lifecycle where this process is most effective –

1. As soon as software is being written before any validations are done on it. If time permits and experts are available to review, doing it this early ensures any obvious logical flaws or gaps in feature expectation are met very early before time is invested in other activities (like unit test, static analysis, complexity analysis, etc.)
2. After software is written, all checks (like static analysis, complexity, unit tests) are successfully done but before code is committed to the SCM. For experts or reviewers to have all checks done while reviewing is invaluable to ensure they have complete insight on the software and its associated artefacts.

Assuming all of the above are in place, the next step is to harness the above information and automatically determine expert reviewers.

There are different mechanisms to derive experts in a particular area, and most of these require the following details –

- Past reviewers and committers of all features and bug fixes: the time period can be determined based on change or commit velocity
- Past review comments handling. i.e. – were the comments good or bad, accepted or rejected or ignored.
- Time between various events. i.e. – time taken to review, turnaround time of modifications after review comments were provided, volume of deferred valid comments.
- Quantum of changes between review cycles for a single change. i.e. – how many lines were modified / added between the first and subsequent revisions. This will give an instant indicator on whether the first change put up was not implemented accurately due to lack of understanding by author or if a version of code was put up for review that was not ready.

Using the above with time series analysis, it is possible to find experts in a particular area. An interesting paper on this is *Search-Based Peer Reviewers Recommendation in Modern Code Review* (Ouni, et al, 2016).

A data driven approach to using the code review meta data to identify reviews is in the paper *A Large-Scale Study on Source Code Reviewer Recommendation* (Lipcˇak & Rossi, 2018).

Code Coverage From Testing

An important measure during DevOps is the extent of Code coverage from the tests, and further if the most relevant areas of the software being covered. It is easy to get side-lined by tracking just the percentage of coverage (i.e. lines of code covered by test over total lines of code) while overlooking if some of the most relevant branches in the software are uncovered in this process. As an example: consider the following block of code with multiple branch statements, with the 'default' block (which could be considered as the exception block) having high test coverage.

Code coverage is a measure of the number of lines of code and the different scenarios (or branches) in the code exercised by testing. Typically, this is achieved by any system that keeps track of all the runtime entities covered during testing and associating that information to the source code. This activity is an extremely important measure in the product development lifecycle. As tests are developed against features, this measure allows teams to understand the efficacy of testing & the potential risk of a release. For historically HotSpot areas, this gives good insights into prioritization of tests.

To understand how code coverage metadata can be used for code analytics, it is important to understand how and why coverage is measured; the following three sub-sections go into the details of the same.

How Coverage is Measured

Take a look at the illustration below, where green lines indicate the lines covered by test and red indicates those not covered yet.

Example snippet can seen in Figure 4.

There is clear indication in the example above that the tests have not exercised the core areas of the block (i.e. test for actual cases) and only the default section has been done. This kind of insight allows teams to understand very early in the development process on gaps in testing. This progressively becomes more complex as code complexity increases (a largely convoluted control flow graph of the code).

See References section for common / popular code coverage tools and solutions.

Figure 4. Code fragment depicting a switch statement

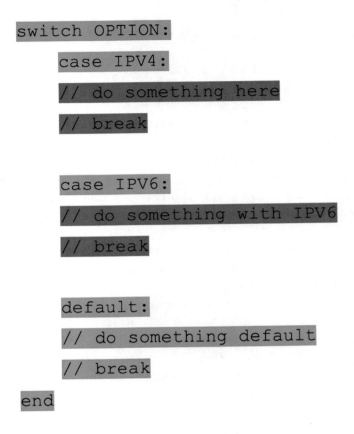

```
switch OPTION:
    case IPV4:
        // do something here
        // break

    case IPV6:
        // do something with IPV6
        // break

    default:
        // do something default
        // break
end
```

Why do we Need to Measure Coverage?

Code coverage measure is important (but not limited to) for the following reasons –

1. While static analysis uncovers a lot of coding or static errors, real testing aided by coverage is the actual activity that uncovers most of the runtime errors.
2. Analyzing a detailed coverage report helps determine multiple conditions in a block of code that are not covered, especially those driven by runtime variables or inputs / parameters from external systems.
3. In a large team or organization with lot of ambiguity on definition of good testing, this measure provides an unbiased view of test stability in a system.
4. Code coverage is more than just a number, it provides a holistic view of a system's risk profile.

How do we Measure Coverage?

Typically, there are two broad categories of software –

1. dynamically compiled & executed at runtime
2. statically compiled & executed at runtime

In the former case, tools exist to capture coverage without much effort needed, with just the overhead of instructing what you want to track for coverage.

In the latter case, there is a need to (in most cases) inject some specific code during compilation to indicate to a runtime coverage environment that coverage collection is necessary and in which specific parts it is desired.

There are broadly three approaches to measuring code coverage –

1. **Source Code Instrumentation:** This approach is common in embedded systems development and relies on adding some instruction to the source code (either before or during compilation).
2. **Intermediate Code Instrumentation:** This approach deals with already compiled classes and instrumentation is achieved by adding bytecodes to compiled artefacts
3. **Gather Runtime Information:** This is the process of actually collecting information from the runtime environment (during and after test runs) to determine coverage

TYPES OF COVERAGE

There are many dimensions to code coverage, with a few detailed as follows –

Statement Coverage

Statements are instructions in a program that have an intent of an action (for example: initializing a temporary variable, reading a variable value, referencing a function, etc.). In reality, this is useful as a simple metric and is considered as only an initial measure of lines being covered.

Function Coverage

An interesting measure in code coverage is a count of functions or methods being covered. By definition, a function or method is a logical block of code that is written with the intention of being used repeatedly. An example of a function is a means to capture age of a person today given their date of birth. Knowing function coverage is important since by definition it implies reusable modules.

Branch Coverage

Branch coverage is a measure of all the decision or control points in a source graph. Consider the figure 5.

Here the tests need to cover two scenarios – one if *honesty_factor* is above the *honesty_factor_threshold* and the other would be the vice versa scenario. This aspect of coverage yields details on the extent of test detailing available.

Condition Coverage

An important aspect of testing and test coverage is condition coverage which indicate whether all conditions of a Boolean statement are exercised. Consider the figure 6.

Figure 5. Code fragment depicting branch coverage example

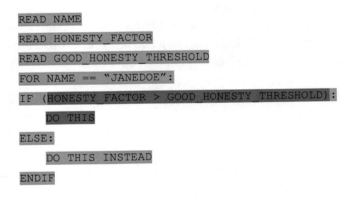

```
READ NAME
READ HONESTY_FACTOR
READ GOOD_HONESTY_THRESHOLD
FOR NAME == "JANEDOE":
IF (HONESTY_FACTOR > GOOD_HONESTY_THRESHOLD):
        DO THIS
ELSE:
        DO THIS INSTEAD
ENDIF
```

Figure 6. Code fragment depicting a condition statement

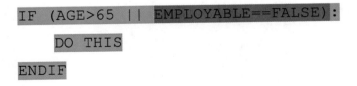

```
IF (AGE>65 || EMPLOYABLE==FALSE):
        DO THIS
ENDIF
```

In this example, it is required to exercise both Boolean statements of age being greater than 65 or if the employable check is false. Condition coverage provides details on if all Boolean conditions are exercised.

A study that validates the importance of these different types of coverage metrics is *Examining the Effectiveness of Testing Coverage Tools: An Empirical Study* (Alemerien & Magel, 2014).

Code Analytics recommends the aspect of paying close attention to these elements rather than just relying on some quantitative numbers. It is possible derive insights on efficacy of tests and understand what to change in order to exercise the red parts of the code fragment (from a coverage perspective).

STATIC PROFILING OF SOFTWARE

One of the most overlooked elements in software development is the importance of Static profiling of software and what these insights provide very early in the software development lifecycle.

Static profiling is the ability to understand some key behavior of your software even before you compile and/or build. Areas like code complexity are derived from this process (a future section delves into this), in addition to possible predictive insights around which areas could run out of memory, illegal assignment of variables, possible memory issues, etc. Understanding and reacting to these are critical since one significant issue that creeps out to the customer could effectively damage the entire reputation of the software provider.

There are multiple commercial and open-source software that helps measure code complexity and provide means to keep track of its trend over time and the references section has pointers to a few of the more popular ones.

Static analysis is typically the equivalent of someone reading through every single line of code and performing some analysis on fundamental failures, bad practices, poorly written code (in terms of complexity), possible security defects and more. This action is typically performed prior to software being pushed for quality analysis and verification.

Static Analysis Techniques

Static analysis tools typically employ following techniques during analysis –

Data Flow Analysis

This technique is performed in a static state and is used to collect dynamic run-time information about data in a software. It captures information about all possible values used or impacted at various points in a block of code.

Typically, most tools or solutions that perform data flow analysis perform a combination of two steps –

- **Forward Analysis**: This calculates each set of points of definition that may help a program reach a specific point. See example in Figure 7.

From the example above, value of z depends on values for x and y. Hence if value of y is assigned or set to be greater than 0, then the else is not exercised.

- **Backward Analysis**: This calculates points in a program by performing variable analysis in a backward fashion for entities that are read before a subsequent write. This helps in identifying and eliminating dead code.

Control Flow

The image in Figure 8 shows an abstract representation control graph for a software . Static analysis performs a check on the number of entry and exit points, directed edges in the graph are used to represent the jumps between blocks.

Static Analysis Value

A few reasons for running static analysis (compared to dynamic analysis which is runtime dependent and is generally later in the software development cycle compared to development) are as follows.

Figure 7. Code fragment depicting a variable assignment based on specific conditions

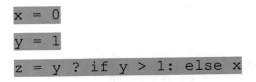

Figure 8. Control flow graph example

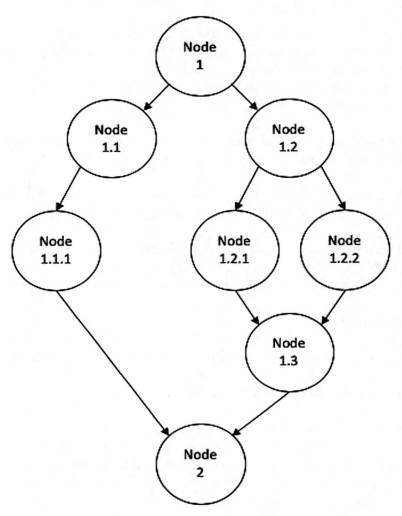

Runs Quickly and Early

Typically, static analysis runs quickly (prior to running actual tests) and is a good quality gate for validating code. This scales well in most scenarios and can be run repeatedly. An effective practice around this is to plug this into commit workflows (ensuring it is run on every commit) and CI/CD workflows (ensuring it is run one to many times a day on the tip of the branch).

Provides Good/Better Understanding Of Code

The aspect of finding basic or elementary flaws leads to developers and reviewers understanding code and inherent risks better.

Detects Critical Security Vulnerabilities Early

It is very effective in automatically finding many issues with a high degree of confidence. In embedded systems programming, it is very good at finding basic security vulnerabilities like memory leaks, SQL injection flaws, buffer overflows and more.

An important aspect of this is static analysis is good at finding Backdoors (or application backdoors) compared to dynamic analysis. Backdoors by definition are functionality added intentionally or inadvertently by developers either with the intention of bypassing security for administrative action of for nefarious or malicious actions later. In either case, the action of finding them is paramount before customers are given access to the software.

Leverage Checks from the Wider Usage Community

Most of the solutions or tools that perform these analyses are designed to learn and adapt from increased usage across different customer sites (much like how anti-virus software solutions work). This ensures that software is guarded against recent vulnerabilities.

LIMITATIONS OF STATIC ANALYSIS

Static analysis is effective in mostly finding basic issues, especially in the security realm. There would have to be a supplement of specific vulnerability profiling and detection tools. It also fails to find non-source code issues or gaps like configuration issues. It also fails when profiling requires compiling code (building software) and all the relevant dependencies like libraries are not available all the time or if it requires some expertise level.

There are two other major concerns or issues around static analysis –

- **False Positives**: These are issues reported as a result of the tool being unsure of integrity of data when it traverses the code and is incorrectly marked as positive ones. The outcome is that engineers may be misled to invest a lot of time on unnecessary areas.

- **False Negatives**: At times, static analysis tools can result in vulnerabilities not being reported when in fact it is. This can happen if there are runtime or external dependencies and this fact is not available during compilation.

Effective Use of Static Analysis

Static analysis is useful if employed as follows –

1. Prior to every code commit (to prevent issues going into the branch)
2. On committed code periodically (like nightly runs or other frequency periods)
3. On cumulative targets or platforms to capture inter-dependency issues
4. Actively working to keep issues out of the system
5. Constantly monitoring the static analysis profiles or checkers being used and updating them when necessary

In summary, this category ensures a lot of issues are fixed early and more importantly avoided before being reported. It is important in the context of code analytics to track and fix specific types of static analysis defects that are applicable to the software under development.

STATIC PROFILING OF SOFTWARE

Cyclomatic complexity is a measure of code complexity developed by Thomas J McCabe Sr. It's an important measure to understand the control flow of a program and determine if the ability to maintain this software will be easy or difficult. For the code fragment in *Figure 9* below, the complexity is derived from the following control graph of the fragment.

Mathematically, complexity is defined in Figure 10.

Details about the McCabe analysis process can be found at - http://www.mccabe.com/pdf/mccabe-nist235r.pdf

Code complexity calculation is important for the following reasons –

1. Knowing state of software and potential effort to maintain it: development teams can use this to determine review effort and prioritization. Additionally, it can be used to forecast cost of supporting older software features.
2. Determining how many test cases are needed to maintain the software: quality assurance or test teams can use this to determine how many test cases they need to write, forecast and invest additional time in high complex areas.

Figure 9. Control flow graph of the switch statement

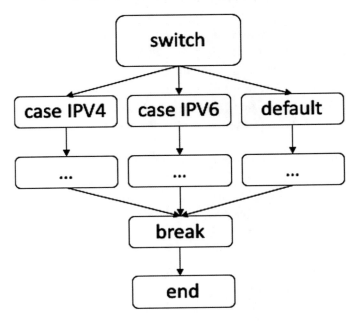

Figure 10. Cyclomatic complexity definition

```
C = Ne - Nn + 2cc

where C -> complexity

Ne -> Number of edges in the graph

Nn -> Number of nodes in the graph

cc -> Number of connected components in the graph
```

3. Estimate risk in the software: determine where risk is high since traditionally high complex areas are also high hotspot areas. Fix high complex areas to address high hotspot areas.

This is widely discussed in the paper *The Correlation among Software Complexity Metrics with Case Study* (Dr. Yahya, et al, 2014). This paper shows that there is a strong correlation between Code complexity and the number of defects that originate in that software. It is therefore imperative to ensure that code complexity is contained over time, especially during early stages of software development.

There are multiple commercial and open-source software that are quoted in the References section.

Effective use of complexity analysis is achieved when it is constantly monitored, and efforts are taken to ensure that it is contained, and early action is taken. Typical actions include modularizing the code further, reducing the number of branches in the code, re-visiting the design for the module or block. If the complexity has to be maintained (at a higher rate), then investments should be done in sound code peer reviews and more importantly on test automation for getting 100% coverage in those areas.

Consider the code flow graph in *Figure 11* that has a high complexity measure against it.

The consideration should be to revise this call flow to something that is less complex and easily manageable.

Figure 11. Convoluted call graph example

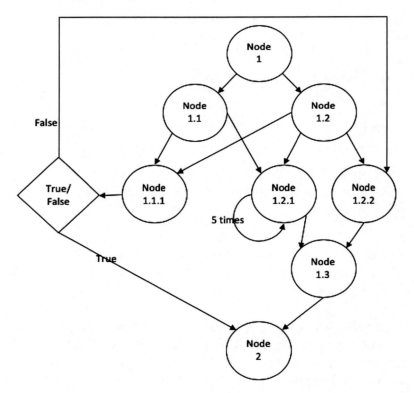

From a code analytics perspective, code complexity and related measures have a huge role to play in the eventual stability and maintenance of a system. These have to be assessed in a phase contained manner and early measures are necessary for the long-term health of a software pack.

DEVOPS, META TRACKING AND GATING CRITERIA

Every enterprise or start-up looking to scale and roll out software releases rapidly need to have robust DevOps process. Having well defined checks and balances in this process is paramount. The ability to orchestrate builds (compilation / packaging / dependency generation / etc.), tests (validation of behavior) and other necessary criteria (like Code reviews, complexity check, tracking of source size, etc.) is available with many popular DevOps systems today. Additionally, using the meta data generated by these processes to infer and improve gating criteria for commits needs to be harnessed. As an example, knowing which of your builds / tests are flaky (flapping between success and failure), areas of software that are vulnerable to certain test conditions, complexity of certain areas that are growing outside the stability range, reviews in areas or by people that are resulting in constant customer defects, etc. need to be closely watched and derived

What is DevOps?

DevOps or Developer Operations is a philosophy of providing sound practices, tooling and solutions between developers building software and customers who will ultimately receive and use the same. A common terminology in the industry for this is also the CI/CD (Continuous Integration / Continuous Development) pipeline that gives insights during code development, test, review, commit, customer validation and customer deployment, eventually creating a feedback loop on customer usage.

An effective and successful DevOps model is one where software development, testing / validation and operations teams are brought together. Members from these various teams work together across the application lifecycle with the constant goal of generating consistent, reliable and secure application behavior in rapid time. This model also requires setting up a pipeline or stack that allows for quick insights, telemetry across various phases and more importantly an easy way to use the different processes or solutions required.

There are some very intuitive and obvious benefits of having well defined DevOps in an enterprise, some of which are as follows –

- **Rapid Application Delivery:** DevOps primarily aims rapid application delivery by allowing quick insights into latest developments across different members in a team and across different dependent modules. It allows for different teams to contribute their tests and checks in the process (like special code review rules, change based testing, etc.) and makes it available for everyone to use without actually having to know the details.
- **Reliability**: Reliability of various artefacts is a key principle of DevOps. These artefacts include Building (or commonly known as compiling) code, executing tests (unit, integration, sanity, regression), packaging of modules and much more. Much of the reliability of these are uncovered or tested when you have sound DevOps in place.
- **Stability**: Stability is a major factor when you have a rapidly scaling application or product. Knowing how newly developed code will perform in a 'near-production' environment is made possible in DevOps.
- **Co-Development**: When there are dependent modules being developed, DevOps allows quick and more pertinently accurate development across teams and owners. It also encourages better accountability and ownership across different teams.
- **Visibility**: One of the greatest advantages from DevOps is the visibility into the progress, stability & risk of everything that is being developed or fixed. Right from having the ability to see real time details, drill down to specifics and to go back in time to see historical information, there is a great deal of transparency that is made possible.

Meta Types in DevOps

The following are some of the additional meta data that is available from DevOps, and how they are useful –

Granular Details of Every Change in a Release or Given Time Frame

When a team or group has robust DevOps process and system in place, then granular details of every change (commit, review, static analysis, validations, unit test, sanities or functional tests, extended regression tests and more) are made available. Knowing how each engineer is performing around each commit and extended details around which tests failed to catch issues or which code reviews failed to do the same, are very critical details that are possible here.

Quantum of Changes in a Release or Given Time Frame

This when profiled for patterns will quite quickly yield details around the volume of changes going into feature commits, complexity of these features, potential gaps with respect to design or requirements, security & reliability of the feature, some sort of inter-operability of modules and much more. Extending this profiling to see the same measures for bug fixes or defects or customer reported gaps will give an insight into potential risks in the software release as they are progressing.

Quantum of Test Coverage and Test Stability

Section **3** has articulated the importance of Code coverage from different flavors of testing and the means to collect and analyze the different types. A DevOps system allows this measure to be harnessed significantly by allowing teams to generate the quantum of test coverage for a release in addition to generating at every commit or change level. Having the ability to track incremental progress and using it to get a measure of test stability and test performance is another important facet that DevOps provides.

While the primary value from this is looking at code stability over a release or a given time frame, a more meaningful use of this is also to understand the efficacy of testing during the lifecycle of the release in the form of the following –

1. How many existing test scripts are already scaling to exercise new feature code being developed?
2. How many existing test scripts are still catching errors or the defect density from these scripts?
3. How are the new scripts performing relative to existing scripts in terms of code coverage?
4. How effective are test script engineers in the new release relative to prior releases?

All and many more questions are answered by looking at the meta data being generated in the DevOps CI/CD pipelines. This helps release teams truly understand –

1. The progressive quality of software from a test coverage perspective
2. The progressive quality of test scripts from a test organization perspective

Significant expenses in test processes and infrastructure can be avoided by reacting quickly and appropriately to indicators emitted from DevOps

Approval Criteria and Failures Being Bypassed

A major aspect of the DevOps CI/CD paradigm is having a commit criteria checklist that every developer's commit is subjected to and is fundamentally based on the changes being made by each developer. A sample checklist of criteria would be as depicted in figure 12.

Analyzing commit criteria for all commits going into a release, and especially those that had a manual override, when failures follow gives considerable insights into which criteria are the most effective and those areas where overrides are leading to degrading quality.

A fundamental question that can arise here – why allow manual overrides for any of these criteria?

Figure 12. Table of sample commit criteria

Category	Check	Manual override allowed?
Peer review	At least 2 reviewers to sign off	Y
	Reviewers from list **[A, B, C, D]** if any change is made to one of **[foo, bar]**	N
	No pending open review comments	Y
Test coverage	Minimum of **X% coverage** for all new code	N
	Any functions with code complexity greater than **N** to have at least **Y%** coverage	N
	All new unit test scripts to be compliant with code coverage	Y
Builds	All builds should compile for the product with the build list as **[A, B, C, D]**	N
	For new features, build time from the new commit should not exceed average build time by over **5%**	N
Test	Tests should have a **100%** pass rate for all commits except when changes are in **[M, N, O]** in which case pass rate has to >= **95%**	Y
Code sizes	All new functions should have a cyclomatic code complexity (ccm) of **< N** with absolutely no override	N
	All commits should have a code size (lines of code) less than **5000** lines	Y
	All files (new or old) should not exceed a total size of **10000** lines	N

There are multiple reasons a manual override may be allowed – lack of experts available in a given time frame, open review comments that are not critical and can be deferred in the interest of getting a feature committed, some test scripts that cannot be candidates for coverage based runs due to this action interfering with the behavior of code, some tests being inconsistent while test teams try to get to the root cause, some commits having to be of considerable size because dependent modules have to be committed together so as not to break the branch, and many such more.

Knowing from history which overrides lead to considerable increases in breakages or defects and also from which overriding user helps profile who should have override privileges revoked (probably due to lack of risk profiling insights or ability from those people).

Most successful enterprises or teams are those that are able to consistently tweak commit or gating criteria frequently based on incremental analytical insights from this category of meta data.

Failure Density per Software Module or Engineer

In section **1** under the *Phase contained defect density* module, we saw the importance of assessing defect density in the release lifecycle. An effective variant of this in the DevOps workflow is the ability to look at **Failure density** per software module or per engineer. The figure 13 details some of these areas.

Figure 13. Table of sample patterns of failure density

Failure category	What to look for	How it is useful
Consistent failures in tests	Are the failures infra specific	Isolation between test infra and software (either code or test software)
	Are the failures test script or test case specific	Isolation of bad test artefacts
	Intermittent behaviour	Could indicate scenario specific problems in software
Failure patterns during builds	Are failures engineer change specific	Bad design or development practices
	Obvious failure that should not have come up	Poor coding and/or poor code review
Failure patterns after commits	Specific failure root causes repeating	Complex software area that needs to be rewritten
	Specific failure root causes repeating after commits from specific engineers	Bad development or design, incorrect analysis or poor experience

The table describes how valuable DevOps meta data is and to some extent how it can be used for effective Code Analytics.

IMPORTANCE OF CODE ANALYTICS

As can be seen from the previous sections, code analytics plays an extremely important role and there are plenty of indicators that can be harnessed for this purpose. It is important to apply many of the techniques described against each section and leverage the ability to have a clean and fast CI/CD pipeline for development.

SAMPLE EXAMPLE

The image (Figure 14) illustrates a typical DevOps flow and some of the major steps in it.

Figure 14. Typical DevOps CI/CD Workflow

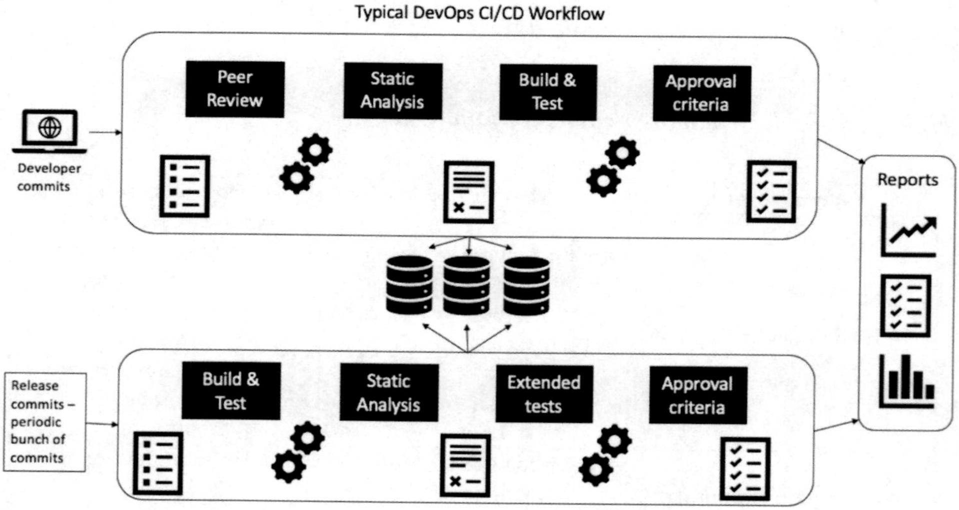

FUTURE DIRECTION

Analytics driven and guided development is the future of software development and Code analytics harnessing increasing data from DevOps is the direction of many enterprises

SUMMARY

This chapter has shed light on the following –

1. Commit history definition and how it can be used for BugSpots/HotSpots analysis, defect density determination & its usage and how 'phase-contained defect density' can be an extremely useful measure of software quality & stability. This is backed by research in *BugCache for inspections: hit or miss?* (Rahman, et al, 2011)
2. Importance of peer code reviews and how over time this info can be used to determine & identify experts in specific areas of software. This is backed by research in *Search-Based Peer Reviewers Recommendation in Modern Code Review* (Ouni, et al, 2016) and *A Large-Scale Study on Source Code Reviewer Recommendation* (Lipcˇak & Rossi, 2018).
3. Definition of code coverage from testing and its different types, how & why to measure and an effective way to use it for test stability analysis. This backed by research in *Examining the Effectiveness of Testing Coverage Tools: An Empirical Study* (Alemerien & Magel, 2014)
4. Use of static analysis and its need, an efficient use of it to significantly reduce cost of quality and the different mechanisms to derive and use it. This is backed by research in *The Correlation among Software Complexity Metrics with Case Study* (Dr. Yahya, et al, 2014).
5. Complexity analysis and its determination, and its use in profiling software in correlation to HotSpots and the eventual means to reduce or keep it in check.
6. Importance of data available in DevOps (CI/CD pipelines – Continuous Integration / Continuous Delivery pipelines) and some insights on how this data can be used for effective code analytics.

In closing, meta data from DevOps is worth its weight in gold and can be the defining difference between sustained success and accelerated failures for teams and enterprises

REFERENCES

Lipc̆ak. J., & Rossi, B. (2018). A Large-Scale Study on Source Code Reviewer Recommendation. Academic Press.

Ouni, A., Kula, R. G., & Inoue, K. (2016). *Search-Based Peer Reviewers Recommendation in Modern Code Review.* doi:10.1145/2025113.2025157

Rahman, F., Posnett, D., Hindle, A., Barr, E., & Devanbu, P. (2011). *BugCache for inspections: hit or miss?* Academic Press.

Tashtoush, Y., Al-Maolegi, M., & Arkok, B. (2014). *The Correlation among Software Complexity Metrics with Case Study.* Academic Press.

Tashtoush, Y., Al-Maolegi, M., & Arkok, B. (2014). *Examining the Effectiveness of Testing Coverage Tools: An Empirical Study.* Academic Press.

Watson, A. H., & McCabe, T. J. (1996). *Structured Testing: A Testing Methodology Using the Cyclomatic Complexity Metric.* Academic Press.

KEY TERMS AND DEFINITIONS

BugSpots/HotSpots: It is the area of a software that churns or has a lot of code commits done to service bugs or defects.

Code Analytics: The area of study that relates to applying data driven analysis techniques to understanding and predicting how software would perform right from development, testing, deployment all the way to usage by customers.

Code Complexity: It is the area of work that defines and deals with a measure of complexity for a software which can then be used to forecast stability of that software when deployed/used by customers.

Coverage Analysis: This pertains to the application of data driven techniques to data collected from multiple test/validation phases of a software. It also dwells into the various techniques and methods to capturing and harnessing test coverage meta information.

Static Analysis: This deals with the aspect of static profiling of software prior to actual testing, and the various techniques to use the same for code analytics.

Related Readings

To continue IGI Global's long-standing tradition of advancing innovation through emerging research, please find below a compiled list of recommended IGI Global book chapters and journal articles in the areas of software development, software engineering, and machine learning. These related readings will provide additional information and guidance to further enrich your knowledge and assist you with your own research.

Abramek, E. (2019). Maturity Profiles of Organizations for Social Media. In R. Lenart-Gansiniec (Ed.), *Crowdsourcing and Knowledge Management in Contemporary Business Environments* (pp. 134–145). Hershey, PA: IGI Global. doi:10.4018/978-1-5225-4200-1.ch007

Abu Talib, M. (2018). Towards Sustainable Development Through Open Source Software in the Arab World. In M. Khosrow-Pour, D.B.A. (Ed.), *Optimizing Contemporary Application and Processes in Open Source Software* (pp. 222-242). Hershey, PA: IGI Global. doi:10.4018/978-1-5225-5314-4.ch009

Adesola, A. P., & Olla, G. O. (2018). Unlocking the Unlimited Potentials of Koha OSS/ILS for Library House-Keeping Functions: A Global View. In M. Khosrow-Pour, D.B.A. (Ed.), *Optimizing Contemporary Application and Processes in Open Source Software* (pp. 124-163). Hershey, PA: IGI Global. doi:10.4018/978-1-5225-5314-4.ch006

Akber, A., Rizvi, S. S., Khan, M. W., Uddin, V., Hashmani, M. A., & Ahmad, J. (2019). Dimensions of Robust Security Testing in Global Software Engineering: A Systematic Review. In M. Rehman, A. Amin, A. Gilal, & M. Hashmani (Eds.), *Human Factors in Global Software Engineering* (pp. 252–272). Hershey, PA: IGI Global. doi:10.4018/978-1-5225-9448-2.ch010

Amrollahi, A., & Ahmadi, M. H. (2019). What Motivates the Crowd?: A Literature Review on Motivations for Crowdsourcing. In R. Lenart-Gansiniec (Ed.), *Crowdsourcing and Knowledge Management in Contemporary Business Environments* (pp. 103–133). Hershey, PA: IGI Global. doi:10.4018/978-1-5225-4200-1.ch006

Anchitaalagammai, J. V., Samayadurai, K., Murali, S., Padmadevi, S., & Shantha Lakshmi Revathy, J. (2019). Best Practices: Adopting Security Into the Software Development Process for IoT Applications. In D. Mala (Ed.), *Integrating the Internet of Things Into Software Engineering Practices* (pp. 146–159). Hershey, PA: IGI Global. doi:10.4018/978-1-5225-7790-4.ch007

Bhavsar, S. A., Pandit, B. Y., & Modi, K. J. (2019). Social Internet of Things. In D. Mala (Ed.), *Integrating the Internet of Things Into Software Engineering Practices* (pp. 199–218). Hershey, PA: IGI Global. doi:10.4018/978-1-5225-7790-4.ch010

Biswas, A., & De, A. K. (2019). *Multi-Objective Stochastic Programming in Fuzzy Environments* (pp. 1–420). Hershey, PA: IGI Global. doi:10.4018/978-1-5225-8301-1

Callaghan, C. W. (2017). The Probabilistic Innovation Field of Scientific Enquiry. *International Journal of Sociotechnology and Knowledge Development*, 9(2), 56–72. doi:10.4018/IJSKD.2017040104

Chhabra, D., & Sharma, I. (2018). Role of Attacker Capabilities in Risk Estimation and Mitigation. In R. Kumar, A. Tayal, & S. Kapil (Eds.), *Analyzing the Role of Risk Mitigation and Monitoring in Software Development* (pp. 244–255). Hershey, PA: IGI Global. doi:10.4018/978-1-5225-6029-6.ch015

Chitra, P., & Abirami, S. (2019). Smart Pollution Alert System Using Machine Learning. In D. Mala (Ed.), *Integrating the Internet of Things Into Software Engineering Practices* (pp. 219–235). Hershey, PA: IGI Global. doi:10.4018/978-1-5225-7790-4.ch011

Dorsey, M. D., & Raisinghani, M. S. (2019). IT Governance or IT Outsourcing: Is There a Clear Winner? In A. Mukherjee & A. Krishna (Eds.), *Interdisciplinary Approaches to Information Systems and Software Engineering* (pp. 19–32). Hershey, PA: IGI Global. doi:10.4018/978-1-5225-7784-3.ch002

Dua, R., Sharma, S., & Kumar, R. (2018). Risk Management Metrics. In R. Kumar, A. Tayal, & S. Kapil (Eds.), *Analyzing the Role of Risk Mitigation and Monitoring in Software Development* (pp. 21–33). Hershey, PA: IGI Global. doi:10.4018/978-1-5225-6029-6.ch002

Dua, R., Sharma, S., & Sharma, A. (2018). Software Vulnerability Management: How Intelligence Helps in Mitigating Software Vulnerabilities. In R. Kumar, A. Tayal, & S. Kapil (Eds.), *Analyzing the Role of Risk Mitigation and Monitoring in Software Development* (pp. 34–45). Hershey, PA: IGI Global. doi:10.4018/978-1-5225-6029-6.ch003

Fatema, K., Syeed, M. M., & Hammouda, I. (2018). Demography of Open Source Software Prediction Models and Techniques. In M. Khosrow-Pour, D.B.A. (Ed.), Optimizing Contemporary Application and Processes in Open Source Software (pp. 24-56). Hershey, PA: IGI Global. doi:10.4018/978-1-5225-5314-4.ch002

Ghafele, R., & Gibert, B. (2018). Open Growth: The Economic Impact of Open Source Software in the USA. In M. Khosrow-Pour, D.B.A. (Ed.), Optimizing Contemporary Application and Processes in Open Source Software (pp. 164-197). Hershey, PA: IGI Global. doi:10.4018/978-1-5225-5314-4.ch007

Gilal, A. R., Tunio, M. Z., Waqas, A., Almomani, M. A., Khan, S., & Gilal, R. (2019). Task Assignment and Personality: Crowdsourcing Software Development. In M. Rehman, A. Amin, A. Gilal, & M. Hashmani (Eds.), *Human Factors in Global Software Engineering* (pp. 1–19). Hershey, PA: IGI Global. doi:10.4018/978-1-5225-9448-2.ch001

Gopikrishnan, S., & Priakanth, P. (2019). Web-Based IoT Application Development. In D. Mala (Ed.), *Integrating the Internet of Things Into Software Engineering Practices* (pp. 62–86). Hershey, PA: IGI Global. doi:10.4018/978-1-5225-7790-4.ch004

Guendouz, M., Amine, A., & Hamou, R. M. (2018). Open Source Projects Recommendation on GitHub. In M. Khosrow-Pour, D.B.A. (Ed.), Optimizing Contemporary Application and Processes in Open Source Software (pp. 86-101). Hershey, PA: IGI Global. doi:10.4018/978-1-5225-5314-4.ch004

Hashmani, M. A., Zaffar, M., & Ejaz, R. (2019). Scenario Based Test Case Generation Using Activity Diagram and Action Semantics. In M. Rehman, A. Amin, A. Gilal, & M. Hashmani (Eds.), *Human Factors in Global Software Engineering* (pp. 297–321). Hershey, PA: IGI Global. doi:10.4018/978-1-5225-9448-2.ch012

Jagannathan, J., & Anitha Elavarasi, S. (2019). Current Trends: Machine Learning and AI in IoT. In D. Mala (Ed.), *Integrating the Internet of Things Into Software Engineering Practices* (pp. 181–198). Hershey, PA: IGI Global. doi:10.4018/978-1-5225-7790-4.ch009

Jasmine, K. S. (2019). A New Process Model for IoT-Based Software Engineering. In D. Mala (Ed.), *Integrating the Internet of Things Into Software Engineering Practices* (pp. 1–13). Hershey, PA: IGI Global. doi:10.4018/978-1-5225-7790-4.ch001

Juma, M. F., Fue, K. G., Barakabitze, A. A., Nicodemus, N., Magesa, M. M., Kilima, F. T., & Sanga, C. A. (2017). Understanding Crowdsourcing of Agricultural Market Information in a Pilot Study: Promises, Problems and Possibilities (3Ps). *International Journal of Technology Diffusion*, 8(4), 1–16. doi:10.4018/IJTD.2017100101

Karthick, G. S., & Pankajavalli, P. B. (2019). Internet of Things Testing Framework, Automation, Challenges, Solutions and Practices: A Connected Approach for IoT Applications. In D. Mala (Ed.), *Integrating the Internet of Things Into Software Engineering Practices* (pp. 87–124). Hershey, PA: IGI Global. doi:10.4018/978-1-5225-7790-4.ch005

Kashyap, R. (2019). Big Data and Global Software Engineering. In M. Rehman, A. Amin, A. Gilal, & M. Hashmani (Eds.), *Human Factors in Global Software Engineering* (pp. 131–163). Hershey, PA: IGI Global. doi:10.4018/978-1-5225-9448-2.ch006

Kashyap, R. (2019). Systematic Model for Decision Support System. In A. Mukherjee & A. Krishna (Eds.), *Interdisciplinary Approaches to Information Systems and Software Engineering* (pp. 62–98). Hershey, PA: IGI Global. doi:10.4018/978-1-5225-7784-3.ch004

Kaur, J., & Kaur, R. (2018). Estimating Risks Related to Extended Enterprise Systems (EES). In R. Kumar, A. Tayal, & S. Kapil (Eds.), *Analyzing the Role of Risk Mitigation and Monitoring in Software Development* (pp. 118–135). Hershey, PA: IGI Global. doi:10.4018/978-1-5225-6029-6.ch008

Kaur, Y., & Singh, S. (2018). Risk Mitigation Planning, Implementation, and Progress Monitoring: Risk Mitigation. In R. Kumar, A. Tayal, & S. Kapil (Eds.), *Analyzing the Role of Risk Mitigation and Monitoring in Software Development* (pp. 1–20). Hershey, PA: IGI Global. doi:10.4018/978-1-5225-6029-6.ch001

Kavitha, S., Anchitaalagammai, J. V., Nirmala, S., & Murali, S. (2019). Current Trends in Integrating the Internet of Things Into Software Engineering Practices. In D. Mala (Ed.), *Integrating the Internet of Things Into Software Engineering Practices* (pp. 14–35). Hershey, PA: IGI Global. doi:10.4018/978-1-5225-7790-4.ch002

Köse, U. (2018). Optimization Scenarios for Open Source Software Used in E-Learning Activities. In M. Khosrow-Pour, D.B.A. (Ed.), *Optimizing Contemporary Application and Processes in Open Source Software* (pp. 102-123). Hershey, PA: IGI Global. doi:10.4018/978-1-5225-5314-4.ch005

Kumar, A., Singh, A. K., Awasthi, N., & Singh, V. (2019). Natural Hazard: Tropical Cyclone – Evaluation of HE and IMSRA Over CS KYANT. In A. Mukherjee & A. Krishna (Eds.), *Interdisciplinary Approaches to Information Systems and Software Engineering* (pp. 124–141). Hershey, PA: IGI Global. doi:10.4018/978-1-5225-7784-3.ch006

Kumar, N., Singh, S. K., Reddy, G. P., & Naitam, R. K. (2019). Developing Logistic Regression Models to Identify Salt-Affected Soils Using Optical Remote Sensing. In A. Mukherjee & A. Krishna (Eds.), *Interdisciplinary Approaches to Information Systems and Software Engineering* (pp. 233–256). Hershey, PA: IGI Global. doi:10.4018/978-1-5225-7784-3.ch010

Kumar, U., Kumar, N., Mishra, V. N., & Jena, R. K. (2019). Soil Quality Assessment Using Analytic Hierarchy Process (AHP): A Case Study. In A. Mukherjee & A. Krishna (Eds.), *Interdisciplinary Approaches to Information Systems and Software Engineering* (pp. 1–18). Hershey, PA: IGI Global. doi:10.4018/978-1-5225-7784-3.ch001

Lal, S., Sardana, N., & Sureka, A. (2018). Logging Analysis and Prediction in Open Source Java Project. In M. Khosrow-Pour, D.B.A. (Ed.), Optimizing Contemporary Application and Processes in Open Source Software (pp. 57-85). Hershey, PA: IGI Global. doi:10.4018/978-1-5225-5314-4.ch003

Latif, A. M., Khan, K. M., & Duc, A. N. (2019). Software Cost Estimation and Capability Maturity Model in Context of Global Software Engineering. In M. Rehman, A. Amin, A. Gilal, & M. Hashmani (Eds.), *Human Factors in Global Software Engineering* (pp. 273–296). Hershey, PA: IGI Global. doi:10.4018/978-1-5225-9448-2.ch011

Lenart-Gansiniec, R. A. (2019). Crowdsourcing as an Example of Public Management Fashion. In R. Lenart-Gansiniec (Ed.), *Crowdsourcing and Knowledge Management in Contemporary Business Environments* (pp. 1–19). Hershey, PA: IGI Global. doi:10.4018/978-1-5225-4200-1.ch001

Lukyanenko, R., & Parsons, J. (2018). Beyond Micro-Tasks: Research Opportunities in Observational Crowdsourcing. *Journal of Database Management*, 29(1), 1–22. doi:10.4018/JDM.2018010101

Mala, D. (2019). IoT Functional Testing Using UML Use Case Diagrams: IoT in Testing. In D. Mala (Ed.), *Integrating the Internet of Things Into Software Engineering Practices* (pp. 125–145). Hershey, PA: IGI Global. doi:10.4018/978-1-5225-7790-4.ch006

Mansoor, M., Khan, M. W., Rizvi, S. S., Hashmani, M. A., & Zubair, M. (2019). Adaptation of Modern Agile Practices in Global Software Engineering. In M. Rehman, A. Amin, A. Gilal, & M. Hashmani (Eds.), *Human Factors in Global Software Engineering* (pp. 164–187). Hershey, PA: IGI Global. doi:10.4018/978-1-5225-9448-2.ch007

Memon, M. S. (2019). Techniques and Trends Towards Various Dimensions of Robust Security Testing in Global Software Engineering. In M. Rehman, A. Amin, A. Gilal, & M. Hashmani (Eds.), *Human Factors in Global Software Engineering* (pp. 219–251). Hershey, PA: IGI Global. doi:10.4018/978-1-5225-9448-2.ch009

Mookherjee, A., Mulay, P., Joshi, R., Prajapati, P. S., Johari, S., & Prajapati, S. S. (2019). Sentilyser: Embedding Voice Markers in Homeopathy Treatments. In A. Mukherjee & A. Krishna (Eds.), *Interdisciplinary Approaches to Information Systems and Software Engineering* (pp. 181–206). Hershey, PA: IGI Global. doi:10.4018/978-1-5225-7784-3.ch008

Mukherjee, S., Bhattacharjee, A. K., & Deyasi, A. (2019). Project Teamwork Assessment and Success Rate Prediction Through Meta-Heuristic Algorithms. In A. Mukherjee & A. Krishna (Eds.), *Interdisciplinary Approaches to Information Systems and Software Engineering* (pp. 33–61). Hershey, PA: IGI Global. doi:10.4018/978-1-5225-7784-3.ch003

Nandy, A. (2019). Identification of Tectonic Activity and Fault Mechanism From Morphological Signatures. In A. Mukherjee & A. Krishna (Eds.), *Interdisciplinary Approaches to Information Systems and Software Engineering* (pp. 99–123). Hershey, PA: IGI Global. doi:10.4018/978-1-5225-7784-3.ch005

Omar, M., Rejab, M. M., & Ahmad, M. (2019). The Effect of Team Work Quality on Team Performance in Global Software Engineering. In M. Rehman, A. Amin, A. Gilal, & M. Hashmani (Eds.), *Human Factors in Global Software Engineering* (pp. 322–331). Hershey, PA: IGI Global. doi:10.4018/978-1-5225-9448-2.ch013

Onuchowska, A., & de Vreede, G. (2017). Disruption and Deception in Crowdsourcing. *International Journal of e-Collaboration*, *13*(4), 23–41. doi:10.4018/IJeC.2017100102

Papadopoulou, C., & Giaoutzi, M. (2017). Crowdsourcing and Living Labs in Support of Smart Cities' Development. *International Journal of E-Planning Research*, *6*(2), 22–38. doi:10.4018/IJEPR.2017040102

Patnaik, K. S., & Snigdh, I. (2019). Modelling and Designing of IoT Systems Using UML Diagrams: An Introduction. In D. Mala (Ed.), *Integrating the Internet of Things Into Software Engineering Practices* (pp. 36–61). Hershey, PA: IGI Global. doi:10.4018/978-1-5225-7790-4.ch003

Pawar, L., Kumar, R., & Sharma, A. (2018). Risks Analysis and Mitigation Technique in EDA Sector: VLSI Supply Chain. In R. Kumar, A. Tayal, & S. Kapil (Eds.), *Analyzing the Role of Risk Mitigation and Monitoring in Software Development* (pp. 256–265). Hershey, PA: IGI Global. doi:10.4018/978-1-5225-6029-6.ch016

Persaud, A., & O'Brien, S. (2017). Quality and Acceptance of Crowdsourced Translation of Web Content. *International Journal of Technology and Human Interaction*, *13*(1), 100–115. doi:10.4018/IJTHI.2017010106

Phung, V. D., & Hawryszkiewycz, I. (2019). Knowledge Sharing and Innovative Work Behavior: An Extension of Social Cognitive Theory. In R. Lenart-Gansiniec (Ed.), *Crowdsourcing and Knowledge Management in Contemporary Business Environments* (pp. 71–102). Hershey, PA: IGI Global. doi:10.4018/978-1-5225-4200-1.ch005

Pohulak-Żołędowska, E. (2019). Crowdsourcing in Innovation Activity of Enterprises on an Example of Pharmaceutical Industry. In R. Lenart-Gansiniec (Ed.), *Crowdsourcing and Knowledge Management in Contemporary Business Environments* (pp. 58–70). Hershey, PA: IGI Global. doi:10.4018/978-1-5225-4200-1.ch004

Pramanik, P. K., Pal, S., Pareek, G., Dutta, S., & Choudhury, P. (2019). Crowd Computing: The Computing Revolution. In R. Lenart-Gansiniec (Ed.), *Crowdsourcing and Knowledge Management in Contemporary Business Environments* (pp. 166–198). Hershey, PA: IGI Global. doi:10.4018/978-1-5225-4200-1.ch009

Priakanth, P., & Gopikrishnan, S. (2019). Machine Learning Techniques for Internet of Things. In D. Mala (Ed.), *Integrating the Internet of Things Into Software Engineering Practices* (pp. 160–180). Hershey, PA: IGI Global. doi:10.4018/978-1-5225-7790-4.ch008

Priyadarshi, A. (2019). Segmentation of Different Tissues of Brain From MR Image. In A. Mukherjee & A. Krishna (Eds.), *Interdisciplinary Approaches to Information Systems and Software Engineering* (pp. 142–180). Hershey, PA: IGI Global. doi:10.4018/978-1-5225-7784-3.ch007

Rath, M. (2019). Intelligent Information System for Academic Institutions: Using Big Data Analytic Approach. In A. Mukherjee & A. Krishna (Eds.), *Interdisciplinary Approaches to Information Systems and Software Engineering* (pp. 207–232). Hershey, PA: IGI Global. doi:10.4018/978-1-5225-7784-3.ch009

Realyvásquez, A., Maldonado-Macías, A. A., & Hernández-Escobedo, G. (2019). Software Development for Ergonomic Compatibility Assessment of Advanced Manufacturing Technology. In M. Rehman, A. Amin, A. Gilal, & M. Hashmani (Eds.), *Human Factors in Global Software Engineering* (pp. 50–83). Hershey, PA: IGI Global. doi:10.4018/978-1-5225-9448-2.ch003

Saini, M., & Chahal, K. K. (2018). A Systematic Review of Attributes and Techniques for Open Source Software Evolution Analysis. In M. Khosrow-Pour, D.B.A. (Ed.), Optimizing Contemporary Application and Processes in Open Source Software (pp. 1-23). Hershey, PA: IGI Global. doi:10.4018/978-1-5225-5314-4.ch001

Sanga, C. A., Lyimo, N. N., Fue, K. G., Telemala, J. P., Kilima, F., & Kipanyula, M. J. (2019). Piloting Crowdsourcing Platform for Monitoring and Evaluation of Projects: Harnessing Massive Open Online Deliberation (MOOD). In R. Lenart-Gansiniec (Ed.), *Crowdsourcing and Knowledge Management in Contemporary Business Environments* (pp. 199–217). Hershey, PA: IGI Global. doi:10.4018/978-1-5225-4200-1.ch010

Sedkaoui, S. (2019). Data Analytics Supporting Knowledge Acquisition. In R. Lenart-Gansiniec (Ed.), *Crowdsourcing and Knowledge Management in Contemporary Business Environments* (pp. 146–165). Hershey, PA: IGI Global. doi:10.4018/978-1-5225-4200-1.ch008

Sen, K., & Ghosh, K. (2018). Designing Effective Crowdsourcing Systems for the Healthcare Industry. *International Journal of Public Health Management and Ethics*, *3*(2), 57–62. doi:10.4018/IJPHME.2018070104

Sen, K., & Ghosh, K. (2018). Incorporating Global Medical Knowledge to Solve Healthcare Problems: A Framework for a Crowdsourcing System. *International Journal of Healthcare Information Systems and Informatics*, *13*(1), 1–14. doi:10.4018/IJHISI.2018010101

Sharma, A., Pal, V., Ojha, N., & Bajaj, R. (2018). Risks Assessment in Designing Phase: Its Impacts and Issues. In R. Kumar, A. Tayal, & S. Kapil (Eds.), *Analyzing the Role of Risk Mitigation and Monitoring in Software Development* (pp. 46–60). Hershey, PA: IGI Global. doi:10.4018/978-1-5225-6029-6.ch004

Related Readings

Sharma, A., Pawar, L., & Kaur, M. (2018). Development and Enhancing of Software and Programming Products by Client Information Administration in Market. In R. Kumar, A. Tayal, & S. Kapil (Eds.), *Analyzing the Role of Risk Mitigation and Monitoring in Software Development* (pp. 150–187). Hershey, PA: IGI Global. doi:10.4018/978-1-5225-6029-6.ch010

Sharma, A. P., & Sharma, S. (2018). Risk Management in Web Development. In R. Kumar, A. Tayal, & S. Kapil (Eds.), *Analyzing the Role of Risk Mitigation and Monitoring in Software Development* (pp. 188–203). Hershey, PA: IGI Global. doi:10.4018/978-1-5225-6029-6.ch011

Sharma, I., & Chhabra, D. (2018). Meta-Heuristic Approach for Software Project Risk Schedule Analysis. In R. Kumar, A. Tayal, & S. Kapil (Eds.), *Analyzing the Role of Risk Mitigation and Monitoring in Software Development* (pp. 136–149). Hershey, PA: IGI Global. doi:10.4018/978-1-5225-6029-6.ch009

Sharma, S., & Dua, R. (2018). Gamification: An Effectual Learning Application for SE. In R. Kumar, A. Tayal, & S. Kapil (Eds.), *Analyzing the Role of Risk Mitigation and Monitoring in Software Development* (pp. 219–233). Hershey, PA: IGI Global. doi:10.4018/978-1-5225-6029-6.ch013

Shilohu Rao, N. J. P., Chaudhary, R. S., & Goswami, D. (2019). Knowledge Management System for Governance: Transformational Approach Creating Knowledge as Product for Governance. In R. Lenart-Gansiniec (Ed.), *Crowdsourcing and Knowledge Management in Contemporary Business Environments* (pp. 20–38). Hershey, PA: IGI Global. doi:10.4018/978-1-5225-4200-1.ch002

Sidhu, A. K., & Sehra, S. K. (2018). Use of Software Metrics to Improve the Quality of Software Projects Using Regression Testing. In R. Kumar, A. Tayal, & S. Kapil (Eds.), *Analyzing the Role of Risk Mitigation and Monitoring in Software Development* (pp. 204–218). Hershey, PA: IGI Global. doi:10.4018/978-1-5225-6029-6.ch012

Srao, B. K., Rai, H. S., & Mann, K. S. (2018). Why India Should Make It Compulsory to Go for BIM. In R. Kumar, A. Tayal, & S. Kapil (Eds.), *Analyzing the Role of Risk Mitigation and Monitoring in Software Development* (pp. 266–277). Hershey, PA: IGI Global. doi:10.4018/978-1-5225-6029-6.ch017

Srivastava, R. (2018). An Analysis on Risk Management and Risk in the Software Projects. In R. Kumar, A. Tayal, & S. Kapil (Eds.), *Analyzing the Role of Risk Mitigation and Monitoring in Software Development* (pp. 83–99). Hershey, PA: IGI Global. doi:10.4018/978-1-5225-6029-6.ch006

Srivastava, R., Verma, S. K., & Thukral, V. (2018). A New Approach for Reinforcement of Project DEMATEL-FMCDM-TODIM Fuzzy Approach. In R. Kumar, A. Tayal, & S. Kapil (Eds.), *Analyzing the Role of Risk Mitigation and Monitoring in Software Development* (pp. 234–243). Hershey, PA: IGI Global. doi:10.4018/978-1-5225-6029-6.ch014

Tolu, H. (2018). Strategy of Good Software Governance: FLOSS in the State of Turkey. In M. Khosrow-Pour, D.B.A. (Ed.), Optimizing Contemporary Application and Processes in Open Source Software (pp. 198-221). Hershey, PA: IGI Global. doi:10.4018/978-1-5225-5314-4.ch008

Trad, A. (2019). The Business Transformation Framework and Enterprise Architecture Framework for Managers in Business Innovation: Knowledge Management in Global Software Engineering (KMGSE). In M. Rehman, A. Amin, A. Gilal, & M. Hashmani (Eds.), *Human Factors in Global Software Engineering* (pp. 20–49). Hershey, PA: IGI Global. doi:10.4018/978-1-5225-9448-2.ch002

Vasanthapriyan, S. (2019). Knowledge Management Initiatives in Agile Software Development: A Literature Review. In M. Rehman, A. Amin, A. Gilal, & M. Hashmani (Eds.), *Human Factors in Global Software Engineering* (pp. 109–130). Hershey, PA: IGI Global. doi:10.4018/978-1-5225-9448-2.ch005

Vasanthapriyan, S. (2019). Knowledge Sharing Initiatives in Software Companies: A Mapping Study. In M. Rehman, A. Amin, A. Gilal, & M. Hashmani (Eds.), *Human Factors in Global Software Engineering* (pp. 84–108). Hershey, PA: IGI Global. doi:10.4018/978-1-5225-9448-2.ch004

Vasanthapriyan, S. (2019). Study of Employee Innovative Behavior in Sri Lankan Software Companies. In M. Rehman, A. Amin, A. Gilal, & M. Hashmani (Eds.), *Human Factors in Global Software Engineering* (pp. 188–218). Hershey, PA: IGI Global. doi:10.4018/978-1-5225-9448-2.ch008

Zaei, M. E. (2019). Knowledge Management in the Non-Governmental Organizations Context. In R. Lenart-Gansiniec (Ed.), *Crowdsourcing and Knowledge Management in Contemporary Business Environments* (pp. 39–57). Hershey, PA: IGI Global. doi:10.4018/978-1-5225-4200-1.ch003

Ziouvelou, X., & McGroarty, F. (2018). A Business Model Framework for Crowd-Driven IoT Ecosystems. *International Journal of Social Ecology and Sustainable Development*, *9*(3), 14–33. doi:10.4018/IJSESD.2018070102

About the Contributors

Girish Babu has extensive experience in Architecting DevOps and prominently around using data from DevOps in deriving effective Code Analytics insights that largely help organisations develop software with high quality.

Jason Cox majored in computer science at the University of Tulsa and later worked in civil engineering, helping transition from manual engineering and drafting to CAD. He spent several years using technology to design and build public infrastructure and residential subdivisions. He later co-founded a local internet service provider and web hosting startup, managing datacenters and business operations. He eventually relocated to California and took a job at Disney where he is currently leading several SRE and platform software engineering teams. Jason is a champion of DevOps practices, collaboration, curiosity, automation, agile and lean methodologies. He has spoken at many conferences and has co-authored several papers on DevOps topics. He is the author of iCurlHTTP, an iOS app for those who want to cURL on the go. He currently resides in Los Angeles with his wife and their four children.

Andrew Glover is the Director of Delivery Engineering at Netflix. He and his team own and operate Spinnaker, the Continuous Delivery platform that is facilitating Netflix's rapid global expansion. He is the founder of the 2009 Jolt award winning easyb Behavior-Driven Development framework and is the co-author of a number of books including 2008's Jolt award winning Continuous Integration, Groovy in Action, and Java Testing Patterns.

Dulani Meedeniya is a Senior Lecturer in the Department of Computer Science and Engineering, at the University of Moratuwa, Sri Lanka. She holds a PhD in Computer Science from the University of St Andrews, United Kingdom. Her main research interests are Software modelling and design, Workflow tool support for bioinformatics, Data Visualization and Recommender systems. She is a Fellow of HEA(UK), MIET, MIEEE and a Charted Engineer registered at EC (UK). https://orcid.org/0000-0002-4520-3819.

Brendan Murphy is a Senior Principal Researcher at the Microsoft Research Centre in Cambridge UK. Brendan's research area is Empirical Software Engineering focusing on Continuous Software Deployment and Security. Brendan has spent a number of years researching software development practices at Microsoft, prior to joining Microsoft he worked at DEC.

Chris Parnin's research spans the study of software engineering from empirical, human-computer interaction, and cognitive neuroscience perspectives, publishing over 60 papers. He has worked in Human Interactions in Programming groups at Microsoft Research, performed field studies with ABB Research, and has over a decade of professional programming experience in the defense industry. His research has been recognized by the SIGSOFT Distinguished Paper Award at ICSE 2009, Best Paper Nominee at CHI 2010, Best Paper Award at ICPC 2012, IBM HVC Most Influential Paper Award 2013, CRA CCC Blue Sky Idea Award 2016. He research has been featured in hundreds of international news articles, Game Developer's Magazine, Hacker Monthly, and frequently discussed on Hacker News, Reddit, and Slashdot.

Charitra Patil is a Solutions Architect at MNP LLP, based in Kanata, Canada. She has over 10 years of experience in Software industry. Proactive, multi-tasking professional with experience in .NET Technologies, Testing, Reporting Services, Microsoft dynamics CRM and Integrating services. Involved in full life - cycle projects from requirement gathering, coding, testing, designing and preparing unit test cases to user training in a multi - project environment. Adept at planning and delivering various successful deployment activities. Excellent communication, process knowledge, strong analytical and problem-solving skills.

Indika Perera is a senior lecturer at the University of Moratuwa, Sri Lanka. He holds a Ph.D (St Andrews, UK) MBS (Colombo), MSc (Moratuwa), PGDBM (Colombo) and B.Sc. Eng. (Hons) (Moratuwa). His research interests include research topics of software architecture, software engineering; technology enhanced learning, UX and immersive environments. He is a Fellow of HEA(UK), MIET, SMIEEE and a Charted Engineer registered at EC (UK) and IE(SL). https://orcid.org/0000-0001-5660-248X.

Zachary Pritchard works as a Security Engineer at Riot Game(s) on the Platform Security team. He is a security enthusiast and has worked in many fields in the information security industry, but currently specializes in cloud security. Previously he worked as a Security Engineer on Slack's Platform Security Team, where he focused on securing the code and architecture of the platform.

Iresha Rubasinghe is a postgraduate student at the Department of Computer Science and Engineering, University of Moratuwa, Sri Lanka. She has research experience in Software Engineering, Embedded Systems, Information Security, Image Processing and Computer Vision. https://orcid.org/0000-0001-9232-3648.

Priti Srinivas Sajja (b.1970) has been working at the Post Graduate Department of Computer Science, Sardar Patel University, India since 1994 and presently holds the post of Professor. She received her M.S. (1993) and Ph.D (2000) in Computer Science from the Sardar Patel University. Her research interests include knowledge-based systems, soft computing, multiagent systems, and software engineering. She has produced more than 200 publications in books, chapters, journals, and in the proceedings of national and international conferences out of which six publications have won best research paper awards. She is author of Essence of Systems Analysis and Design (Springer, 2017) published at Singapore and co-author of Intelligent Techniques for Data Science (Springer, 2016); Intelligent Technologies for Web Applications (CRC, 2012) and Knowledge-Based Systems (J&B, 2009) published at Switzerland and USA, and 4 books published in India. She is supervising work of a few doctoral research scholars while 7 candidates have completed their Ph.D research under her guidance. She has served as Principal Investigator of a major research project funded by University Grants Commission, India.She has produced 207 publications in books, book chapters, journals, and in the proceedings of national and international conferences out of which six publications have won best research paper awards.

Michael Stumm received his undergraduate degree in Mathematics (dipl. math.) and a PhD in Computer Science from the University of Zurich, Zurich Switzerland in 1980 and 1984, respectively. From 1984 to 1987 he was a researcher at IBM Research and a Post-Doc at Stanford University's Computer Science Department. He joined the ECE Department of the University of Toronto as an Assistant Professor in 1987, becoming Associate Professor in 1993 and Professor in 1995. Dr. Stumm's research interests are in the general area of computer systems software with an emphasis on operating systems for distributed systems and multiprocessors. While professor, Stumm co-founded two companies, SOMA Networks, and OANDA, a currency trading company. He ran OANDA from 2001 until 2012.

Laurie Williams is a Distinguished Professor in the Computer Science department North Carolina State University (NCSU). Laurie has been the co-director of the NCSU Science of Lablet research center, for over six years. Laurie's research focuses on software security; agile software development practices and processes, particularly continuous deployment; and software reliability.

Index

Purchase Print, E-Book, or Print + E-Book

IGI Global's reference books can now be purchased from three unique pricing formats:
Print Only, E-Book Only, or Print + E-Book.
Shipping fees may apply.

www.igi-global.com

Recommended Reference Books

ISBN: 978-1-5225-5912-2
© 2019; 349 pp.
List Price: $215

ISBN: 978-1-5225-8176-5
© 2019; 2,218 pp.
List Price: $2,950

ISBN: 978-1-5225-7811-6
© 2019; 317 pp.
List Price: $225

ISBN: 978-1-5225-7268-8
© 2019; 316 pp.
List Price: $215

ISBN: 978-1-5225-7455-2
© 2019; 288 pp.
List Price: $205

ISBN: 978-1-5225-8973-0
© 2019; 200 pp.
List Price: $195

Looking for free content, product updates, news, and special offers?
Join IGI Global's mailing list today and start enjoying exclusive perks sent only to IGI Global members.
Add your name to the list at **www.igi-global.com/newsletters.**

Publisher of Peer-Reviewed, Timely, and Innovative Academic Research

www.igi-global.com Sign up at www.igi-global.com/newsletters  facebook.com/igiglobal twitter.com/igiglobal

Ensure Quality Research is Introduced to the Academic Community

Become an IGI Global Reviewer for Authored Book Projects

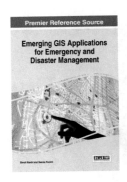

Premier Reference Source

Emerging GIS Applications for Emergency and Disaster Management

Premier Reference Source

Managerial Strategies and Green Solutions for Project Sustainability

Premier Reference Source

Comparative Approaches to Using R and Python for Statistical Data Analysis

Premier Reference Source

Solutions for High-Touch Communications in a High-Tech World

The overall success of an authored book project is dependent on quality and timely reviews.

In this competitive age of scholarly publishing, constructive and timely feedback significantly expedites the turnaround time of manuscripts from submission to acceptance, allowing the publication and discovery of forward-thinking research at a much more expeditious rate. Several IGI Global authored book projects are currently seeking highly-qualified experts in the field to fill vacancies on their respective editorial review boards:

Applications and Inquiries may be sent to:
development@igi-global.com

Applicants must have a doctorate (or an equivalent degree) as well as publishing and reviewing experience. Reviewers are asked to complete the open-ended evaluation questions with as much detail as possible in a timely, collegial, and constructive manner. All reviewers' tenures run for one-year terms on the editorial review boards and are expected to complete at least three reviews per term. Upon successful completion of this term, reviewers can be considered for an additional term.

If you have a colleague that may be interested in this opportunity, we encourage you to share this information with them.

IGI Global Proudly Partners With eContent Pro International

Receive a 25% Discount on all Editorial Services

Editorial Services

IGI Global expects all final manuscripts submitted for publication to be in their final form. This means they must be reviewed, revised, and professionally copy edited prior to their final submission. Not only does this support with accelerating the publication process, but it also ensures that the highest quality scholarly work can be disseminated.

English Language Copy Editing

Let eContent Pro International's expert copy editors perform edits on your manuscript to resolve spelling, punctuaion, grammar, syntax, flow, formatting issues and more.

Scientific and Scholarly Editing

Allow colleagues in your research area to examine the content of your manuscript and provide you with valuable feedback and suggestions before submission.

Figure, Table, Chart & Equation Conversions

Do you have poor quality figures? Do you need visual elements in your manuscript created or converted? A design expert can help!

Translation

Need your documjent translated into English? eContent Pro International's expert translators are fluent in English and more than 40 different languages.

Hear What Your Colleagues are Saying About Editorial Services Supported by IGI Global

"The service was very fast, very thorough, and very helpful in ensuring our chapter meets the criteria and requirements of the book's editors. I was quite impressed and happy with your service."

– Prof. Tom Brinthaupt,
Middle Tennessee State University, USA

"I found the work actually spectacular. The editing, formatting, and other checks were very thorough. The turnaround time was great as well. I will definitely use eContent Pro in the future."

– Nickanor Amwata, Lecturer,
University of Kurdistan Hawler, Iraq

"I was impressed that it was done timely, and wherever the content was not clear for the reader, the paper was improved with better readability for the audience."

– Prof. James Chilembwe,
Mzuzu University, Malawi

Email: customerservice@econtentpro.com   **www.igi-global.com/editorial-service-partners**

www.igi-global.com

Celebrating Over 30 Years of Scholarly
Knowledge Creation & Dissemination

InfoSci®-Books

A Database of Over 5,300+ Reference Books Containing Over 100,000+ Chapters Focusing on Emerging Research

GAIN ACCESS TO **THOUSANDS** OF
REFERENCE BOOKS AT **A FRACTION**
OF THEIR INDIVIDUAL LIST **PRICE**.

InfoSci®-Books Database

The **InfoSci®-Books** database is a collection of over 5,300+ IGI Global single and multi-volume reference books, handbooks of research, and encyclopedias, encompassing groundbreaking research from prominent experts worldwide that span over 350+ topics in 11 core subject areas including business, computer science, education, science and engineering, social sciences and more.

Open Access Fee Waiver (Offset Model) Initiative

For any library that invests in IGI Global's InfoSci-Journals and/or InfoSci-Books databases, IGI Global will match the library's investment with a fund of equal value to go toward **subsidizing the OA article processing charges (APCs) for their students, faculty, and staff** at that institution when their work is submitted and accepted under OA into an IGI Global journal.*

INFOSCI® PLATFORM FEATURES

- No DRM
- No Set-Up or Maintenance Fees
- A Guarantee of No More Than a 5% Annual Increase
- Full-Text HTML and PDF Viewing Options
- Downloadable MARC Records
- Unlimited Simultaneous Access
- COUNTER 5 Compliant Reports
- Formatted Citations With Ability to Export to RefWorks and EasyBib
- No Embargo of Content (Research is Available Months in Advance of the Print Release)

*The fund will be offered on an annual basis and expire at the end of the subscription period. The fund would renew as the subscription is renewed for each year thereafter. The open access fees will be waived after the student, faculty, or staff's paper has been vetted and accepted into an IGI Global journal and the fund can only be used toward publishing OA in an IGI Global journal. Libraries in developing countries will have the match on their investment doubled.

To Learn More or To Purchase This Database:
www.igi-global.com/infosci-books

eresources@igi-global.com • Toll Free: 1-866-342-6657 ext. 100 • Phone: 717-533-8845 x100

www.igi-global.com

Printed in the United States
By Bookmasters